# THE COLLAR

# THE
# COLLAR

*A Year of Striving and Faith
Inside a Catholic
Seminary*

Jonathan Englert

HOUGHTON MIFFLIN COMPANY

BOSTON ▪ NEW YORK

2006

For information about permission to reproduce selections from
this book, write to Permissions, Houghton Mifflin Company,
215 Park Avenue South, New York, New York 10003.

Visit our Web site: www.houghtonmifflinbooks.com.

*Library of Congress Cataloging-in-Publication Data*

Englert, Jonathan.
The collar : a year of striving and faith inside
a Catholic seminary / Jonathan Englert.
p.  cm.
ISBN-13: 978-0-618-25146-9
ISBN-10: 0-618-25146-4
1. Seminarians.  2. Catholic theological
seminaries.  I. Title.
BX903.E54 2006
230'.07'3277594 — dc22  2005021111

Printed in the United States of America

Book design by Robert Overholtzer

MP 10 9 8 7 6 5 4 3 2 1

The author is grateful for permission to reprint the following:
"We live as a constant paradox" by Kristine Malins, reprinted
from *Medical Missionary* 42, no. 6, 1988. Lines from the song
"Packy" by George Gerdes, reprinted courtesy of George Gerdes.
Lines from "The Prayer of the Empty Water Jar" by
Macrina Wiederkehr, from *Seasons of Your Heart,* copyright
© 1991 by Macrina Wiederkehr.

*For J. Carlin Englert and Mary Jani Englert*
*from a very grateful son*

*The Lord has sworn and He will not repent:*
*"You are a priest forever according to the*
*order of Melchizedek."*

— PSALM 110:4

# CONTENTS

*Introduction* 1

1 ▪ ORIENTATION ▪ 6

2 ▪ FALL TO WINTER ▪ 68

3 ▪ BETWEEN SEMESTERS ▪ 158

4 ▪ WINTER TO SPRING ▪ 173

*Epilogue* 295

*Author's Note and Acknowledgments* 299

# THE COLLAR

The Collar had its birth on a rainy autumn evening somewhere between Columbia University's main library and its journalism school. It was the direct product of a plea for vocations at Mass by a seminarian of the Archdiocese of New York and the indirect product of a profound conversion experience in my own life that had seen me move from curmudgeonly agnosticism to the Roman Catholic Church in the space of two years.

The question as I posed it to myself that evening was "Why would a man become a priest today?" As a single Catholic man, acutely aware of the shortage of priests, the question was both personal and universal. Could I imagine becoming a priest and embracing the rigors and sacrifice of religious life? What kind of man would? What was this "calling" that people spoke about? Was it even a question of a calling at all, or was it a conscious decision, even a sense of obligation, to make a commitment at a moment in history that seemed to demand it?

The Collar was born of such questions and never really departed from them. What began with musing and personal reflection soon tidied itself up into a viable journalistic exercise. The initial idea — one that promised a compelling nonfiction narrative with a strong dramatic backbone — was to follow two seminarians through a year or two of seminary. One man would continue on to ordination; the other would not. Their stories would serve as a springboard that would enable me to describe seminary life and education in detail. There had been plenty of books — both liberal and conservative, published by the usual party organs — that dealt with the priesthood and seminaries, but none without a distinct agenda and some hypothesis to be inevitably proven in its pages. My premise was simply to write as clear a story as I could about two men who believed they had a calling and acted on it. Early on, I remember Father Benedict Groeschel, the cofounder of the Franciscan Friars of the Renewal, cautioning me to avoid mere anecdote. This is good advice in general but would have been more applicable if I had been conducting a study and attempting to capture every hill and divot of the American seminary system. That was never my aim.

Over time and many visits to seminaries and seminarians, the idea was refined into a richer concept. The cast of characters expanded, as did the scope, and many of my initial assumptions — both conscious and subconscious — were set aside.

One assumption in particular was not only set aside but firmly and painfully put down. I knew that there would be some reluctance on the part of institutions and individuals to be open to this kind of fly-on-the-wall observation. But I had naively hoped that my larger sense of purpose and commitment in telling what I believed — based on my extensive initial reportage — promised a positive and even inspiring story that Church officials, presumably interested in increasing the number of priests, would embrace. I was wrong.

The book took almost three years to research and report because of access extended and then revoked by two different dioceses. Such obstacles composed a neat parallel to the sexual abuse scandal that enveloped the Church halfway through this process. Each revocation seemed to encompass the same cowardice, lack of accountability, and mere stupidity that plagued the most offending parts of the Church hierarchy during this period. This version of the Church that I encountered (thankfully, not Roman Catholicism's only version) was Church as risk-averse corporate monolith. I found it terribly sad and disillusioning. It was sad because I had met well-intentioned, intelligent men who wanted to share with others what they saw as their liberating and enlightened choice to pursue the priesthood.

The first setback occurred after only four months and was easier to accept than the second, which occurred after more than a year. By that time, I was much deeper into the stories and lives of the seminarians. Although the reasons for my losing access have never been entirely clear, they seem related to a coinciding change in leadership and the effects of the sexual abuse scandal, which began to claim priests within the diocese. I will never forget how, one by one, the seminarians dropped away. First it was phone calls that went unreturned, then visits that were planned but canceled at the last minute, and finally the honest admission by one man, visibly chafing at the restriction, that he had been told in no uncertain terms not to talk to me and advised by others that it was better not to risk saying anything until he was ordained.

While access eroded, I was getting the cheery "You're certainly welcome in our diocese" treatment from the vocation director. Frustrated and sensing I had nothing to lose, I finally pushed the envelope of my supposed access, only to find myself being awkwardly asked to leave a dinner to which I had come with several seminarians. We'll be speaking soon, I was told, as they showed me the door. A year or so before, a prominent Catholic writer had expressed interest in the book's aspirations but doubt about whether it could ever be reported. Now it seemed that he was being proven right.

I did not want to write another book critical of the Church. There had been enough of those, even before the sexual abuse scandal. And although I did not pretend to be objective (if such a state exists among writers), I certainly could not set about fashioning a saccharine vocation story. I believe that a committed priest can do an extraordinary amount of good in the world. But I also know that a vocation, as is the case of all religious experience, is rooted in the reality of the human condition and often emerges from a jagging, uneven road. Some of the stories I wanted to tell would have more in common with Saint Augustine and Thomas Merton, especially as witnessed by his *Seven Storey Mountain,* than the pabulum of the diocesan newsletter. The individual spiritual life also is a metaphor for the life of the Church, flailing at perfection, often well-intentioned, sometimes not. *The Collar* had to reflect these things, or it would be better left unwritten.

Yet two closed doors did not mean the end of the project. Fortunately, the Church is not ruled absolutely by "Vatican central." Although the Vatican exerts a sort of federal power over the dioceses, canon law, the law of the Church, dictates that much power rests with each bishop. Moreover, religious orders, although they might be bound to a diocese and its bishop, typically are outside local authority. The Sacred Heart School of Theology, where I eventually ended up, trains priests for many dioceses but is run by a religious order called the Priests of the Sacred Heart.

I first learned about Sacred Heart one night while I was sitting in the bar of a French bistro in Manhattan's theater district. I started talking with an actor who was finishing a plate of steak and *pommes frites.* I told him about the book, and he insisted that I speak with a priest friend of his who taught homiletics, the art of delivering homilies, at a Catholic seminary in the Midwest. He happened to be in town, and I reluctantly agreed to meet him. Father Andre Papineau was entertaining and insightful, but since his seminary was in Milwaukee, it seemed unlikely that we would meet again. At the time, I had no idea that I would lose my access to my second diocese.

A few months later, the unlikely became a reality. The moment I arrived at Sacred Heart, I had a strange and comforting sense of coming home. The contrast between the Byzantine pall that hung over many of the dioceses of the northeastern United States and the openness at Sacred Heart was dramatic. Fortunately, however, the question of vocation and the process of formation were roughly the same, the latter thanks to the uniformity imposed by the bishop-promulgated "process of priestly formation," which sets the norms for the education of priests in the United States.

At our first meeting, the rector, Father James Brackin, grasped the aim and scope of the book immediately and gave me unprecedented access to every dimension of seminary life. He never wavered during the following year. In addition to having the run of the place, I was allowed to attend faculty and board meetings, and more than once I was alerted to unflattering issues and events that might have effectively been concealed. The access was so straightforward and generous that I would need twenty books to capture the seminary in its entirety.

*The Collar* is an attempt to tell a story of meaning about a seminary and several different men at different points in their priestly formation. The story is both specific to a particular time and place and universal. Sacred Heart is the largest seminary in the United States for second-career, or delayed, vocations. Many of its men have had other careers and families; all of them have lived radically different lives than the one they have currently chosen. Some of them are young, and others are old. *The Collar* follows them through a single year in which two men will leave the seminary, one by choice and the other not; two men will continue on to the next year; and one man will be ordained a priest. It tells the story of a supportive community that fosters the making of priests but also of the limits of this community in a very individual quest. It brings the reader into the classroom with the seminarians; wrestles with questions of theology, Scripture, and celibacy; and delves into the internal world of each man as he judges the meaning of his own calling against the external reality of daily life and what is being required of him in this new life. *The Collar* is a story of redemption and spiritual discovery in the context of both the exigencies of the Catholic Church and the often conflicting values of contemporary society.

# I ✢ ORIENTATION

A T DINNER THE NIGHT BEFORE the new seminarians were to arrive at Sacred Heart, someone suggested that the priesthood is a career like any other. David Placette, who had left a high-paying job and forsaken the possibility of a pension, bristled, and his Cajun drawl quickened ever so slightly. "If I wanted a career, I would have stayed at DuPont. This is a life, a way of life. We're thousand-dollar-a-month men."

Following Christ and serving his Church was a gypsy vision, a wild leap of faith. DuPont was something solid and real. When David had told his crew at DuPont that he was retiring early, giving up his salary and his pension, to become a priest, they had told him he was crazy. Although Placette knew what he had there, he realized that he no longer wanted it. Instead, he wanted the priesthood, even though he wasn't exactly certain what the priesthood wanted from him. Once, during a difficult period, Placette had stumbled upon a passage that described what he felt about this priestly life:

> We live as a constant paradox to ourselves and to the rest of mankind. Ours is the pain of constantly pitching our tent and folding it up again, of befriending strangers and bidding them goodbye, of loving the world but never truly being satisfied with it, of pouring our heart and soul into a project others have begun and still others will finish. If

we would not be torn in two by the tensions of this truth, we must learn to live provisionally — to measure the road well. We need to make the most of occasions when we gather by the roadside to break bread together and compare directions. Joy must be discovered in the going as we never really arrive, not even in a lifetime.

Fifteen new men were scheduled to arrive at the seminary the next day to begin this life of pain and paradox.

Sacred Heart Seminary is almost a quarter of a mile long from end to end. By August 2002, the surrounding countryside was beginning to yield to the vast homes that had appeared across much of the United States during the boom of the previous decade: plywood palaces built to order, faced with brick or timber and festooned with fluted columns and great sloping roofs. Such development had been inevitable. Milwaukee lay just twenty miles to the northeast, Chicago ninety miles to the south. As in the case of so many Roman Catholic institutions built on land acquired long ago, the world had grown up around the seminary and reframed the grounds in much the same way that society had worked on the culture of the Church.

When the seminary building was conceived, vocations to the priesthood had never been more robust. The word "vocation" derives from the Latin *vocare,* meaning "to call." In the secular world, a vocation is most commonly understood as a calling to a particular line of work. In Roman Catholicism, a vocation primarily means a calling to the priesthood or religious life.

In the mid-1960s, American men were flocking to both diocesan and religious seminaries in great numbers to answer the Church's call. These seminaries responded to the demand by expanding their capacity to train priests and spending vast sums of money to upgrade and enlarge existing facilities or build new ones from scratch. The Priests of the Sacred Heart, a religious order informally known as the SCJs (an abbreviation rooted in their French name, Sacre Coeur de Jesus), had built the seminary in Hales Corners. They purchased the land in 1929 from a group of Dominican Sisters. The abandoned convent on the property served as both the SCJs' American headquarters and a seminary for thirty-five years until it seemed that the times demanded a replacement.

A sprawling and contiguous complex of chapels, classrooms, dormitories, athletic facilities, and dining rooms was dedicated in 1968. A four-million-dollar balloon payment would be due in five years, but vocations had plunged. Religious orders were closing the buildings they had so recently and optimistically erected and selling off their property. At Sacred Heart, only forty faculty members and students took up occupancy in a building that could house and employ several hundred people. The provincial of the SCJs had vigorously pushed for the construction, but now he said that it had been a terrible mistake. The order barely managed to repay the loan and faced the prospect of maintaining a building that far outstripped their needs and resources.

Then they came up with the idea to open the seminary to older men with delayed, or second-career, vocations. These men, usually age forty or older, were from diverse and colorful backgrounds. Historically, the Church had shunned such men in part because of an abundance of younger candidates. The younger men, it was assumed, were more able to adjust to religious life and, by virtue of their youth, promised more years of active ministry. The SCJs, however, had always been open to older vocations. In nineteenth-century Germany, for example, where mandatory military service and perpetual war prevented younger men from entering the seminary, the SCJs had embraced older seminarians. They knew the process worked.

Thus, the Center for Adult Religious Vocations, or CARV, was born. The only other option for training second-career men was at Pope John XXIII National Seminary in Weston, Massachusetts, and enrollment at CARV swelled. Many in the SCJ community, including one young seminarian named Jim Brackin, who would become Sacred Heart's rector twenty years later, were reluctant to open their doors to such men. Despite objections, open them they did, and the program thrived.

★   ★   ★

By five-thirty P.M. on August 18, 2002, the fifteen men who were scheduled to begin new lives at Sacred Heart Seminary had arrived. Most had journeyed there alone, driving great distances in their own vehicles, for some the only significant piece of property they still owned. They had come from Pennsylvania and Florida, California and Arizona, Colorado and Michigan. Some had come after years of planning and preparation, others in a rush. Mike Snyder, who had become a widower two years earlier, had packed the contents of his house into a trailer and driven from Texas to find a nine-by-twelve-foot room and a bed that would not fit his massive six-foot seven-inch frame. Robert "Bob" Brooks, another Texan, had left his big yellow dog with his dad and a $60,000-a-year job as a physician's assistant. His formal acceptance to the seminary had arrived just a few days earlier, and he had packed his pickup in such a hurry that things started flying out the back as he did 70 miles an hour north on the interstate. Ron Kendzierski came from Michigan with his mother. He promptly began to memorize the route from his room to the dining hall and chapel, counting steps, learning the sounds of the space, using all of his senses except his eyes, which had been sightless since birth.

All of the new men arrived early. Admission to the program had been rigorous, but the admissions process at least had been finite, with a concrete result. The end of seminary seemed less defined, bleeding into the priestly life beyond ordination and rigorous for the duration. The men would be dissected intellectually, psychologically, emotionally, and spiritually. They would eat most of their meals in a cafeteria and cram themselves and their belongings into small dorm rooms, some of which had only recently been converted from phone booths.

The new men arrived one after the other throughout the day, stepping out of the scorching August weather into the darker and marginally cooler interior of the reception area, a terrazzo expanse between the library and the rest of the facility, which lay down a long hallway lined with tempera paintings depicting the twenty centuries of the Church. A second-year seminarian was on duty to answer the phones and greet the newcomers. He sent each on his way with a schedule, a folder stuffed with orientation materials, a room assignment, and two keys — the seminarian's room key and another called the "sixteen" key, which opened almost every door in the facility. Sometimes the second-year seminarian manned the desk alone; occasionally other second-year students would gather there to catch up with one another after the summer break. Talking about who was, and wasn't, coming back, they surveyed the new crop.

Dean Haley stepped out of his white BMW and placed a cowboy boot on the hot asphalt of the parking lot. It had been a long drive from East Texas. He found his way inside the massive building. At thirty, he was the youngest man at the seminary that year. The average age of the new arrivals was 44.8, and the oldest one was seventy-one-year-old Philip Kim, a widower with three children. Dean Haley was, in some ways, typical of his generation. He liked hip-hop music, instant messaging, and *Buffy the Vampire Slayer.* He could be glib and impulsive, iconoclastic and opinionated. He was frequently convinced that there was a better way to do something and only he knew it. That was Dean's surface. Why he had chosen a path so radically different from even his religiously faithful peers was a mystery to all but himself.

Having removed his sunglasses, Dean found himself facing a thin man, three-quarters his height, dressed in a Roman collar and clerical shirt. This was Father Jim Brackin, the rector of the seminary. The rector of any Roman Catholic seminary is the man absolutely in charge. It is with him that questions of discipline, advancement, and expulsion ultimately rest — as well as the question of fitness for the priesthood. Dean asked if he could see his room. A gnomic smile played about the rector's lips.

"Oh, no, we can't let you do that," Father Brackin said. "We've had guys see their rooms and leave."

Dean figured the rector meant this as a joke, but either way, he was prepared to stay. He had lived under Spartan conditions as a Marine Corps medic and was ready for a harsh and threatening environment, even eager for it.

Dean took his room key and the folder and went to unpack his car. The folder that he and every new student received upon arrival was neither harsh nor threatening. Decorated with a watercolor of the seminary's façade on its cover, the folder could have been the amiable publication of a bed-and-breakfast. Thoughtful, comprehensive, and overflowing with information, it even contained Milwaukee's *2002 Official Visitors Guide.* Outlined within was everything from the school's policy on absences to a $50 membership deal at a nearby health club. Laundry service was available for $135 a semester, and firearms could not be kept in vehicles or stored on the premises. The address for mail was 7335 South Highway 100. All students were required to have a computer and would be provided with an Ethernet card with which to connect to the seminary's network. Guests were welcome, but guest rooms were limited and had to be booked in advance. Requests for how the nameplate on one's door was to read must be directed to the maintenance department (no nicknames or titles permitted), and absolutely no "pictures, posters, notepads, bumper stickers, etc." were to be attached to students' doors. Walking down the hall to his room, Dean could see as he passed door after postered-over door that at least one rule was not taken very seriously.

The first scheduled meeting was a casual gathering of the new men and those in charge of their orientation in the fourth-floor lounge that evening. A few second-year and older seminarians had volunteered to return early to help the new men adjust to life at Sacred Heart. It was hot in the lounge, even though the windows were open and the big ceiling fans were turning. Snacks and wine were spread out on a long table. The room had a faintly buttery smell from the cinema-style popcorn maker in the corner of its kitchenette. The new men had gathered in the corner opposite the pool and Ping-Pong tables. Most of them wore jeans and T-shirts. One man wore a bright yellow T-shirt from the League of Women Voters. A few of the men wore shorts. They sat on the big, black leather couches or leaned against the walls.

A comfortable-looking man in his forties with the hint of a belly, thinning hair, and sharp eyes appeared in their midst. He welcomed them and introduced himself. This was Jim Heiser, their student council president and a second-year seminarian from Wyoming. He pointed out the older students and gave the new men photocopies of a map showing the seminary's second floor, where most of the business of eating, praying, and studying was conducted. Printed in its smallest legible size, the map of the massive building just barely fit on both sides of a sheet of 8½-by-11-inch paper. Heiser remarked on the building's resemblance to the *Star Trek Enterprise,* a well-worn and fitting joke especially apropos during the long, confining Milwaukee winters when the daytime high was colder than the surface of Mars and few ventured outside.

Heiser looked from face to face. There was so much anticipation and uncertainty in those faces. There were fewer new students than the previous year, and Heiser wondered whether the number of older students was quite as robust as the phone list suggested. That list still included several men who were either on pastoral leave, spending a year working in their home dioceses, or not coming back at all.

Heiser turned the new men over to the tour guides and motioned to the snacks and drinks. "You guys go on your tour," he said. "We'll drink the wine."

The heat had broken overnight, and the new men awoke to a rainy, overcast day. They gathered for their first Mass in the Sacred Heart Chapel.

The chapel is like a fortress: heavy, gray stone expanses are interrupted by arrow slit windows covered with thick, mostly yellow, stained glass that glows at sunrise and at sunset. At other times of the day, the chapel is dark, save for theatrically positioned lights that cast long shadows amid the pillars of the encircling ambulatory and tease the altar out of the darkness. Behind the altar, the textured gold surface of the pyramidal tabernacle gleams in the light of a solitary candle. The chapel is majestic, but the severe angles of its metal chandelier and other such features lend it a touch of science-fiction hokeyness.

Although the chapel can seat several hundred people, contains a pipe organ that is two stories tall, and has a sanctuary large enough for dozens of concelebrating priests, it is technically not a church at all. A church must have an outside entrance, and the Sacred Heart Chapel does not. A bank of thick wooden doors marries the worship space to the school. It is a short walk to the administrative offices and classrooms 1 through 4, where most of the courses are taught. Directly opposite the chapel, across the hotel-like lobby, is the dining hall. At mealtime, the seminarians can smell food the instant they pass through the doors but not a moment before.

This morning, the new men clustered on the left side of the chapel, amid a silence broken only by the occasional rustle of paper or the whine of a jet descending on the foul-weather flight path into Milwaukee's General Mitchell International Airport. Some of the men wore pressed khakis and oxford shirts; others were dressed more casually. Dean Haley had decided to don his loudest T-shirt, which challenged all who sat in the pews behind him to recognize that CATHOLICISM IS NOT A SPECTATOR SPORT.

Father Brackin strode down the aisle from the back of the chapel. He wore a long green robe called a chasuble, the standard attire for a priest celebrating Mass. It is an overgarment made like a poncho. Two other priests accompanied him, as did two seminarians — one bearing a cross and the other a thurible, a small pot, hanging from a chain, that is used to hold burning incense.

When the rector reached the dais, he turned around and looked at the ragtag bunch in the pews. The tall, short, fat, thin, old, and not-so-old all peered intently at him. The rector smiled as he ventured to guess aloud what all of them were thinking: "What the heck am I doing here?"

Everyone laughed, the ice broken. Father Brackin began the Mass with words that were familiar to all of them: "In the name of the Father and the Son and the Holy Spirit," he said, crossing himself. The men crossed themselves and responded, "Amen."

Every day, at every Catholic Mass around the world, whether celebrated in Rome or in a Congolese backwater, two passages are read in one of the nearly three hundred approved languages of the Church. The passages change from day to day and follow a yearly cycle that rotates through three years, yet each day's readings are identical no matter where in the world the Mass is being said. Because of this fact, it was especially noteworthy that the day's second reading seemed tailor-made for the men in the pews at Sacred Heart. A rich young man asks Jesus what he needs to do to have eternal life. He has followed every commandment since youth, he reports. Jesus delivers a challenge: Would the young man give up all his possessions and follow him? The young man cannot do as Jesus asks and leaves wracked with sadness. The parable offers a challenge to all who profess to love God but are hindered in some way from doing his will without reservation. The new men had made the sacrifice that Jesus had demanded. But who could say how much sacrifice, how much service, or how much penitence was enough? Father Brackin had the delicate job of taking the parable's radical demands and translating them into the context of seminary life and priestly formation.

Nearly thirty years earlier, Father Brackin himself had sat as a seminarian in the pews where the new men now sat. He had been wirier then and had known so much less about life, although he had seen terrible things as a medic in Vietnam. What could he tell these men that would bring the Gospel home to them that day, at that moment, having left the familiar behind for this new life? His ten years as rector had provided him with a rough script.

Father Brackin told the men that Jesus was not urging them to a radical material poverty. He said that by far the most difficult thing he had been called to do as a priest was to let go of control of his life. This was the kind of poverty that the new men must embrace.

"Some of the things you decided for yourselves, will be decided for you," Father Brackin said. No one would ask them what they thought about Mass times, mealtimes, or the curriculum. The Church, he said, had already decided the things that are needed to form a priest. The seminarians' input in this matter was neither necessary nor desired. The men before him were coming from a society defined by being the most powerful nation on earth. Living in such a society engendered ways of being that often ran contrary to the values of religious life. What might seem like a normal exercise of self-interest in the world outside Sacred Heart was considered abnormal in their seminary community. Religious obedience was much more than behavior that made the cogs of institutional religion run smoothly. Religious obedience was essential to the spiritual maturation of the seminarian and ultimately to his individual relationship with God.

If the men were to be receptive to God's movement in their lives, Father Brackin concluded, they must give up a little control every day. Seminary would be a constant process of letting go.

"How's things going so far?" Jim Heiser asked the new men gathered in Classroom 1. He received some vaguely positive replies and a few comic groans.

Classroom 1 had a blackboard at the front, a satellite image of the Holy Land on the wall, and long tables arranged in a U shape. It was eight-thirty in the morning, and the salmon-colored schedule had led the new men there to attend something called "Orientation into Community Life."

"It gets easier the rest of the week," Heiser assured them.

"Do you have a room stretcher?" asked Mike Snyder, still struggling to fit both the contents of his trailer and his own giant frame into his room.

Ron Kendzierski said he didn't have Mike's problem; it was good to be short. For emphasis, he rapped his folded cane on the table.

"You guys'll find out complaining is not going to get you anywhere," Heiser said with a grin.

"We're not complaining really," Mike said.

"We'll complain later, then you can compare the two," Bob Brooks added.

"Did you have any success with the desk?" Heiser asked Bob, remembering that he had encountered the seminarian rummaging around the basement in search of a nicer desk.

"No," Bob replied, "but I got a light."

"You can have my light," Ron said. "I don't need it."

The men roared with laughter. Ron knew exactly what he was doing: he had to play the blind guy so that somehow he would stop being seen as the blind guy. This was one reason he had learned to do a near-perfect Stevie Wonder imitation. ("I just called to say I loooove you," he would sing, rolling his head around on his shoulders and waving his cane.) Or why he welcomed practical jokes that played off of his disability. Or why he made a point of saying "See you later." His jokes freed his classmates from pity and him from the effects of their pity.

When the laughter subsided, Heiser began his talk. The lecture was a bullet-pointed hand-me-down from a seminarian who had just dropped out, leaving Heiser with the job of delivering it.

"First topic is friendship. It's crucial to survival in this place. You need to develop some friendships, some close friendships, and not just one or two guys that you're always hanging out with, but try to be a friend to as many people as you can. Sit with different people during your meals. The first-year students — every year, you're in the same classes — so it's a natural tendency to hang out with those guys, talk about class talk, about what's going on. Reach beyond your class and make some friends. Gary was an invaluable help to me last year — with any kind of concern or question I had. I'm gonna miss him next year."

He glanced at Gary Rottman and gave a little nod. Gary was in his final year at the seminary and had been the student council president the previous year. The only man in his final year to volunteer to return for orientation, he was participating in almost all of the events with the new men that August. Heiser's first impression of Gary had been strongly negative: too abrupt, too intense, too matter-of-fact. "What business does this man have becoming a priest?" Heiser had complained to his spiritual director. He simply could not see the pastor in Gary. Heiser had come to realize that Gary's intensity masked a sincere and self-sacrificing commitment to people, and his manner, well, that was just Gary, and you got used to it.

"Here's a good topic," Heiser announced, his eyes returning to the outline. "Gossip. 'Deadly in a place like this. This is a fishbowl. What goes around, comes around.' And it's true. Gossip's a terrible thing. It's gonna happen. Don't participate. That's as straightforward as I can be. It'll come back to haunt you. There's roughly a hundred students, and if you're gonna take part in the gossip, people are gonna know that you're a gossip. It's not a very Christian thing to do."

Heiser continued, "Participation. Number three. You're not just here to go to school and get good grades. We're here to become priests. How well you interact with each other is gonna be a sign of how well you're gonna succeed in the priesthood. It's a very social vocation."

Heiser had almost finished speaking about the importance of prayer, topic 4, when Father Michael McLernon wandered into the room. Heiser had become friendly with Father McLernon the previous spring in the priest's Medieval Philosophy class.

"Gentlemen," Father McLernon said over his spectacles, staring archly at his former student. The priest's voice was deep and gravelly but leavened with humor. "Pay close attention to this man. He is *so* learned."

The men laughed. The interloper seemed professorial, but not forbiddingly so, and playful, interested in a verbal joust, which Heiser provided.

"Because I had Father as a philosophy professor last semester," he joked.

McLernon affected a tone of comic awe and pointed at his former student. "He made such breakthroughs in medieval philosophy. Bonaventure will never be safe.

"Good luck, gentlemen," Father McLernon said as he departed. "Sit at the feet of the master."

Heiser returned to his outline. There was a lot to cover, and he was growing concerned that the bus that was supposed to take the new men on a tour of Milwaukee and to a lakeside picnic might arrive at any moment. The year before, it had pulled around to the wrong entrance, and getting everyone on board had been a fiasco. Heiser scoured the list. He had a casual, easygoing surface, but he liked to get things right. Loading a bus wasn't going to be a fiasco on his watch. What on this list was essential? What should he leave out? Then someone yawned.

"Someone is yawning, and I'm only halfway through this agenda," he observed.

"You *could* read this on the bus," Dean Haley interrupted. The comment seemed rude. Heiser raised his eyebrows.

"We could," Heiser entertained politely, but returned to listing the seminary's prayer offerings nonetheless. "We have community prayer. We have Mass mostly in the morning. We have evening prayer after classes at five-fifteen. You're expected to be there. Sometimes it's something that's very easy to not be at. If you're not there, it gets noted."

A ripple of tense laughter greeted this remark.

When he reached "Bathroom Etiquette and Hygiene," he smiled. The outline began, "There's nobody here named Mom or 'Honey.'"

"If you use the last piece of toilet paper, put a new roll in there. Be considerate of the guys," Heiser advised. "Don't throw the old roll on the floor; throw it in the trash can."

Heiser chuckled. The new men had come all this way to embrace a spiritual life, and here he was talking about toilet paper.

Many Catholics are surprised when they learn that a divorced man like Heiser can become a priest. This ignorance defies immediate explanation, given that for three decades, there has been no bar against such men entering the clergy, provided that their first marriage has been annulled. (Annulment is a process by which the Church, though not permitting divorce, can dissolve a marriage by finding that while a civil marriage did occur, a sacramental marriage did not.) The Catholic Church is rife with such misconceptions among its adherents. Economists have a model for a perfect market-place, which depends on the fluid and comprehensive exchange of information between buyer and seller. The more fluid and comprehensive this exchange, the better informed the decisions of both parties can be and the closer the price of something comes to its actual value. For all of its perceived unity as a well-oiled machine and its centrally organized, Vatican-based bureaucracy and vertically administered authority, the Catholic Church remains a mystery to both Catholics and non-Catholics alike. The information exchange of the ideal marketplace is not only beyond its grasp; it's also tacitly rejected. The Vatican may have a press office and its own Web site, but those operations are powerless to overcome the mystery. It's the universal belief in this mystery, built deep into the core of the Church, that precludes the ideal exchange of information. Reformers of both stripes, conservative and liberal, seeking to iron out the Church's inconsistencies once and for all, have been frustrated by this mystery, although a general belief in the mystery usually accounts for why they remain Catholics despite their inevitable failure to change the Church.

In simple terms, this belief in the mystery is a belief in the proposition that no human limits can be put on God and his capacity for mercy. The Church might attempt to clarify doctrine, but it usually stops short of draconian imposition. More common is a definitive pronouncement, followed, typically years later, by indefinite restatement. It's one thing to say that such and such behavior is not permitted and quite another to openly exclude the person practicing the behavior. Hate the sin but love the sinner is the Catholic touchstone. Although exclusion might be the implication, self-exclusion is the only practical possibility. One bishop might deny Communion to a politician for holding a position that runs contrary to doctrine; ten other bishops might do the opposite. In the trenches, it's the rare priest who will deny Communion to a parishioner on any grounds. An uneasy conscience is better than the indifferent conscience of someone who has rejected the hope of reconciliation. There's also the political reality. An outright confrontation with parishioners about a contentious issue such as birth control, regarding which polls suggest that about three quarters of American Catholics diverge from Church teaching, is not to be tempted.

So the Church seesaws. Even political motivation is rooted in this mystery. For instance, there is a telling story of a bishop urged by an adviser to discipline a wayward priest. Why, the adviser wanted to know, was the bishop so reluctant to punish the man? The bishop lifted a crystal goblet and asked his aide to whom the goblet belonged. "You, Your Eminence." The bishop continued, "And if I drop it and it shatters, to whom will it belong then?" "You, Your Eminence," the aide replied. The bishop had made his point. The shattered wreck of one of his flock was as much his as the soul brought safely home. The mystery of redemption discourages Church officials from taking direct, irrevocable action and encourages the obscure transmission of information that would make the taking of such action mandatory. The mystery of redemption discourages the creation of the kind of uniform clearing-house of information and doctrine that would keep every Catholic up to date. There will never be a "Do's and Don'ts" page on the Vatican Web site, a Vatican-published newsletter helping Catholics to stay on top of the latest institutional trends, or mandatory refresher courses on doctrine and liturgy.

As a result, Catholics tend to learn what the Church is currently permitting on a case-by-case basis. They might meet a man like Heiser, hear his story, and walk away happy knowing that someone like him could now become a priest. A few people remain resistant to the idea of a divorced man becoming a priest, perhaps on the grounds that if he broke his vows once, he cannot be trusted to keep them this time. Most, however, seem to think that it's an advantage for a priest to have been married and had children because he can empathize with parishioners who are spouses and parents.

★　　★　　★

Heiser's life was a story of redemption, but not in the traditional sense. He was not the convert instantly reborn to new life. His life experience was not safely filed away under the label "wild days." Instead, those days had made him more capable of understanding, forgiveness, and mercy. These were qualities that the people in the pews needed. If he thought that his past could help parishioners, he would use it.

Heiser said that he still loved his wife and would have married her again even in light of the wreckage left behind in the wake of the divorce. Heiser also thought that he and his son, Eric, had done pretty well as a single-parent family and that he had made certain not to raise Eric with any bitterness toward his mother. The discord and pain of a broken marriage had been followed by a kind of normalcy, he said, years during which Eric had grown into a man and Heiser had felt the ever more insistent call to become a priest.

When the men returned from their tour of Milwaukee in the late afternoon, they changed clothes and made their way to the main lounge for a reception with faculty and staff. It would be their first encounter with the people who would teach, advise, comfort, and confess them for the next four to eight years. A long table was piled high with various kinds of Wisconsin cheese, and caterers stood behind big bowls of fruit punch. The students were dressed formally; the faculty members were mostly dressed casually, having meandered into the reception from the events of Faculty Day, an annual gathering of Sacred Heart's staff held before the school year begins. The final portion of their exercise had been an American Indian prayer ritual conducted under a scorching sun in the stone pavilion of the Sacred Heart Shrine.

The new men had been assured that the faculty of Sacred Heart would stand behind their aspirations to the priesthood 100 percent, yet they also had been warned that they were under the microscope. Any seminarian in 2002 was familiar with this paradox. New priests were desperately needed. Understaffed parishes were being forced to close or consolidate, resulting in many Catholics being denied ready access to the sacraments, such as baptism, confession, and the sacrament of the sick, or last rites. The number of U.S. parishes without a resident priest had more than quintupled from 549 in 1965 to 3,000 in 2002, as the number of priests had dropped almost 25 percent, from 58,632 to 44,000. Meanwhile, the Roman Catholic population in the United States had increased by 30 percent, from 45.6 million in 1965 to 62 million in 2002.

To meet the need for more priests, some dioceses were openly aggressive about recruitment. One vocation director (the person charged with finding men for the priesthood) had a map dotted with bright-colored pushpins denoting promising leads and recruitment venues, as if he was planning a military campaign. Many of the new men at Sacred Heart had been recruited vigorously. Although the common perception is that dioceses will take any single male with a pulse, the reality is quite different. For instance, Dean Haley had entered the application process believing that any diocese would prize him as a priest candidate. He was young, handsome, faith-filled, and intelligent. Indeed, his diocese had been enthusiastic about recruiting him, but this did not prevent the diocese from delaying his application until he was debt-free. Most of the new men were in similar positions. They knew they were desperately needed, but the environment, especially in the wake of the child sexual abuse scandal that seemed unlikely to abate soon, complicated matters.

The new men stuck together at the reception, making small talk and barely mixing with the faculty. After a while, the group moved into the dining hall. Sunlight flooded through the floor-to-ceiling windows, making the glasses and cutlery on the tables shine. Waiters — tall young men in white tuxedo shirts and suspenders — stood at the ready with fresh plates and pitchers of water.

Father Brackin welcomed everyone and led the group in prayer. The meal, prepared by a French chef hired for the occasion, featured lamb and roasted potatoes. When everyone had finished eating, Father Brackin rose again and ran down a list of faculty, staff, and administration. He referred to the new students as a fine group of men with interesting backgrounds. He said that Sacred Heart valued community and looked forward to the new year.

Then, in keeping with tradition, powder blue strips of paper were distributed to the men. They sang the lyrics printed on the strips to the tune of *The Mickey Mouse Club* theme song:

> What's the name of the place
> We call the seminary?
> S-A-C-R-E-D  H-E-A-R-T
>
> Come along and sing our song
> And learn theology
> S-A-C-R-E-D  H-E-A-R-T
>
> Sacred Heart School
> Sacred Heart School
> What's the name of the place
> That's training you and me?
> S-A-C-R-E-D  H-E-A-R-T
>
> Hey, there! Hi, there! Ho, there!
> You're as welcome as can be!
> S-A-C-R-E-D  H-E-A-R-T

One new man didn't sing. Dean Haley took long gulps of water to cover his — what was it that he was feeling exactly? — anger, annoyance, embarrassment. Damn, it was hard to keep his body planted in that chair. Had he prepared for years, given up a woman and the possibility of a family, and driven thousands of miles for this? Dean had envisioned something more recognizably holy than this silly spectacle. Finally, the song came to an end:

> Come along and join our throng
> For life eternally!
> S-A-C See ya real soon!
> R-E-D Delighted to meet you!
> H-E-A-R-T!

The room broke into prolonged peals of applause and laughter, and the gathering promptly dissolved. Faculty and staff headed for home. Heiser and a few others drove off to Miller Park for a Milwaukee Brewers baseball game. Dean Haley wondered whether he should even bother staying the night.

Dean Haley was one of the tallest men at the seminary, and one of the youngest. He seemed a hybrid of several movie actors. He also had a distinctly active presence. He fidgeted more than most people; he spoke at a dizzying clip; he often gave the impression that he had to be somewhere else and was just barely managing to hold himself back from leaping up and going there that instant. Dean loved the idea of accomplishing two or three things at once. In college, he had worked for a service that supplied class notes to blind students. This allowed him to make money while taking the courses he had to take anyway. At thirteen, he had heard a Viktor Frankl quotation saying, in effect, that the meaning of life is to have a life with meaning. This notion had been driving him relentlessly forward ever since.

Sometimes Dean spoke even faster and fidgeted even more. This happened when he didn't take his Adderall. He had been diagnosed with hyperactivity disorder when he was three years old and attention deficit disorder after college. The second diagnosis had helped explain why it had been so hard for him to get things right sometimes. He refused to think of this dual condition, known as ADHD, as a handicap. It had helped him be successful in sales and as an entrepreneur, where he had seen himself as a driven self-starter. He thought that the attention deficit portion of his condition was a misnomer. There was no deficit of attention when he was off the medication. When he focused on something, he focused. He regularly got into trouble, however, because he wasn't focusing on what everybody else was.

On or off the medication, Dean's personality and his condition were intimately connected. He sought advice but kept his own counsel. He was indiscreet and competitive. He didn't worry about stepping on toes. Having ADHD, he would say, was like being a hunter.

You had to pay attention to every detail and keep your eyes on the prey. The medication dulled that mode of perception. It also had to be taken according to a strict schedule. Forgetting to take a dose at exactly the right time could result in weeklong sleeplessness, followed by a crash. Sometimes Dean felt that taking the medication didn't change him as much as it changed the people around him. In fact, he felt that he didn't really change at all; it was everyone around him who changed. Suddenly, instead of giving him dirty looks because of his ebullience, people would ask him why he was so quiet. Instead of being corrected, he would be complimented. Somehow, the medication had made things better.

Long before, the thirty-year-old seminarian had changed his name from Jody to Dean. He had read something about neurolinguistic programming: if your name imprisoned you within the expectation of failure, you could change it and escape failure. Jody Haley, from an uneducated family in East Texas, would never have completed college; Dean Haley did. Jody Haley would never have been influenced by the vast repository of Catholic information and knowledge; Dean Haley was. His conversion to Catholicism had rested on what he saw as the strong Catholic tradition of intellectual rigor going back to Saint Augustine and the early Church fathers.

Jody Haley avoided challenges; Dean Haley had been a medic in the U.S. Marines and had had Special Forces training. He was shadowed by a military ethic of accountability and expendability with no hard feelings, and he brought this with him to Sacred Heart. Dean had worked in banking and construction; he had sold and serviced oil rig equipment in the Gulf of Mexico. He hated details and bureaucracy. He was a "big picture" man and proud of it: let other people handle the details. In college, he had hired a nursing student to be his personal organizer. She had paid his bills, overseen his schedule, and kept his papers in order. When one of his roommates had disputed something, she had sent him a five-page memo with receipts attached. Dean loved that kind of thing. Computers had helped relieve him of some of this drudgery. He tried to automate tasks as much as possible so he wouldn't have to waste his time on them.

Dean had arrived at the seminary with the belief that a vocation to the priesthood — more than a calling to married or single life — entailed suffering. There was no escape from suffering in this life anyway, he thought, and what finer and purer challenge than the priesthood. He had already suffered to come here. He had received only lukewarm support from his parents and grandparents. His last serious girlfriend, an Evangelical Christian, had told him never to contact her again unless it was to tell her that he had abandoned the priesthood and was free — presumably to marry.

Dean had expected something different at Sacred Heart. The other seminarians were so much older than he had anticipated — older, on average, than his parents, who were in their late forties. Many of the seminarians had had wives and kids. Some of them seemed so comfortable in a pastoral role, as if they were already priests. Dean felt nothing of the sort. As a marine, he had relished the straightforward, grinding regimen of goals and consequences that transformed each recruit into something else, something better. He had come to Sacred Heart expecting to find the Marine Corps's spiritual equivalent and a boot camp esprit de corps. How would he find this challenge in a seminary that began the year with the *Mickey Mouse Club* theme song?

The main focus of the next day was an hours-long academic orientation, which would be followed by a battery of assessment tests. The dean of academics, Father Tom Knoebel, led the orientation, for which only eight of the new men assembled. These were the men who had already earned their college degrees and were at Sacred Heart to study theology. The rest of the new seminarians would be attending Cardinal Stritch University, a nearby college where they would begin a combined program of undergraduate and graduate classes.

Father Knoebel turned to the blackboard and wrote:

SEMINARY SYSTEM — ECUMENICAL COUNCIL OF TRENT
(1545–1563)

Then he asked if everyone had arrived. Dean Haley had not. Father Knoebel had just given up waiting when Dean appeared and found his way to a seat. Dean looked as if he had had a rough night.

"Well, good morning! I think this is called Academic Orientation on your schedules. Let me make sure that's what I do with you," Father Knoebel said, grinning as he fumbled for his schedule. "Yeah, Academic Orientation. Why don't we pause for just a moment with prayer?"

The prayer seemed custom-made for Dean.

"Oh, God, our Father, we place ourselves *again*, this morning, in your presence," Father Knoebel began. "In some ways, this is perhaps the first formal experience of our seminary preparation for priesthood. Each of us comes here having lived in a relationship with you for many, many years. Moments of grace, moments sometimes when we may have wandered, but we've always come back, and you've been calling us and guiding us through it all. So here we are now. Each of us may have many, many reasons why we shouldn't be here or why we could be doing something else. But I suppose ultimately there's only one reason we are here, and that is you. Your will, your desire, your love, your care for us that somehow brought us to this place and this point in our lives. Bless us and bless our efforts in these next couple years. Strengthen us when we need it, challenge us when we need it, and bless us always."

Father Knoebel paused, then said, "We make this prayer through Christ our Lord."

"Amen," the men said.

Looked at through the lens of almost any other academic setting — law, medicine, astrophysics — this official acknowledgment of the participants' potential to waiver and drop out was odd. There is the vaunted law school mythology, à la *The Paper Chase,* where the professor informs his students to turn to the right and then the left and recognize that one or the other person he sees will not become a lawyer. But in the seminary, the culling process is largely internal and self-selecting. Grades matter, but only in the most extreme circumstances do grades get a seminarian expelled.

"Forgive me for my cold," Father Knoebel said with a sniffle. "I think I'm getting better, but most of the people who saw me for the first time yesterday thought I was dying. So maybe I'm not doing as well as I think."

Father Knoebel distributed a handout titled "Academic Orientation," which would serve as the outline for the next three hours. He then explained how the concept of a seminary developed. Referring to the word's Latin derivation, he described how each seminarian would "be placed in a nourishing soil in an atmosphere where you are surrounded by good and healthy people and models who will help you grow and develop into the priest that God wants you to be." This system had been developed at the Council of Trent and had become the approach to forming priests for the past five hundred years — a recent innovation in terms of Church history, Father Knoebel observed. Formerly, priests had been trained during parish apprenticeships, with no formal educational requirements. Father Knoebel pointed at COUNCIL OF TRENT on the board.

"Significantly, the Council of Trent occurred after what major — ?"

"The Reformation," Bob Brooks interjected.

"After the Reformation. It was the Church's response and restatement and adaptations," Father Knoebel confirmed.

Then the priest arrived at an intellectual bridge and began to lead the new men across. The bridge spanned the gap between what the world thought of the formation process and what it actually was. For Dean and most of the students, Father Knoebel's talk was the official beginning of the long process of disillusionment and rebuilding that constitutes the formation of a Roman Catholic priest.

"One of the things that followed upon Trent," Father Knoebel said, "was the seminary system — to try and increase the level of priests. The Vatican, therefore, has numerous documents which have guided seminaries — how we are structured, how we live, and what we teach."

Father Knoebel wrote PASTORES DABO VOBIS on the blackboard.

"Any of you know enough Latin to know what that means?"

No one ventured a guess.

"Oh, gosh," Father Knoebel muttered. The seminarians' ignorance of the language that was once so prominent in the Catholic Church still surprised him. He had been trained as a priest before Vatican II, which in the mid-1960s had mandated that the Mass be said in vernacular instead of Latin.

"'I will give' — that's the *dabo* — and the *vobis* is 'you.' Remember *Dominus vobiscum* from the Latin Mass?"

This time there were a few nods of recognition.

*Pastores Dabo Vobis (I Will Give You Shepherds)* was Pope John Paul II's encyclical directing the formation of priests, Father Knoebel told them. It had exerted a strong influence on how seminaries were run.

"But another document which is perhaps even more specific for the United States is this book with the green cover called *Program of Priestly Formation*, affectionately known as the *PPF*. This version — fourth version — came out in 1992, and it is the official document of the United States bishops. Feel free to peruse it, but you'll see as you read it that it's a description of Sacred Heart School of Theology or Notre Dame Seminary — just about any seminary you could find in the United States. We all follow this document very, very closely."

In addition to the uniformity imposed by the *PPF*, every seminary in the United States now granted a master's of divinity degree. In the past, priests generally graduated from the seminary without any formal degree. Most priests ordained before 1972 did not have such a degree, Father Knoebel said.

"It does demonstrate that you really have gone through the full program and that your professional competency places you on a level with other professionals in other fields. You're not just a pious person who got a call from God and came in out of the fields one day and set up a church and began preaching."

Father Knoebel paused to let this sink in.

"We are a specialized seminary for second-career seminarians, and we have built as much flexibility into the program as possible. Nevertheless, we have a number of people looking over our shoulder. I'm not sure that John Paul II is actually physically looking himself, but he has several agents that do. Then the *PPF*, the United States bishops, the accreditation agencies, plus your bishops and your vocation directors. And if there is anyone else that you know of looking over my shoulder — *don't tell me.*"

One thing that seminary educators like Father Knoebel encountered in 2002 that their counterparts forty years earlier had not was Catholic cultural illiteracy, a deficit of common knowledge. This illiteracy went well beyond ignorance of Latin. The men seeking the priesthood in 2002 often arrived with an inconsistent knowledge of their religion — an uneven patchwork of doctrine, practice, and culture that challenged educators to cover topics that in the past every seminarian would have already known. In 2002, one man might know everything about liturgical practice — the conduct and protocol surrounding the Mass and other religious services — but precious little when it came to basic doctrine such as the nature of Mary, whom Catholics believe to have been untouched by original sin. Another might have read everything about Saint Augustine and be able to quote Saint Thomas Aquinas verbatim, but know nothing about the Catholic practice of sealing a saint's relic in a kind of vault under each church's altar.

The reasons for this were manifold. Some seminarians were converts from other religions and lacked the experience of family-reinforced traditions to balance a book-learned knowledge of Catholicism. Others, born and raised in the faith, had returned to the Church after years of being away from it, during which their knowledge of doctrine and practice had grown vague. Addressing this problem was not really Father Knoebel's job as academic dean, but he knew that the master's of divinity program, at least at Sacred Heart, somehow had to confront this illiteracy.

"The MDiv is a *professional* degree. It's called professional because it requires not only the academic component but also the pastoral, or field education, component and the spiritual formation component. Being a priest is not just a matter of getting a certain number of courses under your belt."

Father Knoebel surveyed all his students' faces. Dean Haley had a young-looking face and intense eyes. Philip Kim had an old-looking face and a quiet intelligence. Ron Kendzierski, rocking his head back and forth, looked straight ahead into space, his lids fluttering over his eyes.

"Many of you have gone through academic programs where that is exactly the only goal: get as many credits done as quickly as possible and get the heck out of there. Every year, there is at least one of you who will bring that attitude into the seminary, and you will say, 'Why can't I take twenty-five hours? I'm sitting around. I'm doing nothing on Saturday morning between eight and nine. That's when I can do that additional course work, and I could be out of here in two years and one month.'"

His voice reached a high note of comic desperation.

"'After all, I'm already *thirty-three.*'"

It was as if he were speaking directly to Dean.

"What I'm trying to say is, it's not just an academic program. If it were, yes, you could pile on all these credits and just get out. But you have pastoral formation; you've got your internship; you've got your spiritual formation; you've got your hours before the Blessed Sacrament; you've got your Masses, your homilies, your days of recollections, your retreats, your bumping shoulders with one another, your wrestling with God — that all takes time. The Church has wisely said the program they normally expect for seminarians is four years. Anything under that you need to explain."

Father Knoebel now turned to address the older men.

"If you discover during the course of your year that you are breaking down physically . . . I don't mean that just as a joke. You're not the person you were thirty years ago, and you can't stay up until two in the morning and cram for that exam the way you did in college. Instead, you may want to say, 'I'd rather get ordained at sixty-two and a half instead of sixty-two and live for twenty years and minister, rather than killing myself here.'"

He paused.

"I don't know the bishop or vocation director that would not say,

'Great! Spend four and a half years and save your health or your emotional health or your spiritual health.'"

Everybody knew the Church needed priests, Father Knoebel conceded, but that was no reason to burn out before you had even been ordained.

Although Jim Pemberton had returned early to assist with orientation, as a second-year seminarian, he didn't need to attend academic orientation. Nor did he have to be reminded how badly the Church needed priests. There was Father Joseph Scantlin back home to remind him.

Father Scantlin had been a fellow seminarian in San Antonio during Jim's first time through the seminary in the late 1940s. Hundreds of men filled the seminary then. Many were veterans of World War II, some were boys virtually pledged from birth to religious service by immigrant parents, and a few, like Jim, were devout offspring of a mixed-faith marriage who had come despite resistance at home. Those were the years before the Second Vatican Council caused a tumult that sent the number of men becoming priests plunging and set an uncertainty loose in Catholicism that still hasn't been resolved.

Back then, seminarians' days were regimented and crammed with activities. They rose at six for morning prayer, then Mass, breakfast, morning classes, lunch, afternoon classes, sports, dinner, study, and lights out at ten P.M. This was called *summum silentium,* the highest silence. Dating was not allowed, and opportunities to violate this rule were few. A seminarian could not venture off campus alone or without an appropriate reason, such as a doctor's appointment. There were proscriptions such as the "rule of three," which encouraged camaraderie by requiring seminarians to socialize in groups of three or more, and the rule against particular friendships, which discouraged other unspoken inclinations. Once a month, on "visiting Sunday," a seminarian could return to his family for half the day. A few times a year, the seminarian could take "town leave" to see a movie or go to a restaurant. From this protected hothouse, priests were sent out into the world with little preparation for the actual work of ministry and scant support for their vow of celibacy beyond an uninformed reliance on grace, willpower, and cold showers.

Jim Pemberton and Father Scantlin, both now in their seventies, had this bond. But they also had another. Jim's deceased wife, Joy, had been Scantlin's sister. They had met while Jim was in the seminary. Joy worked for Prudential Insurance in Houston and lived with her aunt. One year, the aunt invited Joe Scantlin and Jim to her house for Thanksgiving. Although Jim had met Joy before, the attraction really began then. After he left the seminary, he and Joy dated steadily. The couple eventually married and had four children.

By the time Jim arrived at Sacred Heart Seminary, Father Scantlin had been a priest for forty-five years. While Jim was diving headlong into this new life, Father Scantlin was facing the end of his ministry. In "the trade," as he sometimes called the priesthood, priests like him were known as parish hacks. This type of priest was a jack-of-all-trades, whose chief work was in the trenches with the people. Sacred Heart trained exactly this sort of priest, who would be sent out into the thick of parish life.

Father Scantlin's present post at Most Blessed Sacrament Catholic Church in Arlington, Texas, had sixteen hundred registered families. This was not a huge number by the current standards of the American Southwest, but it represented a daunting challenge compared to his early days of ministry, when a parish that size might have had four or five full-time priests. Here, he was the only one.

A registered family is the standard unit of measure of a parish workload — the way a Catholic priest assesses his own obligations and compares them to those of other priests. A single registered family invariably requires an array of sacramental services and other support at every stage of life (baptism, confirmation, marriage, confession, and anointing of the sick). Even with the growth of the lay ministry, this work almost always fell to the priest.

With sixteen hundred families, Father Scantlin, like most parish priests in 2002, had constant demands on his time. But unlike many priests his age, he was vital. His cardiologist had recently told him that he had the heart of a twenty-five-year-old. His father had lived to ninety, and except for the rare bout with arthritis, Father Scantlin didn't take any medication. Seventy-five was the usual retirement age in the Fort Worth diocese, but if a priest was in good health, retirement was negotiable, especially now with the shortage of priests. Even if Father Scantlin retired, he planned to continue his ministry in some way. After all, he would remain a priest until he died.

Father Scantlin loved being a priest. He had been sad to see so many men leave the priesthood during the 1960s and 1970s, in the aftermath of the Second Vatican Council, but he had accepted it. As they said in Texas, the horse had bucked. He had not just survived the transition to a post–Vatican II priesthood; he had flourished.

"Clerical priesthood as I knew it, as I was ordained into it, is gone," Father Scantlin would say. The clerical priesthood, the good-old-boy network, had offered a secure haven, but its lack of transparency had failed the people. He believed that there was a great need for priestly ministry in American culture, and this need had always been his focus. He was known as a priest with a dependable sense of humor who worked tirelessly for his people.

To Jim Pemberton, Father Scantlin was one of those successful priests whose vocation had such depths that the foibles and shortcomings of the institutional Church could not shake it. Father Scantlin did not need a perfect Church to be able to embrace his role as a priest. By now, he liked to say, he knew who he was and what he was supposed to be doing.

Father Scantlin referred to the institutional Church as "the system" and spoke openly about it to Jim. One particular shortcoming of the system had become apparent to Father Scantlin as retirement approached. Once a priest retired from active service, in most dioceses he would no longer be supported beyond a modest pension. "When you're not productive, you're pretty much out of the loop," he observed.

There was a common misperception among Catholics, who generally believe that the Church takes care of retired priests. A corporate employee might face the same problem, but he at least would probably have been able to save for retirement over the years. By contrast, priests' salaries, though recently increased, had never permitted much saving. Father Scantlin had been paid $62.50 a month for his first three years of service. Out of that, he had had to pay for his car and his clothing. The system encourages a financial dependency that Father Scantlin considered unhealthy. Like the military, he observed, the Church gives you room and board, which discourages building equity in a home. For tax purposes, the U.S. government treats priests the same as military personnel. Unlike married military personnel, however, priests often find themselves in the highest tax bracket because they don't have any dependents. The effect of this, Father Scantlin maintained, is to deprive a priest of planning for retirement, when many of the expenses that were covered during his active service suddenly become his own responsibility. As a case in point, a priest friend of Father Scantlin's had recently retired to a ramshackle mobile home in a dusty West Texas pasture because it was all he could afford.

The effects of this dependency were tied to another question that Father Scantlin had about the system. Was it realistic to expect a lifetime of service from men entering the priesthood today when people lived so long and often had several careers? He met young men all the time who couldn't seem to fathom such an expectation.

"Have you always done what you're doing?" a seventeen-year-old boy asked him just after he had celebrated his fortieth year as a priest.

"Yes," Father Scantlin replied.

"Did you ever do anything else?"

"No."

"For forty years?"

"Yes."

Incredible, the teenager seemed to be saying.

Jim Pemberton had known Father Scantlin for his entire priesthood, and Jim weighed these observations against Father Scantlin's life as a priest. On Sundays, people would pull at him as he made his way through the crowd. They would tell him about problems he could do little about — a teenage son in trouble or a marriage on the rocks — but he tried to help the best he could.

"My whole life is people," Father Scantlin would say. "My whole life has been somebody else."

You had to love people not to be worn down by this work. Even so, Jim was impatient for his own ordination. His outgoing nature seemed well-suited to the role of a "parish hack."

After a short break, Father Knoebel yielded the floor to Professor Robert Gotcher, the registrar, who handed out each seminarian's course plan. Unlike other schools, where schedules changed from semester to semester, Sacred Heart, with its significant number of required courses, could map out a plan for each man's entire program and, most dramatically, state when the man would be ordained. The registrar emphasized that the plans were tentative, but each man scrutinized his plan as if it were an exact road map of the years to come.

Dean Haley focused so intently on the piece of paper in front of him that he no longer heard Professor Gotcher. He did not grasp the word "tentative." Instead, he read that he had four years — actually, three years and nine months — before he was scheduled to take his vows as a transitional deacon. Six months later, he would take his vows as a priest. Dean had entered the seminary with a vague idea that he had at least six years to go before that happened. Six years was a long time. Six years was a fifth of his life so far. But three years and nine months . . . He felt a rush somewhere between anxiety and exhilaration, then had a string of panicky thoughts: *Permanent! One thousand days! Three years! I'm still going to be me! Whatever metamorphosis is supposed to happen has to happen in three years! I'm not ready!*

When the young Texan had first started dating his ex-girlfriend, his cousin had warned her not to fall in love with Dean because he was thinking about becoming a priest. At the time, however, Dean was resisting the call. When he had first seen her at a wedding, he had felt strongly enough about her that he had thought, *How can this be happening?* From the start, their religious differences had posed a problem. She was an Evangelical Christian. He had asked her the night they met if she had a problem dating a Catholic. No problem, she'd answered. From time to time, however, she would ask him when he was going to convert.

"To what?" Dean would respond.

"To Christianity," she would answer. She'd always made it sound like a joke.

After they had been dating for a while, Dean had a dream that haunted him. He was in a big, round room, shaking hands with her family. There were hundreds of people milling about, and then an announcement came over a loudspeaker: "Would all those resolved to be a priest, please exit to Room 5 now . . . Room 5 *now.*" Without a moment's hesitation, Dean said, "See ya," and walked out. Soon after he had that dream, they broke up, and Dean began applying to the seminary.

Father Knoebel was speaking once again. "Plagiarism is *the* mortal sin of academic institutions. If there is anything that the priesthood cannot stand, it is priests you cannot trust."

Professor Gotcher passed out the *Handbook for Academic Policies and Procedures in the Master of Divinity Program.* In addition to policy, it was filled with course descriptions. The array of academic offerings excited Dean but may have been intimidating to some of the men in the room, many of whom had been out of school for decades. Dean read: "Selected Figures and Topics in Western Philosophy in the 19th and 20th Centuries," wherein a student was to demonstrate his ability to express correctly the views of Hegel on the "rational" structure of being and Heidegger and Sartre on human existence and freedom. "Introduction to Theology I," wherein a student will show his ability to "analyze some basic scriptural, theological and liturgical issues that will eventually be expanded upon and deepened in later, specific courses." "Church History 1500 to Present," which would explore the "major factors that lead to the Protestant Reformation such as the new learning, state power, and papal abuses." "Human Sexuality," described as having "the specific purpose . . . to give the student the foundational knowledge necessary to hear confessions and to give spiritual pastoral advice" and requiring the student to be able "to discuss knowledgeably the basic principles of the Magisterium in reference to human sexual behavior." "Fundamental Preaching Skills," in which "students will demonstrate their ability . . . to employ the principles of public speaking proficiently. Proficiency includes appropriate use of the voice and the body as a medium of communication."

"Your major challenge isn't academic," Father Knoebel said as if he were picking up on both the trepidation and the enthusiasm in the room. "It is spiritual."

The men would question their vocation and their worthiness, he continued. They would get depressed. All this was normal. The seminarian who did not experience these things was, in fact, the exception.

"Some of you need humility," he said. "Some of you will have humility forced upon you. Please don't leave in the first week. It's taken a lot to get here."

He paused.

"Think about it. If you want to sabotage [God's] plans, you can. You can walk out of here tomorrow, and people have. Stay to January, and if you leave then, you will at least know what Wisconsin is like."

Whenever anyone took a dig at Father Brackin, Jim Pemberton would defend him by saying that the rector was at the bottom of the biggest funnel in Wisconsin. The job of rector meant making tough calls and handling every complaint, crisis, and issue that a school of eighty seminarians could generate. It meant cleaning up messes, facing criticism, and earning little praise.

From those directing the orientation, the new men soon learned about two of the most fabled crises their rector had faced during his tenure at Sacred Heart: the seminarian whose sudden death went unreported for several days and the suicide on the loading dock. What they didn't learn was how these crises had played out for the man at the bottom of the funnel.

According to institutional legend, the first crisis involved a seminarian who had died in his room and had not been discovered for days. His neighbors, baffled by the bad smell, had lit incense and sprayed disinfectant in the halls. The facts were less extreme. The incident had occurred over a three-day weekend when many men had gone away. The seminarian had died on Friday and was discovered on Sunday. The man's neighbors had possibly lit incense, but their main shortcoming was not reporting the smell to Father Brackin sooner.

A sense of failure affected many seminarians after the incident, so Father Brackin had had to reassure the community that there was nothing they could have done for the man. He had died of a massive heart attack. Even if he had been discovered a minute later, he still would have died. Nevertheless, the rector explored how the men could do a better job of looking after one another. Sacred Heart was not run on the strict monastic principles that controlled the movements of students at some other seminaries. The men here were older, and many had diverse obligations outside school. They came and went with a high degree of independence. From that point on, however, Father Brackin decided that if a seminarian didn't see either of his neighbors during the course of the day, he was supposed to check up on them.

The second crisis, the suicide, left a deeper mark on the rector and the community. Father Brackin had told Jim Heely that he had to leave Sacred Heart. The seminarian had an alcohol problem but refused to get help. The formation department had been wrestling with the issue for more than a year. The rector felt that he had no choice but to send Jim home. Even so, he had given Jim a week to think over whether he would reconsider. The day before Jim was scheduled to leave, one of the staff found him hanging in the room next to the loading dock. The staff member told Father Brackin. The rector had a seminarian call 911 and went to the room to see for himself. Even years later, whenever he entered that room, Father Brackin expected to see Jim hanging there. As a priest and as a medic in Vietnam, Father Brackin had experienced death. But he had never been so close to someone who had felt so much despair that he took his own life. He also believed that Jim's suicide was an act of violence against the Sacred Heart community. It was done in a public place; Jim must have wanted to shock.

One thing Father Brackin knew about himself was that he shone in a crisis. He could put aside his emotions — emotions that he would invariably have to deal with later — and do what had to be done for those around him. Fortunately, the seminary had resources to deal with the suicide: classes could be canceled, seminarians could talk it out in formation or counseling sessions, and Catholicism offered rituals that could bring solace and some sense of proportion. Jim was estranged from his family, but Sacred Heart managed to find a sister who would attend his funeral. The school also secured a gravesite. Although people who committed suicide were at one time not permitted burial in a church plot, this was no longer the case. The new thinking was that such a person was generally in such an extreme state of despair that he or she couldn't think clearly and thus lacked the true intent to end his or her own life.

Father Brackin picked up Jim's sister at the airport. He had made certain that Jim's room had not been disturbed, in the event that his family might come. He showed the woman to the room. She took the only thing of monetary value, a Hummel figurine, and left the rest.

Father Brackin asked his group of advisers, called the rector's cabinet, whether anyone would be open to delivering the homily at the funeral. No one offered, and the job fell to him. Afterward, he thought that it had been one of his finest.

"Where were you, God?" he shouted at the pews. "Why did you let this happen?"

In the homily, God answered. God had been with Jim through the whole thing, even in his moments of despair. The image that Father Brackin developed was of Jim on the chair, then kicking the chair out from underneath himself; the cord tightening around his neck, killing him; and God catching his spirit and embracing it. He could never abandon his creation.

The burial was the following day. Father Brackin never blamed himself for Jim's death, because he believed that the seminary had done everything within its power to reach him.

Bob Brooks and Ron Kendzierski sat down at a table with their lunch trays. Jim Pemberton and another man were discussing the importance of a good homily and how many priests missed this opportunity to evangelize. The causes were many: laziness, poor training, an anemic prayer life, a thick accent (more frequent as priests were imported from other countries to fill American ranks). The result was disappointing: the once-a-week chance for the priest to reach out to his people was squandered.

Bob moved the napkin basket as Ron was reaching for it.

"Schmuck," Ron said when the napkin wasn't there.

Somehow the conversation turned to other things. Bob told a story about a collection-robbing priest in Mexico. Ron recounted how his aunt had angrily confronted a priest for driving a Cadillac.

"I'm carrying Jesus," the priest had retorted. "You wouldn't want Jesus driving around in a Ford."

That reminded Bob of a story about a rector who told a long-haired seminarian to get a haircut. The seminarian objected and showed the rector a picture of Jesus.

"Look," he said, "Jesus had long hair."

The rector took the seminarian outside to a swimming pool and pointed.

"Walk on that."

After lunch, the men gathered in Classroom 3 to take their academic assessment tests. All except Ron, who would be taking the test on a computer, had their freshly sharpened No. 2 pencils ready to go. Professor Gotcher informed them that there would be no academic

repercussions from the tests, which included a college English placement test and the Nelson-Denny Reading Test. They would have two
and a half hours to finish. There was also a booklet, called the *Kolb
Learning Style Inventory,* that Professor Gotcher instructed them to fill
out and turn in later to the academic department. The purpose of
this assessment was to determine how each seminarian learned. The
inventory included four main learning styles and various hybrids of
the four. Although the assessment never seemed to have any direct
academic consequences at Sacred Heart, students sometimes used it
to explain some particular academic result or trait. In some cases, it
seemed to help improve a student's study habits or self-confidence.

After the first test was handed in, the men were giddy.

"What was an auk?" asked someone about a vocabulary word on
the test.

"A bird," Bob answered. "When it sees people it goes, *Auk . . . auk
. . . auk . . .*"

Long before the idea of becoming a priest had entered Heiser's
mind, the state of Wyoming was his vocation. This calling began as a
vague notion in a suburban Pennsylvanian's mind. He thought it
would be good to move away from the congestion of the eastern
seaboard, perhaps to somewhere west of the Mississippi, maybe
the Rocky Mountains. Born and raised near Philadelphia in a Ukrainian Catholic family, Heiser had attended Roman Catholic schools
for twelve years. The Ukrainian Church is united with the Roman
Church but differs in many ways. For instance, the Eucharist, both
bread and wine, is served together on a spoon and has the consis-
tency of cottage cheese; the Mass goes on for hours; and priests, but
not bishops, can marry. In the United States, most Ukrainian Catholics live in the East, but even there they often must avail themselves
of Roman Catholic resources, such as schools. Although Heiser attended a Roman Catholic school during the week, his family belonged to a Ukrainian church, where he served as an altar boy and
learned to pray in Ukrainian.

Heiser made a tentative stab at college, attending a local Penn

State satellite, while he tried to figure out what to do with the rest of his life. The idea of going west grew more attractive, and one day he made his way to the college library and dug out some school catalogs. The University of Wyoming sounded good. The out-of-state tuition there was equal to Penn State's in-state tuition, and, more important, Wyoming was the least populated state in the Union. It had a few hundred thousand people but was larger in size than Pennsylvania. There would be room to breathe and space to roam. He transferred without delay.

Wyoming more than lived up to his expectations. He hiked, camped, and hunted with a shotgun and a bow. He met Daniel Ortiz, nicknamed "Danny 'O,'" an Arapaho Indian who became his roommate and friend. He also found a bird dog that lived to chase down pheasants and a landscape that spoke to him in a profound way. Wyoming became his best friend and constant companion — this land where the snow fell so deeply that the highways were lined with measuring poles ten feet high and a pickup truck could be blown off the road by the wind.

Heiser couldn't imagine ever moving back to Pennsylvania. Even the small town where he grew up had a stoplight at every intersection now and a growing population that threatened to outstrip the infrastructure. He definitely didn't miss the stunted horizons, the inability to see for miles, or the sense of being hemmed in by trees and houses.

He had been living in Wyoming for twenty-five years when he arrived at Sacred Heart. He missed it every day, but he knew that he would be going back. He had a postcard of the Teton Range on the corkboard in his room, his pack hung on the back of his door, his pickup truck had a bunk that served for short camping trips, and in every class he sat facing the windows so he could keep an eye on the weather and the doings outdoors.

The next day was humid — mild in the morning, but with the promise of severe thunderstorms that night. At nine A.M., all the new students gathered in the IHM Chapel, the worship space for small groups and seniors practicing how to say Mass. It was tucked into a corner of the sprawling basement and had a provisional look: chairs instead of pews, a movable wooden altar and lectern, a few bright tapestries on the walls. Dean Haley arrived late, to find everyone already sitting in an oval. There was a small table covered with purple and white flowers in the middle. A single candle burned in a glass vase beside a red prayer book.

This morning's event was considered by faculty and students alike to be the high point of orientation week. It was the first and last time that each man would have a chance to share the story of his vocation with his fellow seminarians and the priests and nuns who made up the spiritual formation faculty.

There are really two kinds of formation at a Roman Catholic seminary: the general process of turning a layman into an ordained priest and the internal process of exploring the convergence of the spiritual and practical aspects of being a priest. The latter process is spiritual formation. As at most seminaries, spiritual formation had its own department at Sacred Heart, and its director was Father Martin Barnum, a genial priest from Chicago who, like most of the faculty and staff at Sacred Heart, maintained an open-door policy. It was his job to ensure that the seminarians were developing a balanced priestly spirituality that would later translate into a healthy and effective ministry. Social, psychological, and sexual issues all were within the scope of his work, as was spiritual direction, the development of a seminarian's prayer life through one-on-one consultations.

Today's forum kicked off this process by exploring the basic question of what had brought the men to Sacred Heart. Father Marty told them that if the events of years past were any indicator, this session would be a powerful and intimate witness to faith and result in a bonding of the group before the mystery of their calling. As if to underscore this mystery, the men's and women's storytelling would take place during Mass in lieu of the homily. He urged everyone to be candid and to respect one another's confidences. What was said in the room was to stay there.

"We are here because of a calling," Father Marty said with passion. "We of faith believe it is Providence. Our stories are sacred because they involve God working in our lives."

The Old Testament reading was followed by the Gospel, then one by one, the men and women shared their stories. Some of the stories were straightforward, uncomplicated accounts of people who, long immersed in their faith, found religious life the natural next step. Some told of a chipping away at their resistance until all the internal obstacles to entering the religious life were gone. Some told of external obstacles that suddenly disappeared. One man recounted that while his wife was being lowered into her grave, his sister whispered to him, "Now you can become a priest." Another man fell into silence as he spoke of losing his wife to cancer. A nun spoke of choosing the religious life over romantic love and after two decades reported that she had made the right choice. One seminarian spoke of an angry dialogue he had with God over his choice between the woman he planned to marry and the priesthood.

As each person shared his or her story, the session grew more intense, moving from drama to comedy and back again. When they returned from lunch, the chapel had grown hotter and more humid. A little blue fan was set on a stool, and tiny Sister Lucille lugged a dehumidifier in from her office.

When it was time for Dean Haley to share, he, like some of the others, recounted memories of "playing priest" as a child — holding an imaginary host, saying imaginary words of consecration. But the moment that set him on the path to Sacred Heart came in college. With his marine medic background, he had gotten a job making home visits to a paraplegic student. The student had a girlfriend, a beautiful woman. Dean had to show her how to clean up the man's excrement. He asked if she could do this. She didn't hesitate: yes. Driving home, Dean kept thinking, *I will never find someone who would do that for me. Never. And I never want to settle for a commitment less than that.*

Late that night, four of the more senior seminarians — three second-year students and one nearing his ordination — sat around a table in the dining hall shooting the breeze. The gathering had become an almost nightly occurrence the previous year, when they had stayed up writing papers and smoking cigarettes into the early hours of the morning. In the dining hall, they could talk, grab a smoke outside the nearby door, have something to drink, talk some more, grab another smoke. Except for the exit signs, all the lights were extinguished that night. The lamps that lined the paths and drives outside cast a soft glow on everything, and the lights of the long hallway to the main lounge barely sliced into the dark. The drink machines hummed, and every so often the icemaker made a sound like knuckles cracking.

Perhaps it was the darkness or the vaguely illicit quality of the gathering, but the shadow-sketched men ringing the table — chairs pushed back, legs outstretched, fingers toying with empty Styrofoam cups — were something of a Greek chorus for the institution. The opinions expressed were unvarnished, often petulant, and sometimes prophetic.

"How much do you get?" one of the second-year students asked the man in his final year.

"Fifty dollars," he said, referring to the monthly stipend his diocese paid him as a seminarian. Dioceses differed in how they supported their priest candidates. Some paid travel expenses, usually one roundtrip airfare home a year. Others paid only for books and health insurance.

"Annual salary?"

"Eight hundred fifty a month."

"Is that before taxes?"

The senior seminarian thought for a moment.

"Gross or net?" the second-year student said.

"I guess it's net." The man sighed. "We're not going to get rich doing this, boys." He had been an executive for a Fortune 500 company who had raised five kids on his own. If he had wanted the money, he would have remained in business.

The second-year student changed the subject. Sacred Heart wasn't real, he observed. It was a way station. They were being called not to become seminarians, but parish priests. To get there, you had to keep your head down and your opinions to yourself, and navigate this frequently ridiculous obstacle course.

"It's artificial," he continued. As a Vietnam vet, he saw significant parallels to military life. "It's like what we did in the army. 'Okay, men, we want you to learn how to do this over here — that's why we're *not* going to teach you that. We're going to go over here and teach you this instead.'"

So the way he saw it, they lived in this unreal world during the school year, then moved back into the real world of parish life during the summer — although that life wasn't all that real either, at least not until ordination lifted them above the seminarian caste. One of the men mentioned a seminarian who had spent an entire summer planting a lawn at the rectory where he was stationed. The senior seminarian nodded. He had repaired a fence, cut grass, and cut down four trees during his assignment one summer.

"You get to do what the priest doesn't want to do," he said.

The second-year students questioned the value of formation. They had already been active in parish life for decades. Didn't they know enough to serve as priests without several years of formal education? Sometimes it felt as if they were inmates in a prison, counting the days until freedom. For them, freedom was ordination. Some men even ticked off the days on their calendars.

One thousand four hundred ten days to go, one of them said with a wary smile.

Father Brackin wanted to begin on time, but two of the new men were missing.

"It's not good to be late for the rector's meeting," observed Dean Haley, making a rare on-time appearance himself.

When the stragglers arrived, the rector led the group in a brief prayer. Then he explained why he was dressed in a blue polo shirt and black slacks.

"I apologize, but I had my annual physical, so I didn't have time to change. I hope all of you also are committed to at least annual physicals. I'm fifty-six. I've been doing them since the age of forty, and two years ago next month, because of an annual physical, my prostate cancer was discovered. If I hadn't gotten regular physicals — because I had a very aggressive form of cancer — I might not be here right now. So if you don't get regular physicals, I hope that you do, and particularly get PSA testing."

This revelation was typical of Father Brackin. He was matter-of-fact and practical, and he discussed even something as traumatic as his cancer in such a way that it was at once personal to him and useful to the seminarians. From the beginning, he had involved the students in the details of his treatment, even going so far as to tell them about his temporary use of diapers because of the side effects. He was determined to take advantage of this opportunity to serve as a model of how a Catholic priest should respond to such an illness. In seminary life and the priestly apprenticeship that followed ordination, this kind of thing was often referred to as a "teaching moment." The phrase usually applied to less urgent matters — how to avoid tripping over their robes during Mass; how to appeal to parishioners for increased financial contributions without sounding shrill; how to deal with power-hungry parish council members without alienating them.

In this teaching moment, Father Brackin was saying that a priest suffering from a grave illness should have hope because he believes in eternal life. He should not become absorbed with his condition because that would be selfish, nor should he neglect his health or ignore his condition because that would likewise be selfish. He should be humble and share even embarrassing facts if there was a chance that doing so could help others.

Father Brackin rattled off the men's names and their sponsoring dioceses. He joked that he told each class that if he didn't learn somebody's name in the first two weeks, that man would have to go. This year, he noted, it was easier to learn the names because the numbers were down. He briefly told the men about himself. He had been selected as rector ten years before. Although he had not wanted the job, he had accepted it. His attitude as a religious, he said, had always been to say yes to the community's needs.

"I'm principally chief pastor and chief administrator of the seminary. Hopefully, as chief pastor I am sensitive to your needs, encourage you when you're down. As chief administrator I see my role as creating an environment in which priestly formation can happen."

He told the men that there were no checklists. If they missed Mass, no one would be banging down their doors to find out why they had missed. But there were limits. If they missed Mass for a week, their spiritual formation advisers would probably say something, and, Father Brackin hoped, so would their fellow seminarians.

Father Brackin told them that under canon law, he was required to make a recommendation to a seminarian's bishop regarding the man's fitness for priesthood (a recommendation that the bishop was free to accept or reject). But this meant that he had an obligation to get to know each seminarian so that he could make the recommendation in good conscience. His canonical responsibilities also meant that he sometimes had to play the heavy.

Next Father Brackin tackled a topic that was discussed in confidential — sometimes histrionic — tones around the seminary: end-of-the-year evaluations. Most of the new seminarians had already heard about the student who had been approved for priesthood by a majority of the faculty but had been a few votes shy of unanimity. In fact, some of the new men had actually met him at mealtime. Sacred Heart permitted him to hang around for a few days while he got his things together and planned his next move. The perception was that his bishop had used the lack of unanimity to decide against the man's ordination — after having supported him for four years at Sacred Heart. Most of the seminarians drew the same conclusion: the vote might not be binding on a bishop, but it could have consequences.

The new men listened closely as Father Brackin offered a glimpse into the evaluation process. The director of spiritual formation, the academic dean, and the head of field education (if the student had reached his department) all made presentations. Then there was a general faculty discussion, followed by a vote on whether, and under what conditions, the candidate would be moved forward to the next year or, in the case of his last year, toward ordination. Father Brackin did not tell the seminarians everything. He did not tell them, for example, that he capped the faculty discussion at five minutes, because he had found that if it grew negative, the negativity would build on itself and a clear picture of the candidate would become hopelessly muddied. He didn't speak about how clashing personalities could play a role in souring a faculty member on a candidate. If asked, he would cite the numerous checks and balances built into the system — how the years of reports and assessments, the quiet and informal observation of the candidate as he lived in the community, and the importance of a general consensus worked to counter such subjective problems.

"Usually there aren't any issues during an evaluation," he said. "But one of the things that I will *guarantee* is that you will know, well in advance, of any difficulties before that vote. You meet regularly with your formation adviser. He or she will be raising issues with you as things come up. Things will never be a surprise."

He also countered some persistent scuttlebutt. "Please do not believe students who've been here more than a year who say to you, 'If you have to go to see the rector, there's a problem.'" Father Brackin sounded just the slightest bit annoyed. "Please do not believe that. That is *not* true. There might be an issue, but simply because I have to see you doesn't mean that there's a problem."

He told them that he could count on one hand the number of people whom he had asked to leave the school during his tenure. Nevertheless, there were some big pitfalls that he felt obliged to warn them about.

First was the difference between internal forum and external forum. "Internal forum refers to your relationship with your spiritual director. Whatever you share with your spiritual director is confidential, with three exceptions: one, if you're going to injure yourself; the other is if you're going to injure somebody else; or the third if you have been involved in sexual abuses with minors . . . Those are three things required by law in terms of reporting." Unlike spiritual direction, Father Brackin said, the sacrament of reconciliation, still commonly known as confession, was totally inviolable. If a priest were to reveal anything he learned from a confession, no matter what it was, he would face immediate suspension.

Almost everything else was external forum. That meant watch what you say. "Whatever you might share in the classroom, with your formation adviser, dinner conversation — those relationships are *not* privileged, and so I don't want you to have the illusion that they are. They cannot promise you confidentiality. If you were to come to see me, *I* can't promise you confidentiality. In fact, as the rector of the seminary, I cannot even hear your confession. The only exception to that is the danger of death."

Precisely because of this concern that private information might get out, some of the older seminarians were already telling the new men to bring an innocuous issue, such as organizational skills or time management, to their formation advisers each week just to have "something to work on." In this way, they could avoid discussing more sensitive issues. Whether rumors about such information having been leaked were true or not, this practice was evidence of the calculating way some of the seminarians approached the formation process. It was as if they saw their time at Sacred Heart as a prolonged job interview. One could not really say to one's formation adviser, "No problems here," just as someone asked about his weaknesses by a job interviewer could not reasonably reply, "Weaknesses? What weaknesses?" Father Brackin abhorred this kind of practice.

He continued, "You also need to be aware that in terms of the external forum, anything that I know about you, your bishop has the absolute right to know. That's a responsibility of canon law. Now believe me, I don't have conversations with your bishop daily, but if I know something about your suitability for ministry, I have to share that with him. Any questions?"

The room was silent for a long time. Dean Haley remembered

the diocese's required psychological testing and how he had finally drawn the line when they requested that he take a polygraph exam. "This is the end of the road," he barked into the phone at the vocation director. "No more testing." He had already been required to view photos that included pictures of men, women, children, and lingerie, accompanied by a checklist to rate his levels of attraction. Dean found the photographs strange and menacing. He over-analyzed them, wondering what the psychologists were trying to ferret out. One photo, shot through a window, showed an attractive woman inside a house. Dean wondered what he was supposed to think. If he found her attractive, did the context matter? Would his attraction be understood as voyeurism? As photo followed photo, Dean began to sweat and doubt himself.

The written portion of the test he'd been required to take also had been disturbing. One question asked whether he dressed in women's clothing. Dean had done so once for a pageant in high school, so he answered yes to the question. Later, a psychologist quizzed him on this answer. "So what about your cross-dressing?" Dean fumbled through an explanation. By the time the demand for a polygraph test arose, Dean was fed up. His vocation director heard Dean's determination and brought the matter to the bishop. The demand was dropped.

"One of the reasons the Church is in the critical times it's in with reference to sexual child abuse is because we kept secret too much information," Father Brackin said. "In the past, there were horrible situations where Father X was taking altar boys into his bedroom and Father Y knew he was doing that — he may not have known what he was doing in there — but never said anything."

Father Brackin's voice rose with indignation. "We *do* have a responsibility for one another. So, if you see one of your brothers here in inappropriate behavior that would affect his suitability for ministry, you have an obligation to make that known. Now it's not that we want everybody to be spies, but if you know something, you can't say, 'Well, it's not my responsibility.' It *is* your responsibility."

Father Brackin looked at the men.

"Any questions?"

There were none.

"You're all so obedient."

Then it was on to more mundane matters covered in the student handbook: taking the fire alarm seriously; telling any hunters that firearms were not permitted on the property, even in the trunk of one's car.

Dean leaned forward and said carefully, as if he were testing a parent, "I don't have these items, but can we have bow weapons?"

Father Brackin looked amused. "I need to think about that, Dean," he finally said.

"I don't have these items with me," Dean repeated.

"Okay, don't bring them then."

"I just shoot them for recreation," Dean said. "There's an archery range close by."

Father Brackin reminded them that it was a smoke-free building and about quieting down in the hallways by ten P.M.

"I'll tell you an incident that happened when I was a student here," he said. "It was probably about eleven o'clock at night, midwinter. Do they still have Cold Duck anymore?"

"Wine?" Bob Brooks asked.

"Yeah, wine. When I was a student here, we'd buy Cold Duck. In the winter, we would open up our windows and tie a string to hang the bottle out. We were drinking, and as seminarians will do — and I'm sure you will *never* do this — but as seminarians, we would sit around talking about one another. It was getting a little wild. So Jim Keefe, who lived across the hallway, yelled something, a few expletives to pipe down, but we continued to talk. Jim was really angry, and Charlie Murato was coming out of the stairwell and turned right toward Jim's room, and Jim opened the door and slugged him because he thought he was the one making the noise."

Father Brackin laughed. The men looked a little surprised but laughed, too.

"Oh, yeah, he slugged him," Father Brackin repeated. "We were much younger than you are. Anyway, please quiet down. But even if you don't quiet down, please don't slug anyone.

"Any questions before I talk to you a little bit about God?"

Philip Kim had a question. He could be much quieter, he told Father Brackin with a mischievous smile, if there was a smoking room on the third floor. Was there any chance?

"You know, I hear you," Father Brackin said. "But it won't happen."

"Yes, sir," Philip said.

"I'll help you quit it," the rector offered.

Philip smiled.

Then Father Brackin gathered himself. Instantly, it seemed that he had become more priestly before their eyes.

"You have made this journey to come here because God is moving your life. The Holy Spirit has touched you in such a way to give you an inkling of an indication that God *might* be calling you to priest-hood. The Spirit is stirring, conjuring that path for you. *Please* be faithful to a pattern of prayer. Be committed to establishing a pattern of prayer. It's in that stance of receptivity that you listen to the Holy Spirit.

"Now the academicians don't like me to say this, but believe me, when you leave here as a priest, the people of God certainly want you to have adequate theological knowledge — they do, and they have a right to expect that. But more importantly, they expect you to be a *holy* person. They really expect you to be somebody who is in *love* with Jesus. Someone who is committed to continuing to grow in intimacy with God and who is open to assisting them in their own journeys. You're gonna be tempted to cut short your prayer. I'd just advise you not to do that.

"Don't be so locked into a particular pattern or way of praying that you're going to close yourself off to other ways that God may be calling you to prayer. Be open to being surprised by God. God isn't finished with us until we move through the curtain of death to the eternal."

His voice grew almost combative. "The most divisive thing that can happen to you is if you embrace a spirit of being critical — and I mean critical in terms of judging and evaluating everything. Be open to the process. Let God work with you as you move through this formation process, and don't be so quick to think that you know there's a better way of doing it. Let's just say that the Church has been doing this for a long time, and it's worked out pretty well. Immerse yourself in the process. Try not to go kicking and screaming too much."

His voice grew gentler. "God has been intimately in love with you from the moment of your conception, from the moment he thrust you into created reality. Sometimes we locate our relationship with God in our head. Our relationship with God is in our heart. Studying theology is a head experience, but let that experience also come into your heart."

He surveyed the room. Many of the men were his age or older.

"Given your ages, you've already trusted God, or you wouldn't be here. Some of you have left jobs, left security, and here you are. From the outside, unless people see this as a venture of faith, most people are going to think we're absolutely crazy."

There was a ripple of laughter.

"Otherwise, why would you be moving into a nine-by-twelve room, giving up a certain amount of control of your life? I mean, why would you be doing that?"

That night at the round table in the dining hall, the second-year students discussed the story of the Sacred Heart seminarian dropped by his diocese just before he was to enter his final year. They all knew him. The Vietnam vet gathered himself and thoughtfully clasped his hands.

"We're getting one side of the story," he observed. "A few people have said there were some issues he had. I like him, but . . ."

"They can do anything to you until you're ordained," another man said with resignation.

The vet described how things could go wrong. "One guy has a bad day. Teacher has a bad day. They get into a pissing match. It gets personal. After class, teacher talks to a few other teachers, and they say, 'Hmmm, I'll look out for that.' Ninety days later, you've got three votes against you."

How many votes would be terminal?

"They won't say this," the vet said conspiratorially, then held up five fingers.

"The Church has always been political and always will be," another man observed.

But there was also a different kind of politics. The men talked about how it seemed that the students were, by and large, conservative and the faculty was liberal. This led some students to keep their heads down, lest their ideologically more conservative opinions endangered their chances of becoming priests. But the men around the table were good-humored and nuanced about positions that, in the larger arena of Catholic debate, were often hardened and unmoving.

A case in point was their attitude toward *Goodbye, Good Men,* a book making the rounds at Sacred Heart, which alleged that an essentially "liberal" seminary system was actively preventing more "conservative" candidates — men who adhered to Catholic doctrine and traditional devotional activities such as saying the rosary — from becoming priests. The vet, who was just such a traditional Catholic, rejected the findings of the book and said that a lot of the problems cited had already been cleaned up. He believed that such accusations did not help the situation in the Church and predicted that in the end, flexible Catholics, both liberals and conservatives, would carry the Church forward into the future.

After the sexual abuse scandal of the past year, there was talk that an official review of seminaries would be coming directly from the Vatican.

"The inquisition," one of the men joked.

The vet said that it had been a long time coming, but everyone seemed to agree that any kind of review would be as futile as an inspector general's review in the military.

"You'd call South Carolina and ask for a favor. Can you send one hundred boots?" the vet said. "You'd get the one hundred boots and then send them back after the inspection. The wisdom is that at least once a year, the navy, the army, whatever, is up to snuff."

The vet changed gears and drew the gathering to an informal close with a story that he had recently heard from a vocation director.

The vocation director had a new priest helping him in his parish. The man had been ordained about a year. One day the vocation director returned to the parish after a short trip. The secretary asked him what he planned to do without the new man. Why would he be doing without him? the vocation director inquired. "He's leaving today to get married," the secretary replied matter-of-factly.

"I wonder if God ever breathes between laughing," the vet said, dissolving into laughter himself.

The hallway did not have lines or curves or angles or a visible texture. The hallway was a place outside the door. If the light were brighter, perhaps, it would have appeared as a lighter shadow, a smudge. But what was a smudge in his shapeless world? The sun outside the window was bright enough on certain days to be a lighter shadow. He loved the sun, the feel of the sun. He hated darkness and the short, gloomy days of midwestern winters. The keys had a texture to the touch — cold and jagged — and an order on the ring. First the sixteen key, then the key to Room 301, his room. That was how he could do things so smoothly, because everything was in its place. Solid objects spoke to him with a hush — a change of air around them. The long, cool walls of the hallway leading to Room 301 spoke with the hush if he could hear it over the *tap-tap-tap* of his cane. There were smells, too. On hot days, the pine trees seemed to sweat. On cold days, they smelled altogether different. But his sense of smell had never been very good. Allergies clogged his nose for most of the year.

The promise of radically improved senses — a gift for the loss of one's eyes — how had it been borne out? He could feel the contrast of space. He was set adrift in the expanse of the Sacred Heart Chapel, holding on to the pews like flotsam on the sea. He knew that when (soon, he thought; they always used him for his music) he played his violin in the chapel, he would fill it with a sense of human proportion.

Room 301, his room, was different. It was small enough that he could feel its shape, its squareness. When he entered, the bookshelf and scanner were to his right, the doorway to the bathroom to his left. The desk was at thigh level, the dresser at chest level, and the bed, which divided the room in half, at knee-level. No, not really in half. The bed just seemed to do this, when in fact it abutted the window and the radiator. On the wall beside the bed were bookshelves: books on the top shelf and a boom box in the middle. In this first week, the shelves were nearly bare. Later, a sombrero would be added, and still later, at Halloween, the gruesome electronic witch that cackled and cursed when squeezed.

Harm could appear from out of nowhere. A door left ajar in one's path might come out of the darkness like a fist. Testing and caution were part of his every movement — and his speech. His mind, more than most people's, scrupulously knit together past, present, and future, action and reaction, into a web. Was it a safety net or the thing that kept him from flight? Because there was another man who was not as careful. Someone just beneath the surface, who could be reckless, especially if another needed help. At night his dreams were a chaos of voices without sight. He wrote poetry, sculpted, and composed music. Once when he was doing the dishes, he balanced a teetering casserole dish on the sink's edge. "It's level and even," he muttered to himself, and the words of a poem came to him as he rushed to write them down.

> Just level and even somehow, somehow
> 'cause level and even somehow
> I don't quite know how it's level and even

nor am I acquainted with Jackie and Steven
but something inside me has got me believing
'tis level and even somehow
like sun to moon and dark to light
gray to blue and black to white
up to down and left to right
pain to joy and laughter bright
the secret signs which give us sight

Even as a former Eagle Scout and with two master's degrees, Ron Kendzierski had had to work hard to convince Gaylord, Michigan, to support him. In the end, they had, and Sacred Heart also had come through with a Braille printer worth thousands of dollars. The United States Conference of Catholic Bishops had even picked up the story of this blind seminarian and had featured it in an article on the new crop of American seminarians in 2002.

Just before Sacred Heart, Ron had tried another religious community, the Crosiers, in Minnesota, for a year. He hadn't found them very supportive of his blindness, and the strictures of their religious community chafed. He thought that a diocesan seminary and priesthood would be different — more outward-acting, less inward-looking. After six years of life in and around churches, playing music and teaching kids, this decision felt right.

But already there was friction. His vision of the priesthood was not the vision that was being outlined in the daily orientation sessions or talked about by the other men, whom he had already dubbed "super Catholics" to himself. They seemed far too focused on the idea of priesthood as an end in itself, rather than a means to an end. Ron fashioned his Christianity around social justice. He saw Christ as a liberating figure for the poor. He had memorized his Sunday school Catholicism and promptly forgot it after he passed the tests. He knew what he was supposed to believe: celibacy for priests, no birth control, bodily resurrection for the believer. *But that's just what the Catholic Church teaches,* he thought, not seeing the need to accept these teachings as his own. All the dogma, all the doctrines, all the different kinds of sin — these things seemed inessential to Ron's Catholicism. His vision was of a Church that performed good work, rolled up its sleeves and leaped into the trenches. Church was more about making the world a better place than it was about the preparation of one's soul for any afterlife. Ron would say that he had no intention of pushing dogma down somebody's throat. His was a more amiable model of a priest: a source of comfort for people who needed it; someone to make people smile.

Sacred Heart's focus was definitely not this, and Ron was already beginning to wonder whether he had made a mistake. He knew that his positions were not orthodox, but he had expected much more acceptance than he was finding. Did you really need to study how to say the Mass for a whole semester? Wouldn't it be better to spend the time out in the streets helping people? Ron was suspicious of those he saw as merely coming to church to punch their Christian time-cards. For many Catholics, he thought, going to Mass was kind of like zipping up their flies — just something somebody had told them they had to do. These were the people (his father was one) who were first in line to receive Communion, only to skip out before the closing prayer because they didn't want to get stuck in the parking lot. When he became a priest, Ron vowed, he would replace the pews with tables and chairs, and instead of a homily, there would be a group discussion of the Gospel. He deplored complacent, pious, and cliquey churchgoers. They would be the first to crucify Christ if he returned. Ron believed that the Church needed radical reform. Women should be ordained, priestly celibacy overturned, and everyone — not just baptized Catholics — able to receive the Eucharist.

He knew he would have to endure much that he didn't agree with, and to endure he would have to keep his head down and not broadcast his beliefs too widely. But in these first days, thoughts came out of the darkness like a door ajar to disrupt Ron's peace of mind: *You will have to sell your soul for the chalice. Leave.* But then, in defiance, *If you leave, you won't be able to fix anything.*

\*     \*     \*

"Everything that is out *there*," Father Jerry Higgins informed the new men, "is in *here* in a small way."

Dean Haley already knew this was true. One of the minor semi-narians had been eyeing him and had held the elevator doors open for an even longer look. He heard that the same man had been openly flirting with others. It was the last day of orientation, and all of the seminarians were gathered in Room 200 for a final presen-tation called "Transitions." Father Higgins drove the point home. What had the men expected before they came to Sacred Heart? Did they think it would be a perfect place where everybody prayed all the time and there was no study? Did they think everybody would be lovey-dovey? Did they think they could escape the world? If so, they needed to reexamine their assumptions.

Nervousness, doubt, and fear had shadowed the men during this first week. Each in his own way had probably been caught unawares by something and had suffered for it. But overall, everything was still so tentative and the institution so welcoming and supportive that the reality of their decision to begin life at the seminary had not really sunk in.

Many talked to the group about what they had given up to come to Sacred Heart. Bob Brooks spoke of the difficulty of leaving his dog.

"His name is Huck, and I felt like I had betrayed him, and I couldn't find a place and nobody would take him. None of my friends would take him, and, you know, it was the biggest part of turning my life over to God. I finally caught myself praying, 'You know, God, I think I love an old yellow dog more than I love you.'"

Bob chuckled and looked down at the floor. There was restrained laughter. It was almost as if the other men were waiting to see just how far Bob would go — as if they were taking their cue from him.

"'I don't even know how to love you, God,'" he continued. "'I mean, I don't even know *how*.' And then, you know, I started feeling like, sort of like, this sort of condemnation come out of me, like 'If you love me, you keep my commandments.' And then finally I just kinda felt like Jesus himself got real close to me and sort of whispered in my ear, 'You know, I love that old yellow dog even more than you do.' Getting up here, I cried a few times just leaving everything behind. And since I've been here, I mean y'all have just made it so easy on me. I don't know about the rest of y'all, but I even have to force myself at night to pray for the people back home, because I almost forgot about 'em."

Father Higgins had distributed a handout titled "Stages in Transition." This handout would not make things more real, but it did provide an outline for how things might *get* more real. The outline included four stages: "Before and Beginning SHST," "Now That You've Arrived — and into the Future," "The Dark Night," and "Recovery." Credit was given to Father Andre Papineau, a professor at Sacred Heart, from whose book, *Breaking Up, Down and Through,* it had been adapted.

Under the first stage, there were words such as "idealizations," "enchantments," "illusions," and "fear." Under the second, "transition reality," "let down," "doubt," "Why did I come here?" A little hand-drawn balloon with the word "Perfect" illustrated Stage I. In Stage II, the balloon had burst, "Bang." The placid illustration of a crescent moon and a few stars belied the harsh descriptions of Stage III: "Depression," "Betrayed," "Lost faith," and "Isolation." In the final stage, "Recovery" is achieved by seeking help through prayer and from professors, spiritual directors, and other students. At the top of the page, a jagged line ran from I through IV like the squiggles on a seismograph, calm in Stage I, getting more severe in the chaos and displacement of Stages II and III, and settling down again by Stage IV.

Max, a deacon, shared next. If anyone had worried that Bob had upped the ante for intimacy, they were immediately reassured. Deacon Max sounded the retreat by speaking with gruff resignation.

"We don't have say-so in anything," Deacon Max announced. "Everything's going to be chosen for us, and it's for our own benefit, and we might as well just enjoy the ride."

Such apparent pragmatism in the face of divine will might have seemed reasonable to Deacon Max, but it was unsatisfactory to Father Higgins. He wanted the group to embrace the certainty that things would get tougher and that they would come to doubt almost everything.

"Do not decide your vocation at five to five in the morning," Father Higgins advised. "You're sitting on the edge of your bed and wondering why you are in this. Get up, go have breakfast."

Sacred Heart's near-constant preoccupation with the viability of a religious life did not seem odd to most of those within its walls. The formation faculty understood the struggles of such a commitment. A vocation was not something that could be complacently assumed or secured with platitudes.

There was an ever-present background whisper at the seminary: A successful religious life is like a bumblebee flying. It is something that shouldn't really happen in a broken world, with human nature such as it is, but it does happen, and certain things help make it possible. One of these things, paradoxically, is the acceptance of just how hard religious life can be. If seminary is like boot camp (a comparison Dean Haley was quick to make), there is one crucial difference: the drill sergeant of the seminary is almost exclusively internal — a ranting, excoriating busybody within the seminarian himself. That drill sergeant is prompted by the external reality of Sacred Heart, especially its academic and formation offerings, and by its professed purpose. The drill sergeant will question the seminarian's worthiness, his fitness, his desire for the religious life. Then, just when all of these things seem sorted out, he'll turn right around and demand whether the priestly life is worthy of the man's lifelong commitment or, worse, turn into the sudden atheist and question the existence of God.

"*Fraters, fraters,*" Father Higgins urged, knowing the crises of faith that awaited them. "*Remember* Jesus is God. Mary is his mother. *That* has not changed."

Few of the new men could fathom what the priest meant or imagine how accurate a picture of the future was to be found in the seismographic squiggles on the handout. Dean Haley already had a sense of it. So did Ron Kendzierski.

The weekend between the end of orientation and the arrival of the returning seminarians was limbo. A casual reception with beer and wine, Ping-Pong and pool was held up in the fourth-floor lounge and soon devolved into a drinking party for some of the men, most notably Dean. He had spent the early evening tweaking the DVD player on his laptop for optimal movie viewing. He showed the system to Bobby Rodriguez and Mike Snyder while it played *Training Day* in his cluttered room, where a large plaster bust of Pope John Paul II sat atop an old school desk with heavy drawers and stubby legs. Next to the old desk was Dean's new computer desk, fresh from Wal-Mart and assembled by Mike. Dean told the men that everything on his laptop — his schedules and various other organizational material — would automatically go on his desktop. Everything on his desktop would synchronize with his Palm Pilot.

"Without it, I'm lost," he said.

Mike wondered what would happen if the power went out.

Dean dipped under the school desk and emerged with a red, briefcase-size piece of equipment with a lamp in one corner.

"Juice," Dean said, striking a triumphal note. It was his mini-generator/emergency light, a gift from a parishioner back home.

The next morning, while Dean slept in, Ron, Mike, Bob Brooks, and a couple of others piled into Deacon Max's van for the ride to the Mexican festival at the fairgrounds on the shores of Lake Michigan. It promised to be a hot day. It was already humid inside the faintly moldy van.

"Smart to wear long sleeves," Mike said to Deacon Max.

"I'm as dumb as they come," Deacon Max said.

"No, I *mean* it's smart. I'm gonna burn," Mike said.

When they reached an intersection in downtown Milwaukee, Bob saw a dog.

"What a cute dog!" he exclaimed.

The dog stopped in the middle of the street and, as Bob narrated, relieved itself.

"Right now," Bob said, "we're not seeing its best side."

They waited at the kiosk that would soon start selling tickets. Patrick Smith, a soft-spoken Mississippian in his fifties, wore a wide-brimmed hat, smoked a cigar he had purchased on the Internet, and wandered around looking like a southern sheriff. Ron stood at the center of the small group, hugging the wall of the kiosk to avoid the beating sun. Mike complimented Bob on his tan work boots, worn with shorts and a T-shirt with a big picture of Jesus on the back. Bob said that he had tried to cover up his tattoos with the boots, but he had failed.

"I'm an animal rights activist, environmental activist . . . but I've given it up for Jesus," he joked. He pulled down his sock to reveal more of the swirling tattoo.

"People ask what it means," he said, pointing to the abstract design. "And I say it means I was drunk."

Somehow the subject of skiing came up.

"Do you ski?" Mike asked.

Bob said no, but to everyone's surprise, Ron said that he did. "I haven't been skiing for a few years," he said. "I had some run-ins with trees and poles."

After they made their way through the chaos of ticket holders lined up at the metal detectors and bag checks, Ron made a beeline for the beer tent.

"Where'd he go?" Mike asked, bewildered. Mike had become very protective of Ron over the course of the week and shepherded him about the school. "He doesn't even have his cane," Mike said as he scanned the crowd.

At the bar in the beer tent, Deacon Max bought Miller Lites for himself, Ron, Mike, and Mark, a man about Dean's age who was starting the undergraduate part of the Sacred Heart program.

"I sold my business, got rid of everything," Deacon Max said. "All I have are my two cars."

"That's kind of like diving from the high board and not knowing if there's any water in the pool," Ron said.

Deacon Max shrugged.

Later, some of the men ate, then wandered among the stalls crammed with a confusing array of items for sale. A Virgin of Guadalupe serape shared shelf space with a poster of an armed and bloody Al Pacino from *Scarface,* sweatshirts covered with American flags, Indian jewelry, plastic flowers, and balloons.

Mike and Mark stopped in front of a poster depicting the Aztec god Quetzalcoatl, who was wearing a feather headdress and carrying a limp, bosomy maiden up a flight of stairs to be sacrificed.

"That would look good in Dean's room with the black light," Mike said. Dean had installed a black light on his wall, believing that it would help him sleep more soundly.

Mike's glasses broke, and Mark thought he might have a replacement screw in his pocket. Instead, he found a religious relic. A relic is any object, usually part of the body or clothes of a canonized saint, that serves as a memorial to that saint and is thought by many of the faithful to be especially blessed.

"It's only a third-degree," Mark joked. "But maybe it'll help." A third-degree relic is a piece of cloth that either touched the body of a saint or was brought to a saint's shrine.

"I had a Saint John Stonecraft once," said Woody, a former Wonder bread delivery man who, like Mark, was entering the undergraduate program.

"Wasn't he a wide receiver for the Steelers?" Mark asked, looking perplexed.

"Quarterback."

The fairgrounds were filling up. Deacon Max and Ron ate at the beer tent. There was a saying at the seminary that year: the number of seminarians is down, but our tonnage remains the same. It was taken for granted that most of the men would gain weight at Sacred Heart. There seemed to be a number of reasons for this, but the foremost was the superb cooking and the abundance of food. Desserts were left out all night, and two flavors of soft-serve yogurt were always available. Deacon Max said that it didn't matter anymore if they got fat. Ron, wearing a newly acquired straw sombrero, didn't say much. Patrick smoked his second cigar.

When everyone had finally had enough, they meandered back to the van. They walked past a group of girls. Bob thought one of them was calling to him and swung around.

"He doesn't respond that quickly to us," Patrick observed with a smile.

But no one was calling him at all.

S OMEWHERE NEAR THE END of his twelve-year marriage, after years of trying, Don Malin prayed that his relationship
with his wife might still be healed. He was exhausted, ill, and
overworked. He had been scrambling for years to meet her seemingly endless needs. He felt used up. But he was an earnest husband
who wanted to do the right thing, so he kept on trying. Finally, after
one more painful year, the answer to his prayer came back. It was as
if God was saying: *I can't heal what never lived.* Don filed for divorce.

Many years later, on a Saturday morning in August 2002, Don
drove his Jeep Cherokee through the back entrance of the Sacred
Heart School of Theology. Broken branches, twigs, and leaves covered the road, a result of Milwaukee's recent rains. He crossed the
narrow bridge, which looked as if it had been rebuilt over the summer. The stream below was swollen and muddy. He passed the mausoleum, wound up a small hill, and broke out of the woods onto the
campus of the seminary. Don realized that he had forgotten the
parking place they had assigned him at the end of the previous semester. No matter, he concluded. Most people wouldn't be back yet,
and besides, this was the beginning of his fifth and final year as a
seminarian at Sacred Heart. There weren't too many perks in the formation process; being a little loose with assigned parking in your se-

nior year might as well be one. He drove right up to the back of the dining hall, parked at an angle, and went in through the smokers' door.

Seniority at the seminary was curious and certainly not the kind of thing found at schools with age-based grades. The diversity of ages and experiences at Sacred Heart turned this sense of the word "seniority" upside down. Nevertheless, a distinct sense of seniority existed at Sacred Heart. The men close to ordination tended to be looked up to and deferred to. More than that, they actually seemed to be more mature than the newer men. Indeed, some men who had been married and had children and grandchildren could seem younger than others who were decades their junior. It was as if upon entering the world of the seminary, bereft of the usual markers of a life, each man somehow betrayed his spiritual age and the distance he still had to go to become a parish priest. A man like Don Malin, a consummate example of the formation process, provided a yardstick against which these "younger" men could be measured and also could measure themselves.

Don was returning to school injured, his left hand in a cast. He had broken it in his sleep when his arm flailed about and struck the night table. Don struggled with injuries and sickness. Some came out of the blue. The year before, it had been an aneurysm. Eight years earlier, doctors had discovered a tumor on his thyroid, which was then removed. The operation had injured his vocal cords, a harsh assault on his identity as a singer. Other ailments were chronic. He slept hooked up to a machine to monitor and correct his sleep apnea. He also had mild asthma and bad allergies. Don did not dwell on these things, but they caused him to maintain a balanced routine and take rest and time away from work seriously.

In less than three months, he would be ordained a transitional deacon, empowered to act in place of a priest at most church functions. Like a priest, he would take the permanent promise of celibacy. Then, if nothing intervened, he would become a priest six months later. What made men close to ordination different was a sense that their identity had altered. They were not the same men who had arrived at Sacred Heart. Their lives were no longer their own. They had acquired "priestliness."

Don knew that a priest was formed by subtle, patient, and consistent self-denial — denial even of a personal vision of one's priesthood. A man entered the seminary with certain illusions of what priesthood meant. Some entered with visions of becoming an activist priest; others imagined modeling themselves after Bing Crosby's amiable pastor in *The Bells of Saint Mary's*. If they came with mental pictures of themselves wearing cassocks, the traditional and antiquated garb of seminarians, those images had to die. They might think that when they said Mass, they needed to keep their fingers together, but that requirement had been abolished in 1972. The formation process challenged these ideas and discounted them.

During orientation, teachers and staff told the new seminarians to trust the process, and Don had. He had grown to understand the concept that although he might very well be ordained a priest, it would never be *his* priesthood. This meant that when he was assigned to a parish, it would not be his to do with as he pleased. It would not be his domain; it would be the people's. It was their spirituality, not his own, that he would foster. Too many of the men, Don observed, came to the seminary and wanted *their* faith consecrated so that they could go out and share *their* good news — as if God and the people were fortunate just to have them as priests.

A priest was for the people, and each man had to decide whether his illusions of priesthood were worth keeping or not. Some of the men were disabused of their illusions during their pastoral work. Some arrived at a rectory expecting to find the priest praying all day and living a cloistered life. Instead, they found the pastor watching the evening news and eating popcorn with a beer perched on his belly. At first they resented him, but over the course of a summer, they realized that he was an excellent priest, a selfless man tending to the needs of others. Their preconceptions of what made a good priest would have to yield to reality.

In the second semester of his first year, Don's formation adviser told him, "We don't have to look for things to evaluate you. We don't have to make up tests. Life is a test. We watch how you react, because we're looking for what's underneath the reaction so that we can help you become the best priest you possibly can be." The adviser referred to areas of progress as "growing edges." As much as Don disliked cute terms, "growing edges" resonated. It meant that something — an irksome trait, an annoying habit, a general indisposition, even how one handled chronic illness — had been flagged and ought to be fixed.

A tangible benefit of reaching one's final year at Sacred Heart was the right to a second room. Don had chosen the room directly across the hall. He had decided to turn the new room into his bedroom and what had been his bedroom into an office. Even though Don wouldn't be permitted to move into the second room until October (an odd Sacred Heart rule), he had returned with some extra stuff, so he spent the afternoon of his arrival unpacking and moving furniture. Just after nightfall, as he was returning to his room from the parking lot, he saw a giant figure approaching him out of the darkness. The man's arm was around the shoulders of a much smaller man, guiding him. The giant was Mike Snyder, the smaller man was Ron Kendzierski. Don had already heard about Ron and his talent with the violin. He was eager to get him involved in the sacred music program at the seminary. He wasted no time in recruiting Ron for the monthly Spanish Mass. Even though Ron wasn't sure how deeply he wanted to commit to community music at the school, he gave a prompt yes when Don asked him to join the program. Ron warned that he didn't read music.

By all measures, 2001–2002 had been a very difficult year for Sacred Heart. When someone asked Don Malin about the previous year, he responded without hesitation: "It was hell, of course." The memory of it dampened the return of the old students and the arrival of the new ones, making things tentative and uncertain. People seemed prepared for even worse. The atmosphere had been poisonous, and the disappointments, shocks, and pain had been relentless. Some seminarians had left for good, and their departures had added to the bleakness. Others had gone home for the summer, uncertain whether they would return.

The year had begun innocuously enough with an August orientation similar to that of 2002, except there had been a significantly larger class. Fall classes started without a hitch. Every year, Father Brackin offered an annual theme. The theme for 2001–2002 was "Fiesta." The idea was to emphasize the celebratory quality of a vocation, of a seminary community, and of life. Bright T-shirts embossed with FIESTA were prepared. Barb Haag, the director of food services, put together a fitting menu. Father Brackin organized an inaugural talk. They would introduce Fiesta on the first day of recollection and carry it through the spring term.

The introduction was scheduled for September 11, 2001. Everyone had just exited morning chapel when news began to spread of the attacks in New York and Washington. Father Brackin had television sets wheeled out into the main lounge, and soon everyone was watching the World Trade Center towers burn and collapse. The coverage played throughout the day. Classes were canceled for the rest of the week. Father Brackin asked all the professors to take the attack into consideration and adjust their syllabuses accordingly.

A few weeks passed, and the horror began to fade. Then Father Brackin received a phone call from a U.S. Customs Service agent informing him that the government would be executing a search warrant on one of his seminarians the following day. Agents would be arriving to seize the seminarian's computer because they believed it contained child pornography. The call to Father Brackin was a courtesy; he didn't have a choice. He was instructed not to take any action until the computer had been seized. The next day, the warrant was executed and the computer confiscated. Father Brackin confronted the seminarian, and he admitted the truth of the charge. The rector told him to leave the seminary. Soon after, the former seminarian began serving time in a federal penitentiary.

The fall also was marred by a series of hospitalizations. Ambulances regularly rushed to the seminary, prompting one wag to observe that Sacred Heart had more ambulances than the sidelines of a Pittsburgh Steelers game. In addition to sickness, there was death. During the year, there were four funerals for SCJ priests. The round of wakes and funerals seemed to amplify the pervading grimness.

Before the men were even settled in for the spring 2002 semester, the harshest blow was struck. It began with a series of articles in the *Boston Globe*. The Archdiocese of Boston, one of the oldest and most powerful in the United States, stood accused of shuffling around child-molesting priests long after they should have been suspended or defrocked. Unlike a similar child sexual abuse story that had surfaced a decade earlier, this one seemed to grow by the day. Soon evidence of similar malfeasance was being found nationwide, and the problem — now widely seen as a massive cover-up that had put many children in grave danger — had grown into a major crisis for the Church. What had begun as an inquiry into one diocese's questionable treatment of child sexual abuse claims and suspect priests became a general indictment of the institution and the clergy. In the end, several bishops were forced to resign either over their handling of the situation or because of their own sexual misconduct. Two members of Sacred Heart's own board of directors were brought down by allegations of abuse. Just after the spring semester ended, Rembert Weakland, the archbishop of Milwaukee, resigned over an alleged affair and the payment of hush money.

Into this world-turned-upside-down came "Sean the Baptizer." Sean would earn his nickname for an extraordinary act during a Wednesday morning community Mass in the spring. Father Brackin presided. Sean and another man served. When they reached the place in the Mass where Sean was to pour water over the rector's hands, something went terribly wrong. The rector noticed the large cruet of water that Sean held out to him. It was much larger than the usual cruet. Then Sean poured the water over Father Brackin's head. As the water ran all over him, the rector's first thought — as he mentally stepped out of the reality of a very unreal situation — was that he was a football coach, his team had won the big game, and one of his players had just dumped the water cooler on him in celebration. His second thought was that the man before him required gentleness and prayer.

Sean retrieved the large towels that he had put on the altar in lieu of the customary finger cloth. He offered the towels to Father Brackin, and the rector accepted them. Father Marty then escorted Sean off the altar, and Father Brackin continued with the Mass.

The seminarians did not know how to respond. If there was a temptation to laugh, it was squelched by the strangeness of the act. Father Brackin ended the Mass by asking everyone to pray for Sean, who, he said, was obviously in distress. It was never clear why Sean poured water over the rector's head. He had been wrestling with formation and failing academically. He told one man that he had prepared for the stunt the night before. If the towels had been moved, Sean related, he would have taken it as a sign from God that he shouldn't go through with the dousing. Soon afterward, Sean left Sacred Heart for good. Father Brackin drove him home.

Father Brackin would later say that it was only through the grace of God that he had handled the situation well and had managed to turn it into a teaching moment for pastoral leadership. He was a saint for about a week around Sacred Heart, he joked.

At the end of the school year, some of the men returned to their dioceses to find that priests they had known had become embroiled in scandals. Then in June, the American bishops met in Dallas and drafted a "zero tolerance" policy toward priests accused of misconduct with children. Many in religious life saw the policy as a capitulation to the media. It seemed to strip away a priest's right to be considered innocent until proven guilty. Priests reacted with hostility and disbelief. They saw in it an abandonment by their bishops, who were supposed to be their leaders and defenders. One priest told Don Malin, "The bishops have declared war on their priests."

The loose affiliation of religious orders in the United States did not follow the bishops' lead at their own national meeting. According to one member, the words "zero tolerance" did not belong on any Christian's lips. By late summer, it appeared likely that the Vatican, to which the policy had been sent for review, would significantly water down the Dallas decision. But for many priests and seminarians, the damage had been done. Why had the bishops not punished themselves, holding those in charge accountable, instead of targeting their priests?

This was the backdrop to the year 2002–2003 at Sacred Heart. There was trepidation and bitterness, a deep distrust of Church hierarchy, and priests at a low point of morale. But there was also a strong current of hope and the belief that a better Church would somehow emerge from the wreckage.

"It's identified as the sexual abuse crisis within the Church," Father Brackin said to the men gathered for the first official rector's conference of the year in Classroom 1.

"I think you're all aware that the bishops met in Dallas, developed a zero tolerance protocol in terms of addressing allegations of sexual abuse particularly toward children. That protocol has been sent to the Vatican for review. What that means is that the person not only is removed from ministry but they would be stripped of their priesthood. They would be unable to identify themselves as a priest in terms of celebrating Eucharist. They would not be able to wear clerical garb."

Some of this may very well be an overreaction, Father Brackin said, and the Vatican may overturn the Dallas resolution, but whatever happened, something had permanently changed, and the seminarians must be acutely aware of it.

"Even if the Dallas protocol is not accepted in its form, I would say what I'm going to say to you," he continued. "I don't presume to know my own mind, and I certainly don't presume to know the mind of God. For whatever reason, God has called you to be a seminarian in this historical context."

The men before him were at every level of the seminary. First-year students such as Dean Haley and Ron Kendzierski sat at tables with more senior men such as Jim Pemberton, Jim Heiser, and Don Malin. They all knew how severe an action such as that taken in Dallas was to a priest.

"You are living in a seminary environment that is going to be reflective of what is going on within the Church. Each one of us, and *particularly* seminarians, have to be very vigilant about our behavior, about our conversations, about our relationships."

Father Brackin used an example to get his point across. A hypothetical group of seminarians goes to Tom's Pub for a beer on a Friday night. Later, somebody calls the rector with a report about a seminarian who, the caller said, "was hanging all over this blonde."

There was scattered laughter. "I was there that night," someone joked.

When the laughter died down, Father Brackin drove the point home. "But let's say that's what comes back to the rector. The rector calls you in and says, 'This is what's been reported.' You say, 'That's simply not true. I know the woman. I hadn't seen her in a long time. I simply put my arm around her to say it's good to see you.' Let's say the rector believes you."

In the past, the rector might not have thought it necessary to pass on this incident to the seminarian's vocation director or bishop. Not so anymore.

"Given our uncertain times, this is information that will get passed on," Father Brackin said.

"Wow!" someone exclaimed.

"The rector has no control over how a vocation director or a bishop is going to hear that, but given the circumstances in the Church, our behavior is going to be under a scrutiny that it has *never* been under before," Father Brackin continued.

A decade before, when he was stationed in San Antonio, he had met a priest who had since died. The priest told him that when he was in the seminary, the formation department had instructed them to draw an imaginary three-foot radius around themselves. They were never to step outside that circle or allow anyone else to step in.

"Now unfortunately, he lived his life like that," Father Brackin said. "That is a pretty sterile way of living one's life. Some would say that's plain craziness. I'm not suggesting that we draw three-foot-radius circles around ourselves. That's not the way to enter into ministry. But we have to be vigilant. Comments or behavior that might have simply seemed innocuous in the past, because of the times we live in can be seen differently."

The atmosphere in the room had grown tense. Each man was well aware of the delicate balance between the sacrifice that he was being asked to make for his vocation and the benefit — or at least solace — that one hoped to receive in embracing this sacrifice. The respect and love of parishioners for their priest was one benefit that priests had traditionally been able to expect. Now it seemed that not being treated like a leper would have to be good enough.

"Now I think the protocol is going to be adjusted to ensure that the rights of clergy are protected, but as seminarians, *no one* has a right to be ordained." Father Brackin spoke these words slowly. He tapped the desk with his empty coffee mug for emphasis.

"If your sponsor chooses to withdraw his sponsorship, you have no recourse in Church court or in civil court. As seminarians, you simply do not have a right to ordination."

Even though the times were crazy, he said, he believed that God gave people the grace to endure. Many potential seminarians, for example, were being subjected to criminal background checks. That was just the way it was now.

The men sat silent and pensive.

"How does that make you all feel?" Father Brackin finally asked.

"A little afraid to go outside," Dean Haley said in a pained and resentful voice.

"Almost uncomfortable with being yourself," another man added.

"I'm wondering how we're going to be able to relate to parishioners if we have to live in this fishbowl," a third said.

"Gives you a sense of them and us," someone else added.

One man took the opposite view. "It never came up in the three parishes I worked at this summer."

"And I think that's a good corrective," Father Brackin said. "The people of God are waiting for your ministry. They're not seeing every seminarian and every priest as a potential pedophile."

Someone mentioned the fear of working in situations that could lead to allegations. In a hospital, he continued, a priest often found himself alone with patients. What if something happened then, an awkward situation or baseless accusation? Father Brackin acknowledged the fear but insisted that a priest's obligation to serve must outweigh that fear.

"Ultimately, our responsibility is to make present the compassion of Jesus," Father Brackin said. "Sometimes that means we might be misunderstood. We have to make present the compassion of Jesus, but we also have to be prudent. What's the Scripture verse? 'Be as innocent as doves, but as wise as serpents . . .'"

"As cunning as serpents," Bob Brooks corrected.

Hope was what Father Brackin invoked again a few hours later as he stood on the dais in the Sacred Heart Chapel and officially commenced the school year at the community-wide Mass.

"We begin again," Father Brackin declared.

The rector appeared relaxed. He was dressed in a bright red chasuble that hung loosely on his small frame. Chasubles come in varying colors to signify different seasons or days in the Church calendar. Today was a martyr's feast, and the red symbolized blood. Father Brackin looked at the community gathered in the pews around him. To his left sat the faculty in full academic regalia, long gowns and mortarboards — traditional dress now fully secularized but derived from the religious garb of the clerics who populated medieval universities. Filling all the other pews, in no particular seating arrangement, were the administrators, the men and women from buildings and grounds, the kitchen staff, and the seminarians. The seminarians wore jackets and ties. Those men already ordained deacons were dressed in clerics — black pants and clerical shirts punctuated with the white tab of the Roman collar. Unlike at many other seminaries, students were prohibited from wearing clerical clothing until they were ordained deacons or unless they were already members of a religious order.

"We begin again," Father Brackin repeated. "Hopefully, though, our notion of beginning again is not that this time we will get it right."

He paused.

"Because we're never going to get it right. We are in the midst of a mystery of unfolding. And rather than trying to figure out the meaning of life, we need to embrace the mystery and enjoy the life. For us, it is to participate in the continuing unfolding of this place, of this ministry that we call Sacred Heart School of Theology."

Mass was followed by a semiformal lunch in honor of the start of school. Tables were adorned with white tablecloths and rolled-up blue napkins. In addition to the usual deli and salad stations, a steam table was stocked with garlic bread and a multitude of pastas and sauces. Dean Haley dropped into a seat at a table with Bob Brooks and some others. He had piled three plates high with food but had misjudged how much his appetite would be suppressed by his ADHD medication. He pushed the food aside.

Instead of eating, Dean talked. He was filled with enthusiasm. Father Brackin's homily and the first rector's conference had fired him up about this question of hope and vocation. There was no better time in history to be going into the seminary, Dean insisted loudly. He ticked off the reasons: it was the start of a new millennium; because of this sexual abuse crisis, good priests capable of bringing renewal were in even greater demand; the religious reaction of people to the events of September 11 suggested that they hungered for faith (how amazing, he reminded them, that CNN had actually broadcast Catholic Masses from New York's St. Patrick's Cathedral). And the biggest reason: American society desperately needed help.

"Here's a story that sums up America," Dean said. "Okay, maybe not sums it up, but you judge for yourself."

There was a man driving along, and he spotted a two-year-old crawling alone on the side of the highway. He protected the child from traffic with his car but was too afraid to get out and assist directly for fear that he would be mistaken for a child abductor. Was that sick or what, Dean wanted to know.

Bob interrupted Dean's monologue. Sure, the world was broken and in need of a healing Church, but didn't the Church need to heal itself first? The cover-up was still a problem, Bob insisted, as was the vast amount of money that was now at stake through the raft of lawsuits. Everyone at the table seemed to agree that the bishops had toed the media's line — not a Christian one — by adopting zero tolerance. They talked about how easy it seemed for a priest to be accused and lose everything because of it. Hadn't this just happened to one of the seminarian's pastors back home?

"May you live in interesting times," Bob said, quoting a saying that he seemed to think was positive.

Dean begged to differ. The source was Chinese, and it didn't mean what Bob thought.

"It's actually a curse," Dean said smugly.

Before Father Vince McNally arrived for class, the first-year students had actually begun to believe Sister Marilyn's story. She had appeared, leading Ron Kendzierski, with his special multispeed tape recorder, to his seat, and informed them that she would be co-teaching the class. This wasn't in the course description. Early Church to 1500 was Dean Haley's first class at Sacred Heart, and he sat in the third row with his laptop open in front of him.

"How many of you are first-year students? Second years? Be proud. Raise your hands with vim and vigor," Sister Marilyn cajoled.

"You know, Sister, I have one question," Ron said.

"You have just *one* question?"

"Yes, Sister, but it's a very good question. Maybe one that should be asked over and over again."

"Yes?"

"This guy's an Irishman — where's the keg?"

Stifled laughter greeted the joke. Even if they believed her about co-teaching, there was tension in the air. Something fearsome seemed to be on the way that would snatch up the amiable nun. Father McNally, Church historian and proponent of the historical-critical method, was, after all, known for his fondness of the Hobbesian observation that life is "nasty, brutish, and short." It was for his class that one seminarian, though a veteran of the Vietnam War and running computer systems for casinos in Reno, Nevada, sounded an uncharacteristically timorous note when he decided not to use borrowed books but buy new ones, lest Father McNally be somehow displeased.

"Father McNally will let you know where the keg is when he walks . . ." Sister Marilyn's voice trailed off. Father McNally had arrived.

"Oh, Vince," she said. "They did not know we were co-teaching . . ."

Father McNally was of an imposing height. He wore a tweed jacket over his clerical shirt and carried an enormous gray briefcase. The only dissonant note in his otherwise collegiate-clerical appearance was his footwear: leather sandals. His eyes could be acute and withering. His chestnut beard and mustache were turning white at the edges. A gaggle of red pens poked from his shirt pocket.

"Well, one more surprise," he said. His delivery was crisp and measured, faintly arch. But he didn't seem too put off by Sister Marilyn's performance. The class relaxed ever so slightly. The nun departed to muted laughter and scattered applause. Ron shouted, "Encore!"

Father McNally's opening prayer probably surprised some of the men. The scuttlebutt was that he was something of an apostate.

"In the name of the Father, the Son, and the Holy Spirit," he began and crossed himself. "God help us to become more and more aware of your presence within ourselves and our world so that we may become more and more like Jesus. We ask this in Jesus's name."

Father McNally had the men introduce themselves and supply a nickname by which they would prefer to be called. He asked one of the seminarians to prepare the opening prayer for the next class. Everyone would eventually have a turn. Then he read a paragraph that he believed said what Church history was all about:

"Church history provides an important means of understanding a Christian people and their church. And if it is willing to use the historical-critical method, thereby reveals where Christians have been and gives them self-important clues as to where they go . . . The picture it reveals when it is striving to be critical as well as objective is not always clean . . . Shadows are a part of all people and the institutions they create."

Father McNally looked up from the paper and scanned the room.

"Institutional shadows," he said, then paused. "You guys know what a shadow is?"

"You mean a Jungian shadow?" Bob asked. Father McNally said yes, or in other words, a dark side. Issues like sexual abuse are shadows in the Church.

He continued to read. Institutional shadows could be ignored, but only at a price.

"Ultimately," Father McNally concluded, "such studied ignorance weakens and even kills the human spirit, which in turn fosters apathy and finally institutional irrelevance."

Good history, he said, is messy. This was one of his favorite observations. The inclination — especially in a seminary among seminarians — is to see Church history as needing to be performed within the context of faith, like theology. But history is not dualistic. It is neither sacred nor profane. If one were to call Church history sacred, it would be just another way of saying let's eliminate the shadows. The Roman Catholic Church invented the word "propaganda" with its creation of the Sacra Congregatio de Propaganda Fide, or Sacred Congregation for the Propagation of the Faith.

Ron snickered at this apparent dig at the institutional church.

Father McNally asked whether anyone had gone to seminary before the reforms of Vatican II. Jim Pemberton said he had.

"What does apologetics mean?" Father McNally asked.

Jim said it was the defense of the Church against heresy.

"Which was?" Father McNally continued.

Jim answered cautiously. Did it mean the defense against other religions, perhaps?

"Everyone else," Father McNally confirmed.

Institutions, he said, hate the word "why." Indeed, "Why?" is a dangerous question. A child in the terrible twos asks, "Why? Why? Why?" In a creative household, the question is answered. In an uncreative household, it is dismissed with "because," which translates to "shut up." When he was in seminary, Father McNally said, they used to say, "Keep the rule, and the rule will keep you." This, too, translates to "shut up."

But in this classroom, he said, critical thinking was the rule. Father McNally's imperatives and injunctions found their way onto the several handouts that he supplied to the class. In an eccentric combination of all capital letters, boldface and italic type, and underscores, one handout read: "***CRITICAL* THINKING VERSUS *NEGATIVE* THINKING: AN EXTREMELY IMPORTANT DISTINCTION**" and "**Imagination IS** the most essential and necessary ability/skill of a person who hopes to lead a holy/whole life. By imagination is meant the freely graced ability to use all of our God-given faculties to assist us in forming healthy consciences and well-balanced 'IMAGES' of the concrete world to become critical thinkers. *CRITICAL* thinking is very often confused with *NEGATIVE* thinking, though the two are ***ABSOLUTE OPPOSITES***."

A negative thinker is someone who does not think or refuses to think and thus never asks the question "Why?" Negative thinking is opposed to constructive treatment and sees reality as fixed and final. A negative thinker denies the shadows, and thus even so-called positive thinkers, with their Pollyannaish insistence on seeing only the good, are really only negative thinkers in disguise. A critical thinker always asks why and accepts reality (and, therefore, history) as being messy.

Finally, Father McNally arrived at the overarching reason for all these distinctions: "Critical thinking people, who accept that there are no absolutes except love, are not frightened by such 'MESSI-NESS.' If they are truly people of faith, they believe that by taking the **_RISK_** to look at the whole question, especially the shadow parts, though such a challenge can/will be very frightening, confusing, and even contradictory, that such critical thinking is the only way to bring about the hope of personal and communal growth and change (**i.e., people of _VISION_**)."

Dean wondered what exactly any of this had to do with becoming a priest. Was there a liberal agenda beneath the surface? Was it anti-Church? Was it meant to strip a man of his faith? He wasn't one to reject critical thinking, nor did his vision of the Church reject such an approach. Hadn't the Catholic Church intellectually, if not institutionally, ultimately embraced critical thinking over its long history? He knew firsthand about ignorance and uncritical thinking. East Texas, his home, was dominated by the woozy teachings of fundamentalist Christianity, and he found these teachings deeply unsatisfying.

Jim Pemberton found himself feeling trepidation, although he also was stimulated by the discussion. He would not be like some others who dismissed Father McNally's class as just another hurdle to clear. Jim respected the concept of the historical-critical method, but he could not accept the notion of a Church history that didn't feature God with a prominent role for the Holy Spirit. He was not alone among the men at Sacred Heart when he mused, "There must be something behind the Church's survival for all of these years. All the scandals, the popes with mistresses, the failure to always live up to the message of Christ. You can't approach Church history with pure logic. You can't put humanity in a box. It's hard to get your arms around us. We change. We're different things at different times. We're like mercury. It's wonderful to approach the Church from a rational standpoint — Saint Paul had said you need reasons for your faith — but you won't ever be able to have that type of understanding only. Not logic alone."

*   *   *

To Jim, logic didn't seem to play much of a role in a calling to the priesthood. His vocation had begun during World War II in the statuary-crammed St. Patrick Cathedral in Fort Worth. When he was in second or third grade, Jim concluded that no life could be finer than the life of an army chaplain. He drew pictures and daydreamed. When he imagined saying Mass on the battlefield, waves of excitement passed through him. The war ended and the chaplain image faded, but the vocation grew. It matured as Jim matured. He began to serve at Mass. A young assistant pastor in a local church became the kind of robust model of the priesthood that could inspire a preadolescent.

When Jim turned thirteen, he announced his intention to become a priest. The news delighted his mother, Winnie, a devout Irish Catholic. It had the opposite effect on his father, Jack, a Methodist who never went to church and was a former clarinet player with Eutie Goldberg's traveling jazz band. Winnie told Jack that Jim's seminary training would begin in the eighth grade in San Antonio, 275 miles south of Fort Worth. It would continue, with scant time back home, until his early twenties and end with ordination. Jim was an only child. Jack told Winnie that he would not stand in the way of his son's decision, but he wanted something in return. "Give me another child," he said to his wife.

Two years later, Joseph Pemberton was born. Joe called his older brother Bubba. Both boys called their parents Mama and Daddy. Winnie brought Joe with her on the long drives down to San Antonio to visit Jim. On one of those early trips, a trip Joe was too young to recall, Winnie remembered that she had to keep pulling over to the side of the road because her son was vomiting. Winnie wished aloud that she had a cold washcloth to put on her son's head to make him feel better. She looked up and saw a man holding out a washcloth. She took the cold cloth and put it on her son's head. When she turned around to return it, the man was gone. Although Joe challenged the story when he was older, Winnie only replied, "I know what I saw."

Jim left the seminary after seven years. He had met fellow seminarian Joe Scantlin's sister, Joy. Jim liked her, but it wasn't Joy who prompted him to leave. A near-constant restlessness eventually convinced him that he could not remain celibate for the rest of his life. He told the future Father Scantlin about his decision. He never mentioned Joy.

Jim enrolled at Texas Christian University to study business, something practical that could be used to support a family. Halfway through his education, he married Joy. They lived on the west side of Fort Worth until she became pregnant. Then they moved to the east side to be closer to family.

Meanwhile, Jim's little brother was accompanying their mother on her rounds as a member of the Legion of Mary, one of the few lay apostolates in the 1950s. A lay apostolate is a group of non-ordained Catholics designated to carry out specific work within a church community. The purpose of the Legion of Mary is to bring lapsed Catholics back into the fold. A pastor with a chapter of the Legion of Mary in his parish provides the group with a list of local Catholics who no longer attend church. Members of the group contact these people in an informal, usually nonconfrontational way. In one instance, Joe found himself in the kitchen of a famous Mexican restaurant eating tamales while his mother spoke with the owner about returning to church.

Unlike his brother, Joe had no aspirations to the priesthood. He attended high school locally and went away to college. After college, he taught school. Near the end of college, Joe fell in love with a woman who was a devout Catholic. After almost three years of dating, marriage seemed imminent. One day, however, the woman told Joe something important. I observe you at Mass, she said, and I know that you won't be totally happy unless you are on the altar saying Mass yourself. The statement seemed to throw a switch inside Joe. He knew that what she said was true. Finally, he met with the woman and her family. Although he loved her dearly, he said, he had no choice. He was being called to the priesthood, and he had to answer that call.

By the time Jim Pemberton entered Sacred Heart for his second experience at seminary, his younger brother had been a priest for al-most twenty-five years.

Academics was serious business at Sacred Heart. Despite assurances that the people in the pews would never ask for their grades, the seminarians seemed to be more consistently anxious about their classroom work than about virtually anything else. Heiser, who managed to avoid this general anxiety while maintaining a high grade point average, lamented the emphasis on schoolwork. He thought it distracted the men from other important formation op-portunities. Although the course load could be heavy, especially when combined with field assignments, house jobs, chapel service, and formation duties, most of the intensity seemed to come from the men themselves. They seemed to be fixated on receiving the best grades. It was almost as if, in the absence of concrete standards by which to judge their progress in other areas, the seminarians weren't going to neglect the one area where they could chart their forma-tion. But the ideas that the men encountered in their classes often presented a spiritual challenge, which sometimes threatened to de-rail or discourage their vocations.

After apologizing about the cost of the theological dictionary that the new men had to buy for his Fundamental Theology course, Dr. Steven Shippee began his first class by addressing the heady question of what theology is. Many of the men came to the seminary with an incomplete knowledge of the purpose and nature of theology. It was Dr. Shippee's job to disabuse them of their misconceptions, which often were sentimental holdovers from a childhood faith.

Theology at a Catholic seminary is not an exercise that can be practiced by believer and nonbeliever alike, Dr. Shippee said. Theol-ogy is the province of the insider, someone with a living faith. If this were not the case, the exercise would be merely the study of religion.

"Theology," Dr. Shippee pronounced, "should be done on your knees."

Dr. Shippee's delivery buzzed and zipped. The hand that held the chalk darted through the air like a hummingbird from flower to flower. He told the story of how Reinhold Niebuhr, one of the most famous theologians of the twentieth century, once entered a lecture hall and said, "God," then turned around and left. When Niebuhr returned five minutes later, he announced, "Whatever you thought of when I said 'God' was not God."

The object that the seminarians sought to understand in theology was God, but God was by definition limitless and thus beyond complete understanding. The Church, Niebuhr would later say, did not possess a word about God, but instead possessed God's own self. A person is not saved by the *formula* of Jesus Christ, but by Jesus Christ. The words point to the reality of God but are not the reality themselves. I'm not saved, Niebuhr would say, by having a theological grasp of words. That would be idolatry.

"I can't imagine a better job," Dr. Shippee would regularly effuse about his chosen profession. He quoted Saint Bonaventure on his course outline: "Let no one think that he will find sufficiency in a reading which lacks unction, an inquiry which lacks devotion, a search which arouses no wonder, a survey without enthusiasm, industry without piety, knowledge without love, intelligence without humility, application without grace, contemplation without wisdom inspired by God."

The days of Fundamental Theology were long over for Don Malin. In anticipation of his imminent entry into priestly work, the curriculum of his final year was practical. Father Andre Papineau's Basic Preaching class was especially practical — every priest has to preach. The class was held in a bleak basement classroom with cinder-block walls decorated with two paintings. Individual metal desks were arranged in a rectangle. A large TV on a cart stood in front of the blackboard. A video camera on a tripod, used for recording the students' preaching efforts, occupied the opposite corner, and a lectern stood prominently at the front of the room.

"Unless you're willing to make an ass of yourself," Father Andre proclaimed, "you will be one."

Don Malin, who unlike many of the men followed the administration's instructions and actually wore his nametag, rested his heavily bandaged hand on his desk and watched Father Andre hop onto a chair to point out the implied distance from a high pulpit to the people in the pews. The professor did a riff on a priest he knew who had tics. He demonstrated the disruptive effect this had on his homilies by breaking into a spastic break dance.

Father Andre called preaching "the turnstile of all the other disciplines," and he said that good preaching begins with rethinking oft-repeated words and phrases. It's deadly to make assumptions about the general knowledge of your audience, he said. Many Catholics don't know the meaning of "Immaculate Conception" (the doctrine that holds that Mary was born without original sin). And what about "Good Shepherd"? Doesn't a good shepherd keep his sheep so that he can kill them later? Think, he demanded. To be complacent with language and not to interact with it is fatal for the homilist. A speaker must reappropriate the Word to get the point across. Don't just question the text; let the text question you. After all, the stakes are high. You can either draw the people in or drive them away.

And it's not just spoken language that's important, he said, but also quality of voice, body language, awareness of one's environment, and clever use of acoustics. What good could come of a homily swallowed up by a speaker's ignorance of how sound traveled in his space? The Sacred Heart Chapel was a torturous godsend for Father Andre's Basic Preaching and Preaching Practicum. It's basically a theater-in-the-round built within a stone cavern with an erratic speaker system — a homiletics obstacle course for both initiated and uninitiated alike. In Father Andre's class, each student would have his own stomach-churning turn at the podium on the vast dais, with commentary to follow.

Father Andre knew that he was not working with so many Sir Laurence Oliviers. (The actor's letters congratulating Father Andre on his ordination decades earlier could be found framed beneath glass in his apartment on the other side of Milwaukee.) For many of the men who came through his class, success for him would be a permanent nudge in the right rhetorical direction. Nor did he really want to work with actors, because ultimately these men would be sharing themselves with their parishioners, not adopting a persona. A good homily is not merely the right application of dramatic theory; it's the full realization of the speaker as a man, a priest, and a fellow pilgrim. It is founded on the kind of intimate self-knowledge that is also profoundly universal. Good preaching represents the fruits of a courageous journey into the fearful places of the human condition.

A handout stated: "Being emotionally abused by a parent or spouse and then being admonished to forgive 7 X 70 times is meaningless. What means much more is that there be someone who can express the anger and hurt which the person feels against the one who abused him. Identifying the struggle in the sermon is a way of accompanying the pilgrim through fearful dark places. And it is in these places that the preacher needs to be, not resting at the journey's end on some mountain peak."

Don identified with this image. He had been on his journey of formation for a very long time, and the process of spiritual growth by way of external observation and correction by another was an integral part of his life. He had been under spiritual direction since he was fifteen years old. At Sacred Heart, he had acquired a formation adviser who would work with him on everything from his scheduling decisions to his table manners. He also had friends, both men and women, whom he had explicitly instructed to be candid with him if personal traits or habits not conducive to the priestly life emerged — things a spouse might say: "Stop talking with your mouth full" or "Clip your nose hair; it's disgusting." It might seem strange for a man in his midforties to open himself to such minute scrutiny, but Don saw the process as a natural extension of spiritual humility. As a priest, he would not have the luxury of permitting rough edges to intrude into his ministry. Formation was like sandpaper working on those edges — first coarse paper to smooth the more obvious defects, then ever-finer grades.

Father Andre spoke about the art of the homily, and Don sat in a metal school desk and listened. He was scheduled to begin preaching to the faithful in less than three months.

"We haven't heard Ron play the violin yet," Professor Christian Rich said over the din caused by a herd of visiting schoolteachers lining up for lunch. Outside groups often used the facilities for meetings. But even with a hundred extra people in the dining room, there were still a dozen empty tables. Professor Rich, Sisters Lucille and Wagner, and Don Malin, the members of the Spanish Liturgy Committee, sat at one of the tables near the windows, as far away from the crowd as possible. This was their first meeting of the year.

Everyone at Sacred Heart tended to cluster in the center of the room near the steam tables, and it was customary that anyone who wanted to have a private lunch or meeting ate at the edges. Father Brackin encouraged people to dine with others they didn't know to help build community. A seat at any table was fair game. This encouragement was also intended to prevent cliques. Although this year a table (sometimes two pushed together) of the same group of senior seminarians, mostly men who had been in the military, had emerged, so far no one had said anything about it.

After the committee had revisited how to improve the Spanish Mass and group prayer, as well as how to get people to rehearsals, talk turned to "the new blind student" and his violin. He was rumored to be an exquisite fiddler.

Professor Rich was cautious about the new prospect. Almost every year, he had to work with an entirely new array of musical talent. There was seldom any continuity from one year to the next. Don Malin was an exception — a highly talented musician, classically trained and with a master's degree in sacred music, who had been around for years. But soon Don would be leaving. Already he was planning to diminish his role so others could take over. The struggle to maintain quality forced Professor Rich to accept new musical possibilities. The superb organist of the previous year had departed.

Now on the scene were several guitarists and this violinist. Guitars were always welcome, but a violin, though intriguing, presented a challenge for a Spanish music group.

Sister Lucille acknowledged that no one on the committee had heard Ron Kendzierski play yet. "But everybody that has says his sound is gorgeous," she said. Sister Lucille seemed so excited about the prospect of adding Ron's violin that her voice had an almost conspiratorial tone.

"Is it?" asked Professor Rich, his voice pitched scarcely a notch above mild interest.

"I'm going to listen to him," Don said. "But he improvises. It's very hard for him to memorize notes . . . something to do with seizures. He's taking seizure medication and —"

"Improvisation within the harmony?" Professor Rich asked.

"That's what he does," Don confirmed.

Professor Rich still looked tentative. "A violin . . ."

There was very little in Dr. Richard Lux's appearance to suggest the radical effect he could have on some of his students, especially Jim Pemberton. He was of medium height, had white hair and a white beard, and wore glasses, making him a little like an erudite Santa Claus. He pushed a cart equipped with an electric horn. It bore a heavy cargo of reference books to every class. Dr. Lux used the horn to humor people and other obstacles out of his path and the books to thumb through and clarify one point or another as he lectured. Anything could be pulled from the cart. During football season, Dr. Lux's hand would emerge with an electronic leprechaun that would play the theme song of his beloved alma mater, Notre Dame. The leprechaun would take its place on the corner of the front table and be joined at Thanksgiving by a plastic turkey. Dr. Lux spoke with disarming softness, as if he was perpetually congested. A lilt animated his words, even his occasional sarcasm.

"I'm Dr. Rich Lux," he told Jim Pemberton, Jim Heiser, and the other seminarians who composed his Historical Books class. "This is the beginning of my thirtieth year teaching here. I'm a married Roman Catholic layman. Been married . . ."

A puzzled look came over his face as he tried to recall.

"Thirty-four years," he finally concluded.

Dr. Lux's deep immersion in his area of study was evident in the names of his three sons: Nathan, Benjamin, and Micah (born ten days after Dr. Lux had given birth to his dissertation on the prophet Micah at Notre Dame). He spoke fluent Hebrew and liked to say that he was a vocal friend, admirer, and supporter of the Jewish people. He had been actively involved in Catholic-Jewish relations locally, nationally, and internationally, and he had visited Israel a dozen times over the previous twenty years.

Dr. Lux said that he had a passionate conviction that unless the seminarians immersed themselves in Jewish belief, they wouldn't really understand who they were as Christians. He was awaiting approval of his translation of the Hebrew Scriptures, gathering dust in Rome for the past two years.

Then he asked the seminarians to introduce themselves. As they did, he took sips from his big plastic Notre Dame mug. The introductions by now were almost perfunctory, except for Don Wright, a new man and a deacon, who mentioned that it was the first anniversary of his wife's death. The class was composed mainly of second-year students. Heiser sat — as he always did — with his back to the wall and relished a view of whatever portion of trees and sky he could manage through the windows. Jim Pemberton had all of the half-dozen required books before him already. An open notebook and a highlighter were at the ready.

Dr. Lux spoke more of Christianity's Jewish heritage. One crucial area of understanding is the law. For most contemporary people, the law does not connote good things. The law is harsh and rigid. But the law for Jews is Torah, which means teaching or instruction. The Torah teaches how people are meant to live and treat one another. For Jews, the law is beautiful, not forbidding. It is a joyous part of life. This perception of the law, Lux added, is suggested by the papal tradition of naming encyclicals after their first word or words, as is the tradition with sections of the Torah. Encyclicals are letters composed by the pope that are intended to inform the whole church on some matter of critical importance.

Then Dr. Lux donned a *kippah,* or yarmulke, the traditional headwear of Jewish males at prayer, and commenced to pray in Hebrew. In this course, he told the seminarians, they would begin every class with the first prayer that Jesus learned as a young boy. It was the prayer that his mother, Mary, taught him and the prayer that Jesus, an observant Jew, prayed twice a day for the rest of his life:

> *Shema Yisroel!*
> *Adonai Eloheynu, Adonai Echad.*

As he heard the Hebrew, Jim Pemberton felt thrilled. This was the language in which Jesus prayed, the prayer he uttered. Nothing like this would have occurred at the seminary of his adolescence, where the debt owed by Christianity to Judaism went barely acknowledged and the Vatican had not yet rejected the blood libel, the generational guilt of the Jews for Jesus's death.

> Hear, O Israel!
> The Lord is our God, the Lord alone.

Dr. Lux told the class that he planned to have them attend a service at a nearby synagogue later in the semester. Jim found this news especially welcome. He had been giving a lot of thought to the differences between the priesthood of his youth and the kind of priest he should be at the beginning of the twenty-first century. The more he knew about other religions, the better prepared he would be to face the rigors of the parish and the pulpit.

Jim believed that with the spread of university education, the modern priest faced an intelligent, well-informed Christian community. If the members of this community didn't have ownership of their religion, they would find it difficult to participate. This was a far cry from his youth, when the priest was frequently the most educated person in the community and his pronouncements were usually accepted without contest. The days of blindly accepting the party line were over. If a priest thought he could hide behind the collar like the Wizard of Oz hides behind a curtain, he was terribly mistaken.

As academic work grew apace in the first few weeks, so did other components of the seminarians' education. On Wednesday mornings, Dean Haley and Ron Kendzierski joined Sister Lucille, Father Higgins, and the other first-year students in trudging through the forbidding spiral-bound formation handbook filled with photocopied notes divided into color-coded sections.

Dean had lost interest in this process on the first day, when the instructors had led the group in culling pages that weren't supposed to be in the book. Ranging ahead, Dean had stopped dead at the celibacy section. There was a marker for "Section 10 — Celibacy" but no explanation. The page was blank except for the word "Notes."

It was different for some of these older guys, Dean thought. Some of them had already had wives and kids, and besides they were old. Discussing celibacy couldn't be so urgent for them. It was a different matter for Dean.

Three weeks before he had arrived at Sacred Heart, Father Tom Latham had brought him onto the small stage of the parish center with his back to the curtain. With the exception of a little slip-up about a computer, Father Tom had kept the parishioners' generous surprise a secret. He was Dean's mentor, friend, and housemate. Dean had lived with the priest at the rectory for a year before going to Sacred Heart. He had observed his flaws as well as his kindness and service. They kept in frequent contact.

On that day, the curtain opened to reveal a new laptop computer and software. The parishioners had raised five hundred dollars in cash as well. That meant a lot to Dean because it came from a parish of only 250 families. Even though he suspected that it wasn't all about him (was, perhaps, a consciously positive response to the negativity of the priest sexual abuse scandal), he recognized their sacrifice and the faith they were putting in him. Dean could have found a diocese outside of East Texas to sponsor him as a seminarian. He could have left these dry, dusty environs, with their virulent anti-Catholicism and myopia, behind. But East Texas was home, and the area needed priests. The night of that going-away party, he joked with the assembly, saying that now there was no turning back.

Dean had entered the seminary once before, after college, but he had left after only a week. At that time, he'd thought he had other options — a professional career, a committed life as a Catholic husband and father. But the intervening years and the persistence of the call had changed all that. None of those options would do if things didn't work out at Sacred Heart.

Dean asked the instructors why celibacy wasn't included in the book.

"We don't talk about that," Sister Lucille said, waving her hand as if to push the question away. She explained that it would be covered in the second year, but Dean felt cheated. He kept silent and covered up the last two letters of the word "Notes." It read "Not."

The day Heiser married his wife, Donna, he was absolutely certain that he wanted to remain married to her for the rest of his life. They had met at a factory outside Philadelphia that manufactured nuts and bolts. She was the most beautiful girl he had ever seen. Heiser was working there during a break from school in Wyoming. Donna worked a different shift, and Heiser would see her arrive just as he was leaving. After a few weeks of catching glimpses of her, he changed shifts. Finally, they had a date. She stood him up on their second date, but the next day after work she drove him home, and soon after that they became a couple.

They quit their jobs and moved to Wyoming. Despite a few twists and turns, their relationship survived. Heiser finished college at the University of Wyoming and got a job with the U.S. government, only to lose it due to cutbacks a short time later. They moved back east for a time to live with his parents. He seldom read the horoscopes, but one day he did, and under his sign, Libra, he read, "You will get a job in agriculture." *Unusually specific,* he thought. But he soon landed a job with the U.S. Department of Agriculture (USDA) and was back in Wyoming.

Their wedding took place on August 22, 1980, in the midst of this. It was a great party, with all their friends and family in attendance. There was nothing more that he could possibly want, Heiser thought. He was confident that love would see them through anything. Divorce was not an option. His parents were still married after many years, and Donna had told him that as the child of divorced parents, she knew the pain that the breakup of a marriage could cause and was against divorce. Only years later did Heiser come to see what Donna really meant, although she might not have realized it at the time: she had known the pain of divorce and knew she could survive it.

Soon the couple had a son. They named him Eric. The first four years of Eric's life were probably the happiest of Heiser's. He was married to the woman he loved; they had a wonderful son; he had a good job with the USDA; and they had bought their first home, a two-bedroom, single-level house in Riverton, Wyoming.

Then one day Donna told him that she didn't want to be married anymore. There was no warning. She said that there was no one else. It was just that she was young — Donna had been eighteen when they met, Heiser a few years older — and had never lived on her own. Heiser would have done anything to convince her to stay. He suggested counseling; she refused. In her mind, the matter was settled. When she left, she took all the photographs of them except one, which Heiser found later. When Donna's mother had left her father, he had cut his former wife out of every picture he owned. Heiser assumed that Donna didn't want him to do the same thing to her.

*I don't want to be divorced,* Heiser thought again and again. *I don't want to be divorced.*

But there was nothing he could do. The divorce was final in 1986. They had been married for six years; Eric was five. Heiser requested and received sole custody of his son. It was rare for a father to be granted sole custody, but Donna agreed. Heiser and Eric began life on their own. A few years later, when Donna's situation was a little more stable, she wanted to change the custody arrangement. She retained a lawyer, but that was as far as it went. Heiser made it known that he was prepared to fight to keep sole custody.

Donna lived 160 miles away. Eric spoke with her on the telephone daily and visited her every other weekend. During the summer, he lived with her for six weeks. Donna remarried twice over the years. By the time Heiser entered the seminary, she had two children from her third marriage and lived in Mesquite, Nevada.

Heiser was determined not to poison Eric's mind against his mother. He always told Eric that he had two parents who loved him, even though they didn't live together. Heiser managed to do this not only because he still loved Donna and their son but also because his faith, which had begun to grow in the early days of their marriage, was fast becoming central to his life.

Dean Haley arrived at the first student council meeting of the year in high gear. New man though he was, he was determined not to remain a spectator. Heiser chaired the council. Although he had decided not to let the meeting go a second longer than it had to, he used his gavel sparingly. Don Malin, the vice president, weighed in with his years of seminary experience. JJ, the secretary and treasurer, reported on the council's finances.

When the topic of planning the faculty dinner came up, Don said emphatically, "We need to get that set up early. I don't know if we're going to have time to do that today. How do you guys want to handle that?"

"Well, first of all, the guy next to you is like beaming," Dean said, referring to Bobby Rodriguez, who had already become known as a practical joker and organizer of birthday parties.

"No, no, no, no," Bobby protested.

Don didn't acknowledge Dean. There was a tendency for the older seminarians to keep their distance from the new men until it was clear that they would stick. Don and the others had already seen Dean's rough edges. No one would have bet on his sticking.

"Do we want to do a Halloween party? Can I get a straw vote?" Don asked.

"What about the budget?" Dean asked.

Heiser said that the student council's budget was roughly five thousand dollars.

"Five thousand and sixty dollars," JJ clarified.

Reading from the student council guidelines, Heiser said, "Says these parties cost one or two hundred bucks."

"Sometimes three," Don said. "If you really go crazy."

"It has to do with decorations," Heiser said. Don added that Barb Haag would provide both the food and the decorations.

"Idea is everybody dresses up. There's food and libations and libations . . . ," Don said.

"I believe Halloween is on a Thursday," Dean said, looking up from his PDA.

"We would do it on Thursday," Don said. "Or is that All Souls' Day?"

The discussion moved on to other parties. The Super Bowl party, with beer and snacks, carried unanimously. The Midwinter Follies and faculty appreciation dinner were already slated.

"That's a no-vote thing," Don explained. "It's going to happen."

Then Heiser brought up the matter of Augustine Carillo, who wanted student council sponsorship for his annual poetry reading. His idea was to have the poets of Sacred Heart read from their work, with wine and cheese to follow. The event had worked well the year before, but Augustine had since left the seminary program after realizing that a religious life was not for him. He remained as a day student to finish up his master's degree. Heiser continued to be close friends with him. There was generally no resentment against anyone who chose to leave the program at Sacred Heart, and the student council approved the event without debate.

Mention of Augustine prompted Don to inform the council of a delicate issue. When Augustine had discontinued his studies for the priesthood, he had been offered a job as a live-in manager of Elena's House, a small residence for people with AIDS. Every year, Milwaukee hosted an AIDS walk, and some of the money raised went to support Elena's House. Father Brackin had asked Don to make sign-up cards available to anybody who might want to support the walk, but there would be no official school sponsorship. In years past, this had caused a problem because some of the proceeds, it was said, might have ended up at Planned Parenthood, an organization opposed by the Catholic Church. The issue had caused a lot of dissension at the seminary.

"This issue is so complicated," JJ said with a wince. "Why don't we just give this house — if we've got guys working there — why don't we just give this house a grant? A couple hundred dollars. Not post this stuff. Because we're probably not going to give more than a couple hundred dollars out of this anyway. Why irritate some people about this? I don't think it's the HIV; it's the Planned Parenthood stuff. I mean, there's guys who don't want to be part of it [Planned Parenthood]. I speak for myself. I don't want to be a part of it. I don't want to give them any money. I won't give to United Way for the same reason."

"But I think that within the student body, there are probably people who are interested in walking," Heiser said.

"The other option is to go back to Father Brackin and say we could do a direct grant to Elena's House," Don said.

"That's what I'm saying," JJ said with a faint hint of annoyance.

"We could pose that to Father Brackin and see how he feels," Don said. "But he would have the right of refusal. I mean, we are in a hierarchy here. We'd have to get his approval."

Don observed that perhaps this was a teaching moment and Father Brackin wanted people to have the choice to participate or not. Maybe — as he had seen more than once during his four years at Sacred Heart — the rector wanted to raise the seminarians' consciousness and teach them that sometimes they had to partner with people they were not happy with to achieve a common humanitarian end.

Dean shifted restlessly in his seat. The discussion didn't seem to be getting anywhere.

"Does *this* student council sponsor this event?" Dean asked. "Yes or no?"

"I'm not sure it's a question of sponsoring," Heiser said.

"Are we in favor of it or not?" Dean insisted.

Someone suggested that a collection could be taken up during Mass. Don objected forcefully. "No. Because it would feel like a betrayal."

"To the . . . ?" someone asked.

"To the Church," Don finished. "Doing it within the context of the liturgy."

Don had the last word. Because of the strong feelings evident in the room, he said he needed to take the matter back to Father Brackin. He would report back to the council after meeting with the rector.

The moment Sacred Heart heard Ron Kendzierski play his violin, his relationship with the school permanently changed. His self-effacement, good humor, and academic brilliance had already gone a long way toward eliminating the initial awkwardness resulting from Ron's blindness. His Stevie Wonder impression and blind jokes were one thing, but the violin was a different matter altogether. It added a profound and soulful dimension to what had until then been little more than comic relief.

Don Malin had a master's degree in music. He had been a choir director and had developed an innovative way to teach Gregorian chant. He also had an extraordinary ability to play the guitar. But that was Don; expectations were already high.

With Ron, there were no expectations. He looked awkward in his seat before the assembly gathered in the Sacred Heart Chapel the day of his first performance. He began to rock back and forth. His hand moved jerkily to brush his face. He edged forward in his chair and appeared confused and expectant. In his world, there were no visual cues. Someone would have to touch him on the shoulder to let him know it was time to play. Ron was used to things going wrong and to people forgetting that he needed assistance.

When it was time to play, Ron rose to his feet. His bow poked around wildly in the air until it met the violin. Then all the extraneous motion disappeared. The sound that came from his violin was difficult to describe. It seemed that no matter what Ron played, the notes sounded as if they were ascending, ascending, ascending, then dropping back, regaining strength, and ascending again. The sound was a prayerful, hypnotic cry. It refused to stay within the boundaries prescribed for it and instead snaked around the chapel like incense drifting between the pillars and disappearing up into the darkened eaves.

There was not much school spirit at Sacred Heart — too great a disparity in ages, backgrounds, and opinions. But Ron became a source of pride for the men, as if the whole institution was buoyed up by the music of his violin.

Professor Christian Rich and Ron practiced in the afternoons. Invigorated by the black coffee he constantly drank, Ron would arrive in the chapel with his violin case under one arm. Tap, tap, tap . . . He would race along the dais, getting closer to the edge, until sometimes Professor Rich, too uncomfortable to remain silent, would say, "You're going to slip off again." And Ron would correct.

When they got to the organ, Ron would open his violin case and tune, begging the strings not to break as he tightened. Professor Rich would change into his organ shoes and sit down in front of the Byzantine panel. The great instrument would creak to life. At some point during their practice, someone might slip into the chapel to pray.

Don began to play with Ron early in the semester. *In concertante* — Don would think, to play together, to share your energy with another person. He would tap on Ron's shoulder to keep him in time. When Ron played alone, Don would sit back with his arms wrapped over and around his guitar to prevent it from making a sound. During the Spanish Mass, they kept within the music, but one day before rehearsal, they improvised. Jim Pemberton stopped what he was doing as soon as they began and slid into a seat near the dais where they played. The sound was beautiful. Ron had become an example to all of them, Jim thought. It wasn't just his musical talent either. Jim had never seen him down, and boy was Ron patient, never short and always willing to help. He was wonderfully good-humored and smart. What a great priest he would make.

One day after Ron played for the Spanish Mass, Jim led him out of the chapel by the arm. They knelt before the altar, Jim careful to direct Ron down toward the floor and then lift him up so that his violin case never touched the ground. Then they proceeded up the aisle. The chapel had emptied quickly, as everyone hurried off to breakfast, and only a few men were sitting or kneeling quietly in prayer. The smell of incense hung in the air. Jim and Ron stopped at the baptismal font in the entrance hall. Ron dipped his hand in the cool water, and it skittered, crablike, on the dimpled copper basin. He crossed himself, then stretched out a finger to Jim, who touched it, took some water, and crossed himself in turn. Then they were out of the hushed chapel and into the clatter of the main corridor.

By late October, Dean Haley was really struggling. This struggle had begun in the early days with the *Mickey Mouse Club* theme song and classmates older than his parents. From the start, he had been doing things his own way. He was suspicious of formation. He had strong instincts, which often were on target. One such instinct had involved an older seminarian and a disturbing story.

At one of the parties at the end of orientation, Dean had had too much to drink and found himself badgering Ricardo Vasquez about his sexual orientation. The next day, he apologized, but *in vino veritas*. His gut had told him that things were not quite sorted out for

Ricardo in the sexual identity department, and they should have been, given his proximity to ordination.

A few weeks later, on an otherwise sleepy weekend, word spread that two seminarians from a diocese out west had suddenly been called home and their sponsorship dropped — one man under the cloud of a sexual abuse charge. That man was Ricardo. One minute the two were part of the community — well liked and personable — and the next they were gone. Among the seminarians, the reaction was disbelief. Heiser had often helped one of the men practice his English for half an hour after Mass. Now he returned from a softball game to find the two men's rooms empty.

That weekend, the seminary was wild with rumors. Father Brackin, taking an unusual step, posted flyers informing everyone of a special meeting right after Mass on Monday morning. There he told the men that the allegation was credible. A year earlier, the seminarians might have dwelled on the departure. Now they moved quickly back to their work. There seemed to be a consensus that one of the men had been a victim of guilt by association, fallout from the harsh parameters outlined by the bishops in Dallas. "The truth will set me free," he wrote in a single-line e-mail message not long after his departure, but none of the seminarians heard from him again.

Dean had instincts about many other things as well, and when he found he could not address them, they became frustrations that altered his behavior for the worse. He was growing increasingly uncomfortable with what he was being taught. At every turn, Father McNally's Church History course seemed to be saying the Church was evil. He expected this kind of thing in deeply fundamentalist East Texas, but not in a Roman Catholic seminary. To test his instinct, Dean wrote a paper for the class criticizing the historical Church as a secular power. He was not surprised when he received a favorable response from Father McNally and a note: "Why is this true? Why is this so often the way? For example, the Church-state union meant that the state used the Church for its own purposes to impose state control. Thus religion was just one more way to coerce and control."

Dr. Shippee's theology class affected him in much the same way. As for his philosophy class, Dean enjoyed the classroom experience but never opened a book.

One day, Father Hugh Birdsall, Sacred Heart's legendary professor of interpersonal communications, stood before the blackboard and repeated words just spoken on a video about the dynamics of confrontation, or "carefrontation."

"Many people," he said with his arms crossed, "are unable to move when faced with mixed emotions or anxiety." By early October, this sentence described Dean. He resented what he was learning, he didn't feel particularly close to anyone at the seminary, and his medication regimen was suffering. Father Tom Latham, his mentor from back home, spent time on the phone trying to convince Dean that he had to get his medication regulated. Father Tom had always been a big source of support for Dean. He had even sponsored Dean for the seminary and given him encouragement when Dean had faltered during the application process. But Father Tom was far away now. Sometimes Dean followed his advice, but more often he did not.

Dean could not sleep and found himself spending hours alone in his room in front of his computer, surfing the Net or watching downloaded movie shorts or the DVDs he had been buying with the Wal-Mart gift card given to him by the parishioners back home. Dean disconnected his phone for a while, setting off alarms with his study and prayer group partners. He shaved off his mustache. He stopped wearing a jacket and tie because one of the new men seemed to be making passes at him. Dean was making regular trips to a chiropractor, whose office featured a sign that referred to the waiting room as "a way station to better health." He also began butting heads with his formation adviser, who told him point-blank that he must communicate or consider leaving the seminary.

Seminary was fast becoming a survival test, the boot camp he had craved when he'd first arrived. When Ricardo and the other seminarian left, Dean was actually inspired to stay. He remembered an experience he'd had in the marines. His unit had been on a long march with full gear. Every time someone had dropped out or faltered, one of the guys would shout, "Give me some pompoms, man . . . You're just cheering me the fuck on." Dean hadn't quit. He'd stayed to the end of the march and ended up with feet so badly blistered that he was on crutches for weeks. He recited that line now. "Give me some pompoms, man." He was going to complete this march on his own terms, no matter what Father Tom or any of the faculty at Sacred Heart might say.

Even though Dean was sleeping through Mass and classes, he was certain that his computer-based system of organization would work. What were a few missed community events when you were committing your life to the priesthood? He was here for the grades, and he would deliver. But he needed more space and thought it ridiculous that only those men on the verge of ordination were granted an extra room, especially when there were so many empty rooms in the dormitory. To the bold went the spoils. So one day he laid claim to an empty room down the hall. He would keep the new space as a bedroom where he could sleep undisturbed. As it turned out, someone dropped a hint to the staff after Dean slept through yet another class. He was soon discovered in his squatted room, fast asleep. The next thing he knew, he was summoned before the rector. Father Brackin told him that he had to give up one of the rooms. In the end, he moved into the new room. He was grateful for the leniency and vowed that he would get his act together.

But the frustrations continued. Dean would find himself in class thinking, *I just want to be on a honeymoon in Florida right now.* He didn't really believe that he wanted to get married, just that he wanted to be anywhere but here. He brought his laptop to class and watched movies on its DVD player. He saw *Training Day* against the backdrop of Church history and *Return of the Jedi* against a discussion of the early Church fathers. He watched comic shorts and bloopers downloaded off the Internet. Anyone sitting behind him in class could see, but Dean didn't seem to care.

The other seminarians talked about his behavior. Dean, they agreed, wouldn't be with them much longer.

Dean decided to switch formation advisers. Everyone told him he was crazy — it was like putting a target on his back. But on October 7, he did it anyway.

Canon law governs almost every aspect of the institutional Roman Catholic Church. The law details Church procedures, outlines regulations, and safeguards rights. It was to canon law's protection of a priest's basic rights that Father Brackin looked when he predicted that the Vatican would curb the American bishops' zero tolerance plan.

For Don Malin, canon law served a more immediate purpose. Canon 1036 requires that every candidate for the priesthood write a letter to his bishop requesting candidacy. A man for whom the diaconate is the ultimate goal is called a permanent deacon, but a man who is preparing for the priesthood is ordained a transitional deacon first and then, usually within a few months, a priest. A deacon can perform weddings, funerals, and baptisms; read the Gospel at Mass; and preach. A deacon cannot consecrate the bread and wine, hear confessions, or administer the sacrament of the sick (often confused with the last rites, which is only one of the many rites in the pastoral care of the sick). The permanent diaconate was reinstated in 1964 during the Second Vatican Council after being out of existence for nearly a thousand years. Since then, the number of permanent deacons had grown rapidly, and by 2002 there were more than thirteen thousand in the United States.

Don Malin was set to become a *transitional* deacon that November. He had been skipping the dessert bar and following the Atkins diet, a popular high-protein regimen, to lose weight. He was down to 206 pounds. But the real preparation for the diaconate and priesthood was at the nexus of the internal and the external. To be ordained a deacon, Don was required to formally pronounce on paper the oaths that he would later speak at his ordination. However unique a man's calling to the priesthood, the letter was identical for all. Don had to copy it by hand from a form.

He wrote, "I wish at this time formally to request candidacy for the Diocese of Pueblo. It is my intention to complete my priestly studies and to request ordination for the Diocese of Pueblo . . ."

He paused. He had chosen to write the letter in the solitude of a classroom, and mechanical though the exercise seemed, the years of formation suddenly came alive for him, and the future became palpable. He thought, *It's really going to happen. Nothing now is standing in my way.* A long time ago, when Don was in his twenties, he had approached the Jesuits about becoming a priest, but they had told him that he was not ready to apply. He had taken it as a personal rejection. Soon afterward, Don had married.

But they had been right in discouraging him, Don realized later. Even after the formation process had begun in earnest this time, it was remarkable how much growing he had to do.

He continued to write: "I therefore respectfully ask your permission to receive candidacy here at Sacred Heart School of Theology on October 28, 2002. If this is acceptable, a letter from you is requested granting the Reverend James D. Brackin, the President Rector, permission to accept my candidacy on your behalf. Also on October 29, 2002, those who will shortly be ordained to the diaconate will be making their profession of faith, oath of freedom and knowledge, and oath of fidelity before the President Rector, very Reverend James D. Brackin, SCJ, here at Sacred Heart School of Theology. If it is acceptable that I join this group, a letter is required granting Father Brackin permission to accept my profession of faith, oath of freedom and knowledge, and oath of fidelity on your behalf."

A profession of faith is something that has to be made every time a new ecclesiastical office is received. The profession includes the Nicene Creed (a required part of every Sunday Mass for both lay and clergy, in which the believer recites the tenets of the faith), but it also goes further: "With firm faith I believe as well everything contained in God's word that was handed down in tradition and proposed by the Church whether in solemn judgment or through the ordinary and universal magisterium." *This is the big part,* Don thought. When the average person considers what the Church stands for (more often framed in the popular mind as what the Church is against), he or she is thinking of the magisterium, or the official teaching authority of the Church. There was a time, even after Don had entered the seminary, when he was unsure whether he would be able to make it through because of the profession of faith.

The Church's opposition to contraception and divorce is covered by the magisterium. So is the Church's belief in the Immaculate Conception and the divinity of Jesus, as well as its advocacy for the impoverished. There were things in the magisterium that Don could not get his mind around, but he had known that he would have to overcome this resistance if he was to be ordained. He had been determined not to take the promises dishonestly.

As far as the magisterium went, Don's resistance had been in the area of sexual teaching. The Church clearly opposed birth control, but Don couldn't really accept the Church's position. Somewhere along the way, Don had read Pope John Paul II's *Gospel of Life,* and it had convinced him that birth control, abortion, euthanasia, and the death penalty are part of a continuum. The organizing principle is the sacredness of each human life. To be against one of these principles necessarily meant that a person was against all four. He had reflected on his own marriage in light of this and had become convinced that part of the reason for its failure had been that his wife had never been open to the prospect of children. They had used birth control from the start, and Don now believed that taking the procreative possibility out of the act of making love deprived it of a profound and holy dimension and risked reducing it to a selfish pleasure. Don knew how complicated this area was and how carefully one had to tread — especially as a pastor in a nation where a reported 75 percent of Catholics did not hold the Church's view.

In the silence of the classroom, Don was determined to take his time with the letter and let its significance sink in. He figured that he had been in the process of discernment in some way or another for almost three decades. If there was wiggle room for the potential candidate, the second part of the oath narrowed it with its precise language: "I also firmly accept and hold everything that is proposed by the same Church definitively . . . which either the Roman Pontiff or the College of Bishops annunciate when they exercise authentic Magisterium, even if they proclaim those teachings in an act that is not definitive. So help me God."

*I can do this,* Don thought as he copied. *I'm there.*

". . . in compliance with Canon 1036 of the 1983 Code of Canon Law, I'm petitioning for the Sacred Order of Deacon . . ."

If this had been a film, Don imagined that right now he would hear in the soundtrack a tap on the kettledrum. Then the basses and cellos would begin a long note.

". . . granted your permission I will be admitted to candidacy on October 28th, I have received the ministries of Lector and Acolyte, I have diligently considered the matter before God, and I declare I am impelled by no compulsion or force or fear to receive this order. I voluntarily desire it . . ."

*I voluntarily desire it,* Don repeated to himself.

". . . and I wish to receive it of my own free will, since I believe and feel that I am truly called by God."

*Feel.* The word was problematic. Don believed that he had discerned well during his time at Sacred Heart, but he was also aware of all the bad discernments he had made in his life. How many times had he fooled himself? A positive feeling was not enough. Yet *this* positive feeling had been confirmed by his own contemplation and prayers. It had also been confirmed through unanimous faculty votes and through people back home assuring him that he was going to make a good priest.

". . . and I am aware fully of all the obligations I should contract in the reception of this order, which I freely wish to receive, and I earnestly and sincerely intend to observe them diligently through the whole course of my life. I acknowledge especially that I clearly understand that the obligation of celibacy means that I firmly intend to fulfill it freely and observe it in its entirety to the last day of my life with the help of God."

In his solitude, the words resonated like wedding vows. He was choosing to be the bride of the Church. He was being asked to be faithful to the call of chastity. Although Don had come to the seminary thinking he could handle chastity, he had been challenged once. Now he remembered how he had faced the attraction: *Do I want to have someone in my life for the rest of my life? Am I going to muck things up with the confusion and trouble that would come? I was given the grace to overcome it. But not without sadness, because there is always that sadness when you know you can't do anything about it or don't want to do anything about it, especially if the other person is interested. But I said "no." The life that I have now is the one I have chosen and discerned. This life is the one I want. I was free to leave the seminary, but I knew I wanted to do what I was doing because it was for the sake of God, for the sake of the people of God, for the sake of the call.*

Don continued: "I sincerely promise that I shall obey willingly all commands of my superiors and whatever ecclesiastical discipline requires of me according to the norms of the Canon . . ."

*This comes down to the very question of who I am in the face of God and who I am for the people. I want to be evangelical in my life, so the people will see that I — that guy right there — has chosen to live a certain kind of life. They say that strong currents run deep and weak currents meander. I want a strong current running through my life.*

Don finished: "I ask you to consider my request to be ordained to the Order of Deacon, which will be conferred by you, Bishop Tafoya, on November 23, 2002, at Sacred Heart School of Theology."

He had known the date for a year. He was convinced that the glory of the call, the beauty of the call, and its essential truth were being confirmed all around him. He could rely on profound help from all corners even as the Church was assailed from within and from without. The letter was finished. The hallways were still. Gratitude flooded through Don. Tears filled his eyes.

The 102-year-old man Heiser visited weekly wanted to die. All the people he had known were dead. Florence, on the other side of town, wanted to live, but not badly enough to be brought back to life. She had a standing do-not-resuscitate order. Most of the Franciscan sisters he visited were terminally ill; they would be dead within a few months. Others, those off the official visitation list, had been hanging on for years at the nursing home, their cubicles decorated with religious icons, posters of Jesus and the Virgin Mary, and pieces of personal memorabilia. For one sister, who was slipping into the cloudy world of macular degeneration, constant fatigue, and sourness, a photocopied sheet taped above her bed read, JOY IS THE IN-FALLIBLE PROOF OF THE PRESENCE OF GOD.

These people had become Heiser's responsibility as he fulfilled his second-year field education requirement. At first, it looked like Sacred Heart might not be able to send anyone out for such fieldwork. The consequences of the sexual abuse scandal had leached into everything. Insurance companies balked at covering the hospital visits of priests and seminarians, and health care providers could not afford the risk. This meant fewer religious in places where more religious were needed. But in the end, Father Bob Schiavone, the head of field placement at Sacred Heart, somehow ironed out the details and found a place for Heiser. The seminarian was permitted to make rounds twice a week for three hours at a time.

Visits weren't easy. One moment Heiser was sitting in his truck listening to classic rock, and the next he was watching someone die. He could have done other things, such as teach religious education. But a friend who worked in a hospice had told him that priests are generally not good with death and dying. She saw many priests fumble, behave callously, or bring little comfort to the dying. Heiser had vowed that he wasn't going to be one of those priests. But sometimes a patient made him recoil in spite of himself.

"How would you like it if I cut your dick off?" the old woman in the bed screamed at Heiser's supervisor.

Then she turned on Heiser. "What are you doing with that stupid-looking face of yours?"

She made obscene gestures. She ranted. She grabbed the supervisor's hand and wouldn't let go. There was nothing wrong with her, she insisted. Couldn't they see? Why did she have to stay in the hospital? She felt perfectly fine.

"Get me out of here," she shouted.

Heiser thought that she looked as if she'd had a rough life. She had been living at home with cancer when she had fallen and been brought to the hospital for observation. She had been in the hospital for three days.

After they left the woman's room, Heiser's supervisor told him he thought that perhaps the cancer had affected the woman's brain. More than that, though, she was scared.

*Scared?* Heiser thought. Belligerent, nasty, mean — all of those he could accept — but scared?

Three days later, the woman died.

By late October, two of the patients Heiser had been visiting regularly also had died. But Florence endured. She had an apartment in Luther Manor, an assisted living development. She had a very bad heart; a tube delivered oxygen to her lungs from a machine next to her La-Z-Boy recliner. Photos of her husband and family lined her shelves. A painting of Jesus hung on the living room wall, and a sign near the kitchen said, THIS IS GOD, I WILL TAKE CARE OF ALL YOUR PROBLEMS TODAY.

One rainy day in late October, Heiser brought Florence Communion. He carried it from Sacred Heart in a pyx tucked into the left pocket of his raincoat. He sat down opposite Florence on the sofa, and after some small talk, he held a Communion service. They prayed for the people she knew as well as for those she didn't know. They prayed for peace in the world. Heiser prayed for Florence, who was scheduled to move to a nursing home the following week. Florence was scared about the move — she did not want to leave her familiar surroundings — but she maintained her placid demeanor. Heiser gave her the host, then they sat in silence for a long time. When Heiser left, he told Florence that he would see her soon. As it turned out, he never saw her again. She died hours before the scheduled move to the nursing home.

At the Marian Franciscan Center, Heiser visited a group of nuns who occupied one end of the second floor. Sister Angela never said very much and was frequently asleep when he arrived. Sister Antonice, who lived around the corner, was entirely different. She patrolled the hallway in her wheelchair and had spunk.

"Did you ever think of all the saints in heaven?" she would ask him in a hushed, awestruck voice. "All those people . . ."

Heiser would nod and smile.

"Heaven must be full," she would marvel. "Just think, from the time of Adam and Eve, all the saints in heaven and the poor souls in purgatory. See, when you die and you're not holy enough for heaven, you go to a place called purgatory. Did you ever hear of that? How many people must be up in heaven. All those wonderful people up there."

The thought seemed to make Sister Antonice very happy. She had been a teacher for decades, and she still prayed for her first graders every day even though she could no longer remember their names.

Heiser never told Sister Antonice that the Church's concept of purgatory had changed from time served in a particular place to a purification process that may happen at the instant of death. He didn't want to upset her theology. But the thought of Sister Antonice constantly praying, whether lying in bed or rolling about in her wheelchair, inspired him. *You might never think of Sister Antonice again,* he mused, *but she is praying for you.*

Sister Angela had been a nun for sixty-one years and entirely independent up until a few weeks before Heiser's visit. She said that the doctors had told her that she was doing better, but if that was true, he thought, why was she on his list? For most of her life, Sister Angela had taken care of orphans. Now she lay in bed and worried aloud that she should be more concerned about death. Sometimes she actually tried to be, but she just couldn't.

"You know how great it is going to be," Heiser said. By "it" he meant heaven and seeing the face of God. "It is going to be greater than anything we've ever thought of."

Sister Angela agreed. But today she was a bit worried because one of her orphans had dropped out of contact. Heiser and his supervisor, who was not Catholic, prayed with Sister Angela for this orphan. They also thanked God for her years of service. As Heiser was leaving, she took his hand and told him that she would pray for him to remain in the priesthood. "We need priests," she said with feeling, as if a grand old world was slipping away.

The radio in Heiser's truck played Grand Funk Railroad on the way home: "Heaven help me, Heaven help me . . . although I'm feeling mighty sick . . ." As he pulled into the parking lot back at school, a familiar car with Toronto plates reminded him that they were losing another man. Charles McDermott, who had been at Sacred Heart for three and a half years, had just announced that he was calling it quits and moving back to Canada. It had been a shock to everyone. Charles was telling people that he might return, but that was what everyone expected him to say under the circumstances. Few seminarians ever made a clean break. Jim Pemberton had given him an inspirational book on leaps of faith called *If You Want to Walk on Water, You've Got to Get Out of the Boat*.

When someone like Charles left, it was disturbing on many levels. The seminarians were told that God would give them the grace to get through formation and the strength to meet any challenge. So when someone left, Heiser would wonder, *Did the man have a vocation in the first place? Was the evil one at work drawing him away from his vocation?*

But such thoughts did not linger. Heiser found his fieldwork illuminating and his course load easy to manage. He had just celebrated his forty-eighth birthday, and Eric had sent him a card quoting Mark Twain: "When I was fourteen, my father was so ignorant I could hardly stand to have the old man around. But when I got to be twenty-one, I was astonished at how much he had learned in seven years." Things were going great for Heiser.

It would have been easier if Ron Kendzierski had hated the place, but he didn't. He had grown fond of Sacred Heart and the people there: late-night coffee in the dining hall; pizza and beer at the Charcoal

Grill; impromptu jam sessions in the student lounge; David Placette cooking gumbo for the entire school. He loved spending time hanging around staff offices and talking. When he had been sick earlier in the fall, Joe McDonald had brought lunch to his room, and Bob Brooks had brought dinner. When he had tried to sneak out to get something done in the library, Father Brackin had spotted him in the hall and sent him back to bed.

Halloween was approaching. It was one of Ron's favorite holidays. He bought a plastic witch that made threats and cackled when anyone squeezed it. He put her on top of his bureau. Mary Anne Wheeler, the gardener, had lined the bridge to the library with intricately carved jack-o'-lanterns that were lit at night. Plastic bats hung from the ceiling. The student council had organized a karaoke party.

Ron knew that other men were struggling as the end of the semester approached and the pressure mounted with more papers and projects coming due. He had his share, but it wasn't academics that worried him. Blindness might have seemed like a disadvantage in studying, and sometimes it was. But anyone walking past Ron's room and finding the door open (which it usually was) and Ron inside working (which he usually wasn't) might hear a prolonged chipmunk shriek emanating from a tape player on his desk. That sound was a book being played at the recorder's highest speed. Ron didn't miss a word. Not only could he get through books much faster than the other men, but the papers here seemed short — not like those he had written in graduate school. He would have finished his midterms early, but his paper for Professor Gotcher took him a bit more time because he had to hunt through the *Catechism of the Catholic Church* for the right passages.

Despite his earlier reservations about immersing himself in too many activities, he was committed to playing his violin not only at all the Spanish Masses but also at almost every major service at Sacred Heart. He also played at one Sunday Mass at St. Benedict's across town. Every Thursday, he helped catechize a group of developmentally disabled kids. He had tried to keep up regular exercise on the treadmill in the basement gymnasium after taping Braille markers to the controls. The routine became less appealing after he took a spill off the machine and also learned of the suicide on the nearby loading dock. He had always believed in ghosts.

Ron was immersed and loving it, but now he had a problem. When he had arrived, he had known that he was ideologically at odds with the Catholic Church. But he had framed this difference as a challenge that he would ride out by keeping his head low and his agenda discreet. At that time, he'd had no doubt that he wanted to become a priest. Now he wasn't so sure.

Ron hated being alone. That was why he kept his door open and probably part of the reason he said yes to every activity on offer. That was also why he had left the religious community of the Crosiers. He had thought that religious life would mean good, hard, meaningful work and people to share that work with. He had not found that kind of life with the Crosiers. The men there seemed to disappear into their rooms at night instead of sharing the events of the day with one another. Then Ron thought that he would find a better sense of community in the priesthood. He approached the Diocese of Gaylord, Michigan, because it was pretty close to home and had a population of elderly people. Ron loved working with the elderly. The application process became a struggle because he had to convince the diocese that his blindness was not a bar. In the end, he was accepted.

Ron had focused so much on the struggle to get into Sacred Heart that he'd arrived at the seminary with only a vague understanding of what a priest really does and the kind of life he lives. Ron had not expected the heavy emphasis on a priest's sacramental role. Instead, he had envisioned himself as a priest-activist or priest-agitator, bringing Jesus to the people in new, unorthodox ways. Nor had he realized how transient a priest's life could be and how little control he had over basic decisions such as where he would live and for how long. A priest was at the mercy of his bishop as to parish assignment. The days of a letter turning up without warning and informing a priest to pack his bags and appear at a new parish by such and such a date were largely over. Priests now had more input into the decision, but most generally go where the bishop assigns them. The longer Ron stayed at Sacred Heart, the more disturbing this prospect seemed. He wanted to grow roots somewhere, not have them torn up every six years.

And then there was the matter of returning to an empty rectory at the end of the day. Because of the shortage of priests, few lived together anymore. Ron could live with celibacy, even though he thought it was a dumb rule. But loneliness and isolation? A church musician had recently told him that at the big holidays such as Easter, he would be insanely busy as a priest, surrounded by people, and then when it was over, everyone would go home and he would be left alone. *But I don't want to ditch Sacred Heart,* he thought, so he kept trying to convince himself that he really didn't mind being alone.

When that didn't work, he began to look in a new direction: the diaconate. Deacons could be married and have families. They often stayed associated with the same parish for decades. But Sacred Heart was a place for training priests, not deacons. Even though the diaconate and priesthood shared some qualities, the formation process for the diaconate was totally different. If he wanted to become a permanent deacon, he would have to leave Sacred Heart. This prospect presented a host of problems. There was the problem of his vocation director, to whom he felt an obligation, irrational though it might be, to become a priest. Then there was Sacred Heart itself, and Father Brackin, who had authorized the purchase of the costly Braille printer in the library to accommodate Ron. He felt he owed the school something.

In addition, Ron believed that by becoming a priest, he would acquire a certain amount of power to effect change in the Church. A deacon didn't have the same power. And if he didn't stay the course and show that a blind man could be an effective priest, he would be letting down other blind people. Perhaps he shouldn't leave after all.

He knew that he was a bit wacky, but you have to be a little wacky to consider being a priest, he thought. You can't be mainstream. The next step was unclear.

Ron spoke to Don Malin about his struggle after music practice one day. Don listened carefully but offered no solutions. Ron didn't tell Don about something — or rather someone — else: Tina. When Ron was in graduate school in Kalamazoo, Michigan, a girl named Rachel lived upstairs from him. Rachel was in her final year of college when she became pregnant with her boyfriend Matt's child. The couple struggled. Ron gave them money and maxed out his credit cards filling their refrigerator for six weeks. He helped Matt get a job at a bar where Ron played music. First Matt stopped showing up for work, and then he left Rachel. Rachel moved up north with the baby, but she and Ron stayed in touch. Her daughter, Serena, became one of Ron's many "nieces" and "nephews."

Rachel introduced Ron to Tina, who was in her late thirties. She was like an aunt to Rachel. Ron and Tina began to spend time together. Ron's mom, who had always been protective of him, seemed uneasy with the relationship. Tina had been a party girl, but when Ron met her, she seemed to be getting her life together. Ron liked her, but he didn't realize how much until after he had signed his letter of intent to become a candidate with the Crosiers. At the time, he reasoned, *I can't have two wives, and I've already picked one.* He stayed in touch with Tina, who lived in Cadillac, Michigan, but went to the Crosiers in Minnesota anyway.

Now he was entertaining feelings for her again. Tina had a twelve-year-old son and was struggling to raise him alone. She had some health concerns as well. Ron knew that Tina wasn't the most sensible choice for the wife of a blind man who had no ready ability to earn a living, but he had had feelings for her for eighteen months, and they would not go away. Besides, he liked the fact that Tina was involved in community action. In addition to helping out local kids on her own, she had been working with Head Start and another volunteer group.

If he did leave Sacred Heart, he wouldn't want to sacrifice his life's work for Tina. He wouldn't give up his social justice goals or his need to help people. Whether it meant becoming a deacon or doing that work apart from the Church, Ron needed to be involved. Tina would have to understand that.

Seminarians at Sacred Heart weren't allowed to date, but Ron didn't really think he was doing that when it came to Tina. The phone calls that lasted late into the night were just part of the discernment process, he thought, as was their growing closeness. Right now, he was just talking, kicking ideas around, and weighing a possible future. How could there be anything wrong with that?

There had been no obvious repercussions from Dean Haley's decision to switch formation advisers. Even so, Dean was enduring yet another lecture from his new adviser, Father Donald Krebs. If he wasn't doing his reading for his philosophy class, Father Krebs chided, he was being dishonest — no matter how good his grades were. Dean must abandon his secular attitude toward academics. The seminary was not just a school, the priest insisted. If Dean went through the seminary and didn't follow the syllabus, do the reading, or give himself over to the formation process and was ultimately ordained anyway — well, he wouldn't be a true reflection of what Sacred Heart could produce. Without becoming overly scrupulous, Father Krebs directed, Dean was to go back and do the reading he had skipped.

When Dean got back to his room, he picked up one of his philosophy books and began to read. *Pretty interesting stuff,* he thought. Then and there, he decided to make the effort. If he didn't read it now, chances were he never would.

The next night was Saturday, and he and Bob Brooks had tickets to Yakov Smirnoff. The Russian comedian did not disappoint. Dean laughed harder than he had since arriving at Sacred Heart. When the men walked out of the theater, they found the street filled with revelers dressed in Halloween costumes. The police had closed off the street to make room for the massive party. *Halloween*, Dean marveled. He had forgotten all about it.

Dean felt himself coming alive. He loved to dance, but it was one of the things he thought seminarians had to give up. A bit bolder after three beers, he started dancing. He found himself talking to everyone: men, women, the kind of people for whom a seminary was a distant and foggy concept. *Nourishment*, Dean thought as he and Bob bounced from bar to bar. He felt a twinge of fear that somehow this night out would get back to his vocation director. Luckily, he thought, a little hazily, a lot of people were dressed as priests and nuns. Sometimes he told people with glee that he was a seminarian; other times he kept this to himself. The early hours approached, and although he was careful not to give anyone the impression he was on the prowl, Bob apparently thought otherwise.

"Oh, you're still here," Bob shouted over the crowd, looking puzzled. "I thought you were . . . Well, what did you yell before?"

"We're going back to where we were," Dean replied.

"I thought you said, 'I'm going home with her.'"

"Okay," Dean said in disbelief, "but I'm *your* ride."

Bob apologized. It was just that he had seen women flitting around Dean, and after Dean had had a few drinks, Bob didn't know where he was headed.

"I didn't drive twelve hundred miles to have a one-night stand," Dean said. "Or even a one-year stand."

After that night, things began to change for Dean. He got his meds under control by setting his alarm for an early wake-up. That way, they would work during the day but wear off by bedtime so that he could fall asleep. As a result, he began to sleep regularly. Then he learned that his ex-girlfriend was dating again. Instead of being bothered by the news, as he had expected, he found it liberating. She seemed to be getting on with her life, and by doing that, she was freeing him to get on with his.

Dean's midterm grades were good, and people were starting to ask him to help serve at other churches on Sunday. His Caritas prayer group met every week and had become the cornerstone of his experience at Sacred Heart. Every seminarian had to participate in at least one extracurricular group that incorporated discussion and prayer. Caritas is an international confederation of Catholic relief and social service organizations. The Caritas prayer group ate out once a week at St. Martin's Inn, a restaurant-bar decorated with NASCAR memorabilia. They grilled each other about their vocations: "Where are you right now?" "If the bishop said he wanted to ordain you tomorrow, are you ready?" They said the Angelus, a prayer to Mary. Some of them also made a habit of saying the Divine Office, the daily prayer formula said by the clergy. The lawyers in the group had helped Dean prepare for his meeting with the rector after he had been caught with the second room. Through them he'd learned that many of his fellow seminarians thought that he wouldn't be coming back the next semester. He respected their advice. Joe McDonald delivered wisdom with gentleness. Tom Mescall, a former federal judge, leaned back, thumbs stretching his suspenders, and quizzed Dean as if he were still in chambers. *These guys will keep my ass in line,* Dean concluded. More than anything, Dean began to slow down his head. He realized that his vocation didn't have to be worked out that very moment. He had years.

The pompoms came out again when Deacon Max abruptly chose to depart after lying about the circumstances of an auto accident and the possibility of an alcohol problem. He was said to have been ferrying Ron Kendzierski and other classmates to various locations around Milwaukee while under the influence. Within a few hours, and with no warning to anyone but the administration, he packed up his van, left his keys and a stack of books in his room, and disappeared. From Dean's perspective, a major player — an ordained man, no less — hadn't been able to hack it and had dropped out of the march. The pompoms also made a brief appearance after the rector raised the specter of a troubled seminarian pulling down shower curtains and defecating in sinks on the fourth floor. In response to the news, Dean thought, *I'm not doing so bad. There's someone here who really doesn't have his shit together.*

Dean also experienced a minor academic triumph. He had been foundering on the concepts he was encountering in Fundamental Theology. But clarity suddenly came the moment Dr. Shippee held up a Bible and said, "This is a theology book, not a history book." He gave as an example the two stories of David and Goliath and the different ways Goliath dies in the stories. Neither ending is reconciled with the other. He took this observation to Father McNally's next class. Dean told his professor that he had had his paradigms mixed up. He had been applying a historical approach to theological study and a theological approach to historical study. To Dean's surprise, Father McNally complimented him. He had picked up that crucial distinction very quickly — it was one that most seminarians struggled with. All along, he had been certain that he was behind the curve.

Of course, he still got upset with the occasional Church historian who might suggest that Roman Catholicism risked marginalization in the modern world. If that was true, objected Dean, becoming a priest in the Catholic Church was like asking for a job on a sinking ship. That concept irked him. He was being asked to give up things (such as the possibility of marriage) that were here now but would not be here tomorrow for something (the Church) that he had been sure would be here tomorrow but now was being told might not be.

When Archbishop Timothy Dolan, the new head of the Church in Milwaukee, visited the seminary for the first time in mid-November at the invitation of the Knights of Columbus, Dean was inspired. At the reception for Dolan, the archbishop shared a beer with one of the pre-theology students and backslapped and hugged his way through the crowd. Dean was taken with his congeniality but more impressed by something the archbishop said: Young men will commit their lives to a mystery, but they will not commit their lives to a question mark. The sinking-ship model of the Church was the question mark, and Dean refused to believe that was the final word on his vocation to the priesthood.

The school's Halloween party in the dining hall followed his own outing by a week. It reinforced Dean's turnaround. There was a keg of beer, a karaoke machine, general frivolity, and dancing. Ron

Kendzierski wore a big plastic football on his head. Mary DeSantis, a consecrated virgin who taught Spanish, and some of the nuns danced. Dean grabbed the mike and, hoping to surprise everyone, tried to perform an Eminem song. But they only had an uncensored version, and he found himself singing, "Can't say that, can't say that, can't say that" over and over. Around midnight, fifteen seminarians crowded onto the small stage, spilling off its edges, and managed to do one last song, "American Pie." For a moment, the great fishbowl, the forum of scrutiny and correction that was Sacred Heart, seemed to disappear, and Dean at last felt that he was starting to belong. The mystery was emerging from behind the question mark.

"You don't intend to baptize. You don't intend to baptize," Professor Christian Rich repeated to the men as they prepared to perform a practice baptism.

It was vital for the men to remember that this was merely practice. Baptism is, to quote the *Catechism*, "the basis of the whole Christian life, the gateway to life in the Spirit." It could be done only once. Through baptism, a human being is freed from all sin, is reborn as a son or daughter of God, and becomes invested in the mission of the Church. Baptism requires the simple Trinitarian formula ("I baptize you, in the name of the Father, and of the Son, and of the Holy Spirit") and a simultaneous pouring of water on the head. It was this formula, along with some additional words and actions and a little chrism oil, that Don Malin was about to use on a real baby in the Sacred Heart Chapel for his Deacon in Liturgy course.

"I don't intend to baptize. I don't intend to baptize," Don repeated to himself. Dr. LoPresti and his wife stood before him with their baby. The baby's actual baptism would take place the following Sunday, but the LoPrestis had allowed a group of soon-to-be-deacons to use their newborn for baptism practice. The sun streamed in yellow bars through the stained glass of the tall, narrow windows. It shouldn't have mattered even if Don did intend to do the real thing.

Unless the baby was dying, a valid minister was needed. Some of the men had their albs on backward. Albs are white tunics worn during many Catholic rituals. Dennis Cloonan performed the ritual in English, and the baby was fine. The next man used English, too, but the baby cried. Don decided to try Spanish. He checked that his alb and stole were on the right way. He had the books for the ritual in both English and Spanish. There was a problem, though. One of the parents needed to unbutton the baby's shirt. But this became a struggle, and as they were trying to open the baby's shirt, Don could only stand there, with chrism oil threatening to drip off his thumb onto both mother and baby, waiting for it all to come together. "This is just practice," he finally said. "We'll just skip it." But Mrs. LoPresti insisted that they proceed.

"Did I get the right chest?" Don asked the couple afterward.

By early November, Don's diaconate ordination was only a few weeks away. In late October, he had been admitted to candidacy for the priesthood. The ceremony had been brief but powerful, because in it he'd promised to be celibate, to fulfill the office, and to profess that he believed everything that the Church taught in the magisterium. He had gone out for drinks with Father Marty and some of the other men afterward. So far, the fall had been good to him. He had been healthy, except for one severe bout of allergies that seemed to have been brought on by scented candles or incense being burned by another student on his floor. Invitations had been sent out for his diaconate ordination, and he was expecting a large crowd, including his spiritual director from Colorado and his father from California. He was still trying to follow the Atkins diet.

The prospect of his ordination made him giddy. Knowing that his time at Sacred Heart was limited, he enjoyed everyday things like sitting around the table talking during meals, driving twenty-five miles north to play music for a Mass or a party with friends, even stopping by Father Marty's office for advice on figuring out First Corinthians.

"You know, Paul calls us dumb idiots if we believe in the Resurrection, and it turns out it isn't true," Don observed.

"I like that," Father Marty replied. "Dumb idiots . . . putzes."

"Schmucks," Don said. He smiled and dipped his hand into the basket on Father Marty's credenza which contained little laminated pieces of paper bearing a single word of inspiration: peace, truth, release. These were Father Marty's angels. Don's read "release."

"Christian tarot," Don declared.

Father Marty laughed and said he was looking forward to Don's sermons.

One night Don was fine-tuning a PowerPoint presentation for a class when Carl Hellwig, known to all as Wiggy, wandered in for a chat. Wiggy was a second-year student and Sacred Heart's resident funnyman. When Wiggy had returned in August, he dressed in Hawaiian shirts, shorts, and sandals. Beads of sweat often rolled down his wide face. He wore a towel rolled into a tube around his neck because of his unusually heavy perspiration, a condition he labeled "sweatmata." Even in November, he favored Hawaiian shirts, although the sweating, the towel, and the battery-powered fan that he had bought from a late-night television shopping program had all disappeared. Some of the men took Wiggy too seriously and were offended by him. He would return from his home parish in Palm Beach, Florida, with reports of marital counseling performed on the StairMaster at the gym and his work with what he called the "Mission for Wayward Strippers." He seemed to be experiencing a near-perpetual discernment crisis — speaking almost incessantly about leaving the seminary but turning up back there semester after semester.

He didn't offend Don, who believed that it wasn't a bad thing for a seminarian to lay his struggles and doubts out for all to see. It was worse when these things were left hidden and unexplored. Don didn't see anything wrong with Wiggy heaping scorn on the holier-than-thou types who act perfectly pious in public but dress up like Catwoman in private, or wondering whether the only men God was calling to the priesthood were wounded or only wounded men thought they were being called. Wiggy reported that when he'd told an elderly female parishioner that he did not think he would ever be one of those holy priests, the woman had replied, "We don't want holy; we want real."

Wiggy watched Don work on his presentation without speaking. Finally, Wiggy mentioned to Don that he had to write something that involved condensing monthly spiritual exercises into daily ones.

"Ignatius has done it already," Don pointed out, referring to the Jesuit founder's spiritual guide, which enables a reader to practice daily meditations.

"See, this is how I get through seminary, picking the brains of people smarter than me," Wiggy said.

Each deacon candidate — there were three to be ordained that fall — could choose one man from the seminary to serve at their ordination Mass. Don had chosen Heiser.

Heiser felt that he was on academic easy street for the rest of the year. He had only a handful of assignments due for the fall semester, and the spring semester would be light, with only fourteen credits. He was getting good grades. His paper for Dr. John Gallam's philosophy class came back with glowing comments. Heiser's final sentences defended Descartes's ontological argument for God: "But inherent in our concept of God is perfection; God is perfect. If something is perfect, it must exist (please refer to Bill Clinton's definition of 'is'). Things that don't exist can't be perfect, they can only be nonexistent. (Did I really write that?)" Dr. Gallam responded with a brief note written in a compact script: "No one is more amazed than I — NOT? A really excellent in-your-own-words defense of the ontological argument. Can I quote you?" Dr. Gallam gave the paper an A.

Dr. Gallam had been a seminarian himself at Sacred Heart in the 1970s but had left to earn his Ph.D. in philosophy. Eventually, he'd married, had children, and returned to teach at Sacred Heart. In almost three decades, it was rumored, he had not received a single negative evaluation from a student. With a wiry, athletic build and an urgent delivery, Dr. Gallam would dart around the classroom and wave his arms in the air, pushing and pulling from above to below, from outside to inside, as if he were kneading the ideas around him. He would say "faith" and hold both hands together. It was as if the question of faith were a small ball that could be compressed between them. In the midst of an involved discussion of empiricism, rationalism, or Kant, he would suddenly go off on a fascinating tangent. Class would inevitably run overtime, Dr. Gallam would mutter about needing to catch up, and Heiser would exit with the others, feeling as if he had discovered another room in his brain.

Heiser was being challenged in another course as well, but not academically. His human life reading forced him to endure stories of abortion, adoption, miscarriage, and childbirth and to reassess his beliefs. He read of a college girl who put her baby up for adoption and found it to be such a traumatic experience that when she became pregnant again eight months later, she had an abortion. Another woman was reminded of an abortion clinic every time she heard a vacuum cleaner. Heiser concluded from all of this that counseling had to be foremost in the mind of any priest ministering to these women, either before or after they had an abortion. The priest must bring God's mercy to them, not his condemnation. Although his reading didn't change his mind about abortion being wrong, it did challenge some long-held beliefs regarding the moment of conception. Heiser was incapable of seeing the world in black and white. Ironically, his son, Eric, who was not particularly religious, saw no nuances in the question of abortion. He was fiercely against it. When someone told Eric that he wouldn't be against abortion if he hadn't been brainwashed by the Catholic Church, he exploded. It had nothing to do with the Church, he said. He knew deep in his heart that abortion was wrong.

Heiser was usually slow to judge others. Wiggy had tried to pin him down during a formation class by implying that Heiser was probably the kind of conservative who would automatically be against married priests.

"I come from the Ukrainian Church," Heiser replied. "I was baptized by a married priest. My parents were married by a married priest. And the pastor of the church that I go to in Milwaukee is married."

Heiser also knew that there were already some 250 married Roman Catholic priests in the United States. Married Episcopalian priests who converted to Catholicism were allowed to stay married and become Catholic priests. The thought of "Father" being out there in the dating world was a little too much for Heiser to swallow; he hoped it would never come to that. The wife of a Ukrainian pastor had once given him some perspective on the issue when she told him about a warning a friend had given her before her husband-to-be became a priest. He would have constant demands on his time, the friend had said, and it would be tough on the marriage. All of this, the pastor's wife told Heiser, had turned out to be true. She had to work outside the home to help support their three kids, and her husband was always busy attending to his parishioners' needs.

Wyoming was never far away from Heiser's thoughts. It had been difficult coming back to Sacred Heart in August; he had felt like a resistant schoolboy. Now they were more than halfway through the semester, and Heiser knew that he would be returning to Wyoming for more than a month in early December. Meanwhile, Wisconsin had experienced a string of warm days, and the Internet told him that the weather in Wyoming was the same. He could just imagine it: the air perfumed with sage, the silence broken only by the wind and the crackling of the undergrowth.

Heiser liked to take long walks in the woods around Sacred Heart. The first time he had met Dr. Shippee was in the woods behind the school. It was a day of recollection, and Dr. Shippee was sitting on a log, rolling a cigarette, and thinking, perhaps, about systematic theology and the need for a communitarian approach to studying it. Heiser seemed to appear out of nowhere, making no sound as he passed through the brush. He was looking for buck rubs — peeled bark, evidence that a male deer had been scraping its antlers on a tree to mark its territory. Dr. Shippee was originally from urban New Jer-

sey and was not well versed in country things. Heiser told him about
the basics of animal tracking and how even these woods, wedged between a suburban development and a highway, were full of invisible
life.

Still, his mind went back to Wyoming. He missed the smell of
sage and kept a small bag of it in his room. He thought often of a
quote he had read long ago in *National Geographic*: "The smell of
crushed sage on a hot summer's day. As rich as a drug and every bit
as heady."

The smell of sage reminded him of his Arapaho friends. He had
recently received a letter from Danny "O," who was in the federal
penitentiary in Tucson, Arizona, where he was serving 12.3 years on
an aggravated sexual assault charge. Heiser had strong doubts about
the truth of the charges and sometimes found himself thinking that
Danny's imprisonment was just another case of the white man putting an Indian in jail.

Heiser had attended a sun dance festival on the reservation over
the summer. Danny's nephew Ryan had danced. He was painted red
and black. Twelve poles surrounded a central pole at the site of the
dance. Ryan was both an enrolled member of the tribe and a Catholic. Heiser learned that the twelve poles symbolized the twelve Apostles. Ryan spent four days fasting and in deep prayer. As he danced,
he occasionally put a pouch up to his nose and inhaled deeply. Heiser
guessed that the pouch contained sage and later asked Danny "O"
about it. Danny wrote: "This sage is known as 'mother plant.' It is sacred to all traditional people. We believe that the Creator gave it to
native people to use in whatever way we need . . . Now Ryan could
have kept some sage in his pouch so when he was feeling down he
could inhale the sage to give him strength to focus on his vow. You
don't EAT it OR drink it, you smell it. You might consider this psychological. It's just what we believe."

Danny "O" had made Heiser a leather rosary pouch and covers for
his prayer books. He said that leatherwork helped keep him sane. He
also had a talent for carving and had once etched an intricate wildlife

scene in a bar of soap at Heiser's house. In his room at the seminary, Heiser kept two sacred possessions in trust for his friend: an eagle feather and an eagle claw. According to federal regulations, it was illegal for a white man to possess these objects but permissible for a Native American. Heiser planned to return them to Danny "O" when he got out of prison.

Heiser had done some of his first hunting in Wyoming with Danny "O." He had learned many things about reading the land from his friend. He couldn't wait to return home, put on his boots and hunting jacket, throw Packy — his half-deaf hunting dog — into the back of his truck, and get out in the woods with his gun.

As Ron Kendzierski's ultimate departure from Sacred Heart seemed more and more inevitable, the sense of community he found there became harder to bear, especially when he saw how much the people cared for him. This was apparent at a formal dinner that followed a Mass for the ministry of acolyte. The rite had invested a handful of second-year seminarians with the power to serve the priest at the altar. Ron sat at a table with Don Malin, with whom he had played music for the service. Joining them were Mary DeSantis and Rose Stinefast, a former nun who was the director of continuing education at Sacred Heart. Ron's face was swollen and mottled. Someone asked him what had happened.

"I hit a door really hard," Ron explained.

"I bet you know where that door is now," Rose said.

"No," Ron lamented. He had been late to class and was rushing down the classroom hallway. The coordinates of the offending surface were still unknown, liable to swing out of the darkness again. "You see, the thing is, the door was wide-open — all those doors are wide-open in the hallway. I had overshot; I had gone past where my room was. I was late."

"You thought you were being punished," Don said, laughing.

"I think so," Ron muttered.

There was a pause, and beneath the clatter of banquet plates and

silver, he almost heard a collective, happy sigh. Ron had heard it before at Sacred Heart — a welcoming, loving, communal embrace,
tinged, perhaps, with possessiveness. Rose spoke, seeming to capture
this collective emotion: "I admire your sense of humor, Ron."

"Well, thanks," Ron replied.

"Really," Mary echoed.

"I appreciate that," Ron said, using a response that he employed
when someone plugged in his recorder for him in class or brought
his tray to the scullery. He said it a lot.

"If you can't laugh . . . ," Ron mused, struggling to minimize their
compliments. "Life's short enough as it is."

There was another pause. Things were getting a bit too emotional
for Ron's liking. "Well, it's good to be here," he said finally.


"For those of you leaving in three semesters, this will not affect you,"
Father Brackin said. "But for those of you who are going to be here
beyond that, *you* will be breaking in another president rector. It's not
a difficult task."

The seminarians laughed. The rector had just informed them that
he would be leaving his post at the end of three semesters.

Although the new rector would probably take a fresh look at the
ministry, Father Brackin emphasized that faculty contracts were usually not just year-to-year affairs, so there was some built-in stability
against sudden upheaval. The staff also would be protected — if not
contractually, then practically. A new rector, Father Brackin said
from experience, would be reluctant to dismiss the old hands who
knew how the system worked.

"Any questions?" Father Brackin asked. The room was silent.

"Anyone going to ask me what I'm going to do?" There were a few
rumbles but no formal questions.

"Oh, thank you," he said.

Father Brackin answered his own question. He was finally going
to take the sabbatical he had never taken — Hawaii sounded good.
But he wouldn't remain idle for long. He thought he might do something in gerontology or perhaps become a pastor, since he had never

done that either. Then Bob raised his hand. He had a pained look on his face.

"I know this is really private," Bob said gingerly. "But are you going to be okay?"

Father Brackin looked amused. "I'm not getting ready to die tomorrow," he said. "But thank you for asking that."

Tom Mescall wondered aloud if the next step for Father Brackin was bishop. The rector said he would never be offered such a position.

"I am sure that there is a note on my file at the Vatican that says 'I don't think so,'" Father Brackin said. No, he wanted to go somewhere warm for his next assignment. Of course, if he was sent to South Dakota, so be it.

When one had lived the religious life long enough, with all its comings and goings, the joy of settling in and then the upheaval of reassignment, a certain sense of circumspection developed that would appear like cynicism if it had been marked by a greater quotient of bitterness. Although Father Brackin had spent much of his time and energy at Sacred Heart constructing a legacy for the school, he would now be leaving the direction of the seminary to someone else, and he would have little say in its future. He had been exacting and tireless about building a sense of community, but perhaps his successor would have different values. He thought of the Hummel figurines in his office, the rosy-cheeked cherubs and the little glazed shepherds, with their expressions of almost pathological innocence. Some pieces were valuable in themselves, others only to him. If he were to die tomorrow, the rector figured, there was a good possibility that they would be swept into the garbage with the rest of his office clutter. In ten years, the people at Sacred Heart might remember him only as that rector who had water poured over his head during Mass. But even if he could not control what came next, the way he left mattered. Father Brackin was determined to provide a model of departure. He felt that he had an obligation to say goodbye to people the right way.

⋆     ⋆     ⋆

"I assume you're going to be thurifer," Jim Pemberton said to Heiser. His voice was hoarse from a bad cough. Everyone at Sacred Heart seemed to be getting sick. Professor Gotcher, feeling as though he was coming down with the flu, was wondering whether he should go home early. One of the older men was in the hospital with a urinary tract infection.

Heiser nodded. He was sick, too. His sinuses had been congested for weeks. At first he'd thought it was an allergy, but now he wasn't sure.

"I'm sorry, I should have let you know," he said.

It was no problem, Pemberton replied. A brief silence followed.

Pemberton had been all set to stand in for Heiser as thurifer, an acolyte who carries the censer during Mass, at Don Malin's ordination to the diaconate. Heiser had been offered a ticket to the Notre Dame game, and he'd deliberated over the decision for four days. Attendance at the ordination was expected but not required, and Heiser was sure that some of the men would not attend. He had asked one of the SCJs for advice, but the priest had said that it was entirely up to Heiser. In the end, he'd decided that it was his responsibility to attend the ordination. After all, Don had asked him, and not someone else, to serve as thurifer. Still, small sacrifices could chafe.

It was late November, and the weather was cold. Heavy clouds made it look like early evening rather than early afternoon. Heiser left Pemberton and walked in the direction of the Sacred Heart Chapel, where Professor Christian Rich would prepare the deacon candidates and the servers for the ordination. Although Professor Rich planned each liturgy down to the most minute detail, he knew better than to expect perfection.

"If you both make the same mistake together," he told the men, "everybody will think you're right."

To LeRoy Schik, who was doing a few practice swings with the censer over the Gospel, he said, "It's okay to hit the chain." LeRoy hit the chain hard, and Professor Rich shouted, "Yes!" as if he had just won the lottery.

Leading the deacons around the ambulatory and toward the main aisle and the altar, Professor Rich indicated the doors. This was their last chance to escape before taking their promises, he joked.

Professor Rich had the three candidates lie prostrate before the altar as they would in a few days. He warned them about the dangers of fainting if they got up too fast. It had happened before. The candidates got to their feet and tried on their gowns.

"That's your color — fantastic!" exclaimed Michael Tynan, the master of ceremonies, stepping back from Eugene Hornung.

"These are dusty," Don Malin said, sniffing the sleeve of his gown. "They need to be cleaned."

Later, they knelt before Professor Rich, who stood in place of the bishop. Professor Rich kept up a steady commentary of guidance. When the men were formally deacons and the consecration commenced, they should make sure to stand far enough away from the altar lest it seem they were concelebrating. Only priests could concelebrate. Professor Rich had a special message for Don concerning the sign of peace, the part of the Mass when parishioners exchange greetings with one another.

"Go into the pews," Professor Rich said, "with this warning, *Don Malin:* you can't shake everyone's hand."

The Mass would be close to an hour and a half long, and the ritual was intricate, but Professor Rich told the men not to worry about what came next in the order of things. "Don't go back to your room and say, 'My God, what did he say?' Just leave it to God and to Michael," he advised.

Don wasn't worried about the liturgy, but sleep had been elusive. More than two decades before, the Jesuits had said "not yet" to his desire to attend the seminary. Yet was now, Don thought. When he arrived at the rehearsal, he thought, *Ah, here it is.* Then he saw the dalmatic, the long, loose, wide-sleeved vestment worn by deacons. This was like getting to a concert early, he thought. The orchestra filters onto the stage, and the individual musicians fiddle with their instruments. The concertmaster calls for silence, then the oboist maintains the A, the violins tune, the winds tune, and the horns tune. Everybody makes sure they're all together. The hall falls silent in readiness for the first piercing note. Don was waiting for that first piercing note.

As Don was leaving the rehearsal, Professor Rich asked him for a lift to pick up his car at the mechanic's garage down the road. Don retrieved his Jeep Cherokee from the lot and picked up the professor at the flagpole on the drive.

"Welcome aboard," Don said. The compass on the dashboard bobbed uselessly above the CB radio. The heat didn't work, and the engine was starting to make an unhealthy sound.

"Thank you," Professor Rich said as he swung himself into the front seat. He told Don that he should get the engine checked before he drove home to Colorado at Christmas.

"They promise a lot," remarked Professor Rich, changing the subject to the ordination. He always got a little emotional when the men took the promises for deacon. "The thing about you guys is that you're a little bit older. I trust you. You guys know what you give up. Not that it's just celibacy, but embracing the whole life. You know God because he's been with you since the beginning."

Don pulled into the service station. It was already dark, even though it was only a little past five, and the weak yellow beams of his headlights lit up Professor Rich's car parked in the corner. The station was closed, but the mechanic had left the keys in the ignition. Don waited until the professor was on his way before turning back to the seminary for the night.

"Ron, do you remember? About conflict?" Dean Haley asked. The two men were seated at dinner. Dean spoke rapidly, not waiting for Ron Kendzierski to catch up.

"Conflict resolution?" Ron suggested halfheartedly.

"No," Dean insisted. "The part about the rhesus monkeys."

Ron didn't remember.

Dean expanded on a reading from Father Birdsall's class about a study that explored what happened to monkeys that were deprived of the ability to fight.

"The monkeys didn't fight, but they didn't reproduce either," Dean said significantly, knowing that Ron had just returned from an antiwar rally.

Ron nodded politely but said nothing. Dean had called him a flaming liberal before, and perhaps Dean was baiting him again. There was always a lot of verbal jousting between the two men, as there was between Ron and Bobby Rodriguez, who sympathized with Dean's political and religious sensibilities. Bobby would drive Ron to the "liberal" church across town to play violin on Sundays. The people there regularly referred to God as "our mother" and "our father," and the liturgy featured alcoholic and nonalcoholic wine. Ron preferred to say "our creator." Dean had told Ron that he would end up a Protestant in three years. In twenty years, he would be one of those guys who said, "Yeah, I was in seminary once. I know what those guys are all about."

Most of the time, Ron baited them back. Once, on the way to church, Ron got Bobby so angry that he missed the exit. From Ron's perspective, aside from being more vocal, Dean was no different from the rest of the students, whom he found to be very conservative, in awe of "Mother Church" and the noxious hierarchy that Ron saw as holding it all together. Ron felt more in tune with the faculty. They at least seemed liberal-minded. But even they, he thought, had to toe the party line or risk losing their jobs. The way he saw it, the bishops ran Sacred Heart, and the bishops wanted a return to the days before Vatican II. If the bishops didn't like what they saw at the seminary, they would send their candidates elsewhere.

Tonight, Ron didn't want a fight. He had a big, very public decision to make soon, and he was feeling anxious.

Dean finally left the table to find his ticket to *Late Nite Catechism*, a one-woman show featuring "Sister," a generic holy terror of a full-habited nun, who evoked every third grader's vision of a religious sister. Dean's room was frigid because he had left the window open in an attempt to prepare his body for the Milwaukee winter that was fast approaching. He had read somewhere that it took seventeen days to acclimate one's body to a new environment. This could be done even more effectively with greater exposure to the elements.

Everything in his room was cold to the touch: the giant car speaker wedged into his closet next to his clothes; the two Audiobahn twelve-inch Kevlar speakers he had bought in his dark period a month into seminary but could not install because they required an expensive amplifier, which he felt too guilty to buy; the military sleeping bag rolled out on his bed; even the cartoon of the Buddhist monk looking at something called the Zen crossword puzzle. The puzzle featured a single white square and the clues "Across 1. Nothing" and "Down 1. Nothing." Near the cartoon was a photograph taken in August of all the new seminarians. Dean was shown with the mustache that he had shaved off soon after the semester began. He looked much younger without it, even when he occasionally stopped dying his sideburns, which had been graying since his early twenties.

August seemed like a long time ago. Dean felt more settled now. He had rearranged his first room six times in a little over a month but was more or less content with the setup of his new quarters. The maintenance staff had made Dean an even better nameplate for his door. He had fastened an ornate silver crucifix above the mantel. When he thought of Ron, it seemed that a strange reversal had occurred. At the beginning of the year, Ron had appeared strong and Dean weak. Now the opposite was true.

Recently, he had received a card from his grandmother. She was not a Catholic, but she had begun to attend Catholic religious instruction, apparently out of curiosity about what Dean was doing with his life. He never would have expected that, and it gave him pause. There were consequences to being an example held up for all to see. Good consequences. Just remaining a seminarian was a powerful sermon. Hadn't Saint Francis of Assisi said, "Preach the Gospel always — if necessary, use words"?

Dean found his ticket and left for the show.

Ron had no show to distract him. He was scheduled to meet with the rector at nine the following morning.

"I've been thinking about it for four or five weeks," Ron told Father Brackin the next morning. "But I didn't have the guts to tell you."

They were sitting across from each other in the rector's office. The sun that Ron couldn't see fell upon Father Brackin's Hummel figurines, making their bow-lip smiles look even cheerier than usual.

Ron hadn't been quite sure what to expect from Father Brackin. He had wanted to be truthful but was afraid of the consequences. Therefore, he'd first confided in Father Marty, the director of formation, who had told him it was time to speak to the rector.

Two things had made him certain of his decision to leave Sacred Heart. The first was Tina. On October 30, Ron had asked her to marry him over the phone. She had said yes. The second thing was doctrine. The longer he remained at Sacred Heart, the more he realized that the doctrine of the Catholic Church presented a huge personal obstacle. *There's doctrine that I know the bishop's going to ask me to swear to that I can't swear to,* Ron thought. *I should leave because (a) don't lie to yourself, (b) don't lie to other people, and (c) don't waste other people's money putting your ass through school. Take your two master's degrees and go home and get a job and do some ministry. But don't live in a palace, play your fiddle, and then leave.*

Ron knew a man who had done exactly what he refused to do. He had studied at Sacred Heart for four years and had been ordained. Nine months later, he quit the priesthood to get married. This wasn't fair to the people of the Church, Ron thought. They were trying to feed their kids. Rome may have a lot of money, but it was the people working on the fruit farms that put their cash in the plate every Sunday and then gave more whenever a second collection was taken up for vocations.

Father Brackin took Ron's first salvo in stride. Then Ron let it all out. He told the rector about Tina. He said that he felt guilty about the Braille printer that Sacred Heart had purchased for him. He worried that his vocation director, who did not yet know of his decision, would feel let down.

Father Brackin told Ron not to worry about any of those things. The Braille printer was a good and necessary purchase for the seminary. It would be used for Steven, a blind master's student, after Ron departed and for others in the future. As for Ron's situation, Sacred Heart was a place to explore where God was ultimately calling him. Ron's vocation director should understand that. Father Brackin told Ron that he should probably leave the seminary and explore the possibility of building a life with Tina.

Ron was always welcome at Sacred Heart, Father Brackin concluded, either as a seminarian or a layman. If he later decided that he was called back to the priesthood, he could reapply. Ron thanked Father Brackin and asked him if he could keep some of his stuff in his room past the end of the semester. It would be difficult to move everything right away. Father Brackin told him that would be fine.

Ron still had to tell his vocation director and Don Malin, but he left Father Brackin's office feeling lighter than he had in weeks. With Don's ordination approaching, Ron decided to wait a little while longer to tell him the news.

Heiser watched the snow coming down outside the window while Dr. Gallam spoke about evil and whether pain and suffering are necessary for virtue. Ron, who had arrived halfway through class because of a delayed rehearsal, rocked back and forth in his chair. Jim Pemberton, his reading glasses sliding most of the way down his nose, took careful notes in his binder. A newly focused Dean Haley typed away on his laptop. No videos played on his computer screen that day. His silver watch faced up on the desk to his left.

As usual, Heiser was positioned along the inside wall with a good view of the weeping willows outside. He took notes in the binder that sat in a neat black zippered case and paid even closer attention than normal. Much of Dr. Gallam's talk was going to be on the final. Still, Heiser's eyes were drawn to the outdoors. He noticed that the willow leaves had thinned out in recent days. He had found many buck rubs in his latest walks but had concluded that only one buck was involved. The snow had begun to fall during the first class session of the day, but so far hadn't done anything but frost the grass and melt on the surface of the parking lot.

In Heiser's previous class, Dr. Shippee had explored the topic of whether the Church had ever been a stable and unchanging institution. He concluded that it had not and that those who believed it had were clinging to a dangerous illusion.

"There is no peaceful, perfect past when there was no conflict," Dr. Shippee said. "We can't underestimate the tensions, but the tensions aren't the final word. The final word is Communion, the banquet."

During a two-minute break, Philip Kim, the septuagenarian who always smelled faintly of cigarettes, stood by the window and watched the snow. He felt like a young man. He had been waiting for this moment for forty-six years, since he'd left Korea as a Buddhist houseboy in the employ of a U.S. Air Force officer bound for San Antonio, Texas. San Antonio had become his home, but its snow was never like that of his native Korea. Texas snow was unsatisfying, light and fast melting. Wisconsin snow was supposed to be different. So far, though, Philip couldn't tell if this was true. He returned to his seat, turned on his tape recorder, and rested his elbows on the table. The tape recorder helped Philip, whose native language was Korean, catch the words of the fast-talking professor.

Already, Dr. Shippee had put up a transparency and was vigorously underlining words: the Council of Chalcedon's "Definition of Faith" . . . Hypostatic Union . . . Nestorius's heresy . . . Christ is "acknowledged to be unconfusedly, unalterably, undividedly, inseparably in two natures" . . .

At one point, Philip turned away from the transparency and stared out the window. Everybody from the North seemed sick of the snow even before it began, he mused. Maybe he, too, would get sick of the snow after a while.

"*That* is a great myth about experience," Dr. Shippee said. "Experience *requires* interpretation. You don't actually have an experience until you've got language and understanding with which to interpret it."

What experience required interpretation? In what language? And to what end understanding? The snow kept falling, but it would soon end in large wet flakes, leaving little evidence of its having fallen except for the boyish joy in Philip's heart and Heiser's heightened desire to be trekking through the Wyoming brush with Packy and his gun.

When Father Brackin arrived to eat his breakfast, the dining hall was empty except for one student and two kitchen staff. It being the weekend, the steam tables would remain in the kitchen, and there would be a cold breakfast for everyone. Barb Haag and a worker were setting up tables for the big meal to follow the ordination. Barb crawled under the tables, making sure each one was level. Father Brackin, dressed as usual in his clerics, got a bowl and filled it with half granola and half raisin bran. He grasped a steaming takeout cup, took his blue tray in the other hand, and sat down alone at a table beside the windows. It was a cold and beautiful morning, but the rector did not pick a table that looked out at the woods. Instead, he sat looking back at the seminary building and his office. He noticed that someone had dropped a napkin on the floor. He bent down, picked it up, and walked it halfway across the dining hall to the garbage can. Then he returned to his seat, resumed gazing out the window, and began to eat. The dining hall was silent. All of Sacred Heart seemed asleep.

Don Malin and two other men would become deacons this day. On Don's desk was a folder labeled "Deacon Stuff." It held relevant announcements and a memo outlining the day before ordination. He had followed the memo in a mad dash all day Friday, greeting guests as they came in from out of town, leaving gift baskets in the rooms of his bishop and vocation director, eating lunch with his father, organizing a tour, attending a pre-ordination conference with both his bishop and his vocation director, and finishing the day with a night prayer for his family and friends. His good friend Jay Jensen, a priest from the Diocese of Colorado Springs who had been a seminarian with Don at Sacred Heart, had flown in and given the homily at the Friday morning Mass. Make no mistake, Jensen had said, this ordination was not about Don or Don's achievements. It was all about God taking possession of Don's heart.

After delivering the baskets, Don had stopped by Father Marty's office. Jay was there. He and Don had been part of a group of friends that had often sat under the stained-glass pane of the Bible that hung in the dining hall. They had called themselves the "liturgy committee" and considered themselves a riotous bunch of wits. They'd usually shared one meal a day together. Then one by one, they had left and been ordained priests. Don was the only one left at Sacred Heart. It was lonely without the others.

"Hello, Your Worship," Don boomed.

"Good morning, Your Prominence," Jay replied.

"Good job this morning," Don said.

"You think?" Jay mused. There had been some visible confusion on the altar, as the final readings had been mismarked. "They moved the ribbons on me."

Don asked where Jay was staying. Not at the seminary, he said, but at a hotel down the road.

"I was in 371 long enough," Jay said. "I don't want to share a john with twenty guys today."

Don fished an angel out of the bowl.

"Beauty," he pronounced.

"That's the same one *he* got," Jay said, indicating Father Marty.

"You've got to pick up the bish," Jay reminded Don. Don said he had that and a hundred other things to do.

Don had felt hurried but happy all day. When his father arrived at the seminary, Don saw him through the double doors down the long bridge. Don ran toward him, past the paintings that visitors sometimes mistook for the Stations of the Cross. His father thought Don would knock him over.

"You don't realize how big you are," he cautioned.

"Yeah, Pops," Don managed to say through his joy. "So glad you came."

In the previous days, Don had made a general confession, part of the Ignatian exercise in which the penitent looks over his entire life, especially lingering over habitual sins, those things that keep coming back. Don believed that his ordination would bring him an abundance of grace, and he wanted to capture that grace with as much of his being as possible. He did not want to stand beneath Niagara Falls with a Dixie cup.

Signs that he was pursuing the right path abounded. The most curious sign occurred in the early morning of ordination day itself. He had brought a box of toiletries with him to the seminary when he began. In the box was some aftershave that his wife had bought for him as a Christmas gift while they were married. That morning, he used the last of it. He didn't realize what he had done until after he had emptied the bottle. Interesting, he thought, that it finally ended there. Don threw the bottle into the garbage. Then he stopped by to see Martín Frias, one of the other men who would be ordained that day. Don needed help fastening a white tab collar into his black clerical garb. The edge of the collar kept creeping above the black lining of the shirt.

The ordination began on time. The Sacred Heart Chapel was filled with the parents and friends of the three men becoming deacons. Behind the altar, preparing to process as Professor Christian Rich had shown them during rehearsal, the men fidgeted and made small talk. Heiser saw Don standing with Michael Tynan. He made his way through the crowd and asked Don a question: "Are you as nervous now as you were on your wedding day?"

No, Don replied. On his wedding day he had had a sense that he was doing something wrong. Heiser's question made him remember how he had looked down the aisle, seen his future wife at the other end, and felt his legs buckle. No, no nervousness now, he said. Not even a trace.

The line began to move, winding up the stairs from the sacristy underneath the altar. The seminarians, dressed in their long albs and bearing the cross and the censer, led the procession. The faculty, dressed in caps and gowns, followed in a great cloud of incense. Shafts of light from the tall windows cut through the haze, making the men's features look vividly frozen, as in a tableau vivant. The faculty were followed by the clergy, the deacons, the officiating priests, and finally Don's bishop, Arthur N. Tafoya, bringing up the rear. The line moved slowly around the ambulatory as the choir sang "Laudate, Laudate Dominum." The faculty filled the pews to the left of the altar. The servers, the participating clergy, and the candidates proceeded toward the main aisle, turning right at the baptismal font. The choir sang: "Exultate jubilate per annos Domini omnes gentes." The men moved slowly but inexorably. Don, Martín, and Eugene Hornung stood beside the first pews of their respective sections. The servers and the clergy filed onto the altar. The cross bearer secured the cross in its stand. The bishop climbed to the chair on the riser above the altar. Father Brackin stood beside him. The music stopped, and everyone fell silent. The bishop spoke: "In the name of the Father, the Son, and the Holy Spirit . . ." The Mass had begun.

"Now do we call you Reverend?" someone wanted to know when it was all over. The new deacons stood just outside the doors to the Sacred Heart Chapel in a receiving line.

"No," Don said firmly. "Call me Deacon Don."

People were sipping drinks and eating hors d'oeuvres. A huge group of well-wishers waited in the line that would bring them past Eugene, Martín, and Don. Many asked for a first blessing, a traditional request of the newly ordained.

The line crept forward. Finally, Ron Kendzierski reached Don.

"Nice job," Ron said. He had played his violin at the Mass. At some point during the service, without any warning, Ron had been overwhelmed by emotion and had begun to cry. He thought it was the music, all the beautiful music — a big sound — and the incense. Ron loved incense.

"Nice job," Don replied. He told Ron that he had heard about his decision to leave.

"Are you at peace with it?" Don asked.

"Yes," Ron answered. But suddenly he thought, *Peace with it? I really don't know.*

Don laid his right hand on Ron's head and blessed him. They hugged. Ron thanked Don for everything Don had done for him that semester.

"We'll have a party, schmuck," Ron said. Laughing a little, he moved on.

Don's father, Leonard, sat on the edge of a sofa across from where the new deacons had gathered in the main lounge. He stared at Don for five minutes and did not stop smiling. When Don was younger, Leonard had discouraged the idea of going to the seminary. He had been in the seminary himself for four and a half years with the Jesuits — minor seminary for high school and then a semester in college. But, as he would later put it, he liked girls and eventually wanted kids. So he went to Loyola University instead and became an engineer. When he had entered the seminary, there were forty men in his class. By college, only six were left, and only two or three were ordained. The way he saw it, they had taken the time and money of the Church and then just dropped out. Better for Don to see life, he had thought. Then he could make a decision.

All along, though, he had perceived Don as ascending to the priesthood. Church music had attracted his son. Leonard was proud of his son's master's thesis, which presented a system for teaching people how to sing Gregorian chant.

Father and son had lost touch for some years after Don's parents had divorced, but they were close again. Leonard was a pilot of small planes and the president of the municipal airport in Yucca Valley, California, where he lived with his second wife. When Don visited, they would fly together, sometimes doing the twenty-minute flight up to Big Bear Lake for breakfast. Don usually visited at Christmas, but that would be ending this year, with Don's ordination to transitional deacon and the beginning of his official duties in Pueblo. Don would be returning home as a deacon invested with the powers to preach, baptize, marry, and bury. Christmas was a busy season for the clergy; Don was now commissioned to carry part of the burden.

Don's spiritual director, Father Robert Hagan, SJ, had flown in from Colorado to attend the ordination. He was sixty years old, but there were many priests in the diocese older than he, and he knew how important the ordinations of Don and Martín were. In a few years, the number of priests in the Diocese of Pueblo was expected to be cut in half. The diocese covers a region that measures three thousand square miles, twice the size of New Hampshire. Much of it is mountainous. In Trinidad, where Father Hagan had gotten to know Don, they had closed two parishes and five missions in the past decade alone. They simply did not have the manpower. The diocese was preparing Pueblo's Catholics for a time when there might be only a handful of priests, and permanent deacons would have to shoulder many clerical responsibilities. When Don decided to apply to the priesthood, Father Hagan was leading him through the Ignatian Spiritual Exercises.

Don had felt equally drawn to a career in either sacred music or the priesthood. He had recently written a Te Deum, or hymn of praise, for the 125th anniversary of Pueblo's cathedral parish. But Saint Ignatius directed that a person like Don, equally drawn to two very different futures and free from any obligations, such as marriage, that would make a radical commitment impossible, should go in the direction of most need. That meant the priesthood. The need in Pueblo was obvious, especially when a close priest friend of Don's collapsed during the Easter season, leaving his parish searching for a substitute. The latest Vatican document had advised that Catholics be optimistic about the shortage of priests, but optimism wasn't easy in the trenches.

The dining hall filled quickly with the families and friends of the new deacons, the faculty, and the seminarians. Don moved from table to table still dressed in his clerics. The entire Gotcher family attended. Dean Haley held their newest arrival in the palm of his hand. The baby went limp as the seminarian held him.

"That's one relaxed baby," Dean said.

He lifted the infant up and down. Kathy Gotcher watched with a broad smile.

"Dean, I think you're called to daddyhood, not fatherhood," observed Philip Kim, whose grown children still kept in close touch with him.

Kathy disagreed. "The best priests are those who can juggle babies," she said.

"Bishop's homily . . . bishop's homily . . . shrub in your head . . . more shrub in your head," narrated Deacon Don Malin. He and Michael Tynan were in his office shuffling through photographs from the ordination, looking for the slip-ups. "More shrub in your head . . . still more shrub in your head."

"It should be just after that I should have . . . ," Michael said. "Is that *you*?"

"Uh-huh. Let's see, then, the Litany of the Saints. Then we lay down on the floor."

"Right," Michael confirmed.

"There you are," Don said, pointing.

"Yeah," Michael said ruefully. "It should have been just after that that I should have sent you back to get vested."

Thanksgiving had come and gone. The first week of December had arrived, and with it the last week of classes for the semester. Exams were the following week, but many men would be leaving early because of their testing schedules. Don had just received the pictures from his ordination, and Michael was revisiting a mistake he had made as master of ceremonies. The mistake had seemed major to Michael — Professor Christian Rich had hissed his name from the organ to get his attention — but no one else had seemed to notice, least of all the bishop.

"At the end of the Mass, the bishop said, 'Well, we did everything right,'" Michael told Don, laughing. "I said, 'Yes, Bishop.'"

"That's the way you do it," Don replied. "You know there are only two answers that you give a bishop: 'Yes' and 'Yes, Bishop.' He was the one who told me that once."

Don believed in obedience to mainstream Catholic practice and

the chain of command, but he was also deeply committed to a movement that existed on the fringes of the mainstream. That movement
was called Charismatic Renewal, and it emphasized ecstatic and impromptu expressions of faith, the laying on of hands for healing, and
speaking in tongues — none of which was a formal part of Catholic
belief. Saint Paul wrote that such things were evidence of the gifts of
the Holy Spirit, and many Christian denominations had been built
around charismatic practice. Many Catholics were resistant. Even
though the movement had grown considerably, it was still widely
viewed as being not especially Catholic.

Don understood this tension, but he believed that through outreach and dialogue, Catholics would eventually accept Charismatic
Renewal. Don had been involved in some aspect of Charismatic Renewal since his conversion, and he had joined a group in Milwaukee
called the River of Life soon after he had arrived at Sacred Heart. At
first he had been reluctant to assert himself. He was wary of being
seen as intruding on the group's autonomy and did not want to be
perceived as the pushy seminarian coming to teach the laity a thing
or two. But as time passed, Don became an integral part of the
group. He sang and prayed with them on Monday nights and went to
their homes for meals or to get away from the seminary for a while.

Many of Don's guests for his ordination were charismatics. They
gathered with Don in the lounge after lunch. Don invited Ron
Kendzierski to join them, and Ron sat perched on the edge of a chair
with his cane folded. Leonard Malin and Don's cousin Eva sat nearby on a long couch. The charismatics were a comfortable-looking
group of midwesterners dressed in varying degrees of formality.
Most wore suits or dresses; one man wore a bright red tuxedo.

Presents covered the table. A few people stood up and gave
speeches describing Don's effect on their lives. Some people cried.
Then they huddled around the new deacon and began to speak in
tongues. The sound was hypnotic and otherworldly, a melody and
yet too erratic to be a melody, a sound that fluctuated in intensity
like the song of cicadas, rising and falling. It was elusive, like the

words to a song being sung just out of earshot. The Apostles were said to have spoken fluently in languages they could not possibly have known and were thought by passersby to be drunk on wine when speaking in tongues. A few seminarians crossed the lounge to and fro, glancing over at the group as if not quite certain what to make of it. Leonard and Eva looked a bit uncomfortable, as did Ron, who had clapped at their first rousing rendition of "Awesome God" but didn't follow them into tongues. This was certainly not Ron's way of praying. Despite his progressive views, he still liked traditional church music and cringed at anything that came close to Christian rock. He was suspicious of what he saw as the emotionalism of charismatic worship. Ron liked practical, nuts-and-bolts, feed-the-hungry, clothe-the-poor Christianity. He sometimes dismissed charismatic prayer as "sex with Jesus," but then who was he to say; it seemed to work for some people.

The speaking in tongues stopped, and the new deacon's guests began to prophesy, telling Don the things they had seen in their visions. In the background, a handful of voices would occasionally resume the tongues, chantlike or in song.

"'Rise up' keeps coming to me," someone said.

"I see a jet plane distributing pamphlets," someone else added.

"I've walked with you on the journey," a short woman with big glasses sang out in a beautiful voice.

One man said that he saw obstacles, like tangled metal, in Don's path, but they would not be insurmountable.

"I have not taken music away from you," a woman with white hair assured him, relating how she saw God cuddling Don like a newborn.

Then the visions ended, and Don led the group in the "Our Father." Smiling at his role, Don faced the gathering and made a vigorous cross in the air with the blade of his hand as he gave the final blessing. Don's posture toward the group was gracious, but his distance from them was palpable. He was different now that he was a deacon. They recognized and even encouraged that. Don was conscious that his identity had shifted — not as completely as it would when he became a priest, but it had shifted nonetheless. He didn't feel any different, but he recognized that he was being perceived as a leader, a model whose actions and words had consequences. Charismatic Renewal was important to him, but he could see its potential for excess. His understanding of it was now framed within a larger theological and pastoral context: How could a Charismatic Renewal group be incorporated within a parish? How could Hispanics and others who had left the Church because of its reluctance to embrace Charismatic Renewal be brought back?

He began to open gifts, and at some point he leaned over and told Ron that he was proud to be the friend of someone with such sincerity of heart.

"Me, too," Ron replied, once again aware that doubt about his decision to leave Sacred Heart was growing.

It seemed to Ron as if everyone was angry with him. Had his mother really disinvited him home for Christmas? Already Ron missed the cranberry bread they baked together every holiday. Tina seemed upset with him as well. Don's words about being at peace with the decision had been unsettling, and Ron had told her that he was thinking about giving Sacred Heart one more semester. Tina told him that after she had received that news, she had taken the phone off the hook and cried all day long. When he had finally reached her again, he remembered saying:

"Look, you're the love of my life. I'm not abandoning you. I just want you to know that if I've got to go to Bangladesh for a while, I've got to go to Bangladesh for a while — you know what I mean? I'm a busy, getting-things-done, working-with-a-lot-of-people kind of person. That's what you're going to marry if you marry me. You know that I *like* me, and that's the biggest part of me. If I change that part of me, then I'll wither. I've got a Boy Scout troop Christmas party on Saturday. I've got to go to the old folks' home for their Christmas party on Saturday. I had a thing here with ESL today for lunch. I've got retarded kids tomorrow night at St. Veronica's . . ."

Other people's wants and expectations weighed down on him. He couldn't sleep, study, or do much of anything. Everybody seemed to want something from him. His mother wanted him to be careful in his choices. Tina wanted him to leave the seminary and spend most of his Christmas holiday with her.

There were also Ron's father's wants. He held Ron's social activist vision of the Church in contempt. For him, the world would always be rotten; it was the afterlife that counted. Ron wasn't that concerned about the afterlife. He wanted to build the kingdom of God on earth. His father told him that if he left the seminary, he was giving in to temptation and the devil. In response to Ron's decision to leave Sacred Heart, his father suggested that he join the Knights of Columbus, the antithesis of the kind of Catholic Ron wanted to be.

Then there was his vocation director. The man had worked hard to get Ron into the seminary. Not long after his talk with Father Brackin, Ron had arrived back in his room to find a message on his voice mail. His vocation director had gotten wind of his decision not to return. One of the other seminarians from Ron's diocese had told him. He was not happy to have learned of it from someone else. Ron called him back. He said that he wasn't really surprised; Ron had a pattern of not committing. Yes, he had been exuberant, but he didn't know enough of Catholic history and faith, even though his social justice piece was strong. *But it's the social justice piece that makes me want to do it*, Ron thought. His vocation director also thought that Ron might be being hasty with respect to his marriage plans. He had a nephew who had done something similar. The marriage had ended badly. Ron told the director that his father had said he could get ordained, see what the priesthood felt like, and then get married. Ron assured the director that there was no way in hell he would follow his father's advice. Good, his vocation director replied.

One night, Mike Snyder stopped by Ron's room. He began to remove the streamers and balloons that Bobby Rodriguez had hung on the door for Ron's birthday the week before. Mike's gesture was homey, comforting, but also faintly grating, like a big brother doing something helpful that wasn't wanted just yet.

"I kept them up as long as I could," Ron said, referring to the sagging balloons.

"Well, I could leave them up longer," Mike offered.

"No, that's okay."

This made Ron wonder how he could quit a place like Sacred Heart so quickly, after only one semester. The seminary had stretched him; it had made him grow. Ron thought it was premature to jump ship before he had learned more. Staying also would mean that he wouldn't have to move in the snowy months. Not only that, but remaining in Milwaukee through the winter would make it easier for the intergenerational program, a project that he had successfully pitched to a local parish, to get off the ground in the spring. The proposal had been called "Breaking Barriers by Building Bonds: Bridging the Gap Between Young and Old." The idea was to create a program in which Girl Scouts and seniors worked together. "While volunteering at an assisted living facility as part of my preparation for the priesthood," Ron had written in the introduction to the proposal, "I was struck by the awesome need of many of the residents for even the slightest amount of attention."

This decision to leave — it's too final, Ron concluded. He needed to talk to the rector again.

Unlike almost everyone else at Sacred Heart, Dean Haley had decided to spend Thanksgiving break at the seminary. Heiser had flown to Philadelphia to be with his parents and brothers. Jim Pemberton had used frequent-flier miles to journey back to Fort Worth to be with his family. Ron Kendzierski had gone to Minnesota to visit the Crosiers. And Don Malin was spending time with his friends the Essers.

For Dean, staying was a defensive move. A month earlier, he had learned that his ex-girlfriend would be attending a wedding that he was also planning to attend. She had called him herself and told him. The men in his Caritas prayer group advised him to take a pass on the wedding. Maybe in a year, he could negotiate the obstacle, they said, but right now he would be dead meat. He was too vulnerable. "Don't you recognize an old-fashioned setup?" one of the men asked him point-blank.

So Dean stayed at Sacred Heart, roaming the halls and logging even more hours online and watching even more DVDs than usual. The phone became his lifeline: calls to family, friends, and Father Tom. The Saturday after Thanksgiving, he drove his BMW down to the Illinois border and met an old friend he hadn't seen in a long time. They had lunch. She was a feminist now, she told him. Dean thought she was dressed more like a Buddhist. Maybe it was just the place he was in, but lunch did nothing for him. Afterward, he drove back to the seminary. He vowed never to stay at Sacred Heart for another holiday.

Pressure was intense during the last week of school. The final days of classes followed Thanksgiving by only a week. Santa Claus was the subject of a half-serious debate between the faculty and the staff. The faculty was generally against decorations because according to the Church calendar — not the secular and commercial calendar — this was technically Advent and the Christmas season would not arrive until December 25. Nevertheless, the staff put up trees, hung decorations, wore red and green, and held a Christmas lunch.

Ron sat at a table with Tom Mescall, the former federal judge, and Professor Gotcher. Tom's Christmas spirit was subdued by a re-eruption of the sexual abuse scandal in Boston.

"Just when you think you've heard the last of it . . . ," Tom said with a sigh. That morning, he'd seen a photo of a man with a Roman collar on AOL. *What's this?* he had thought. *Vocations up?* Hardly — just more scandal news.

"At this point, I don't see how Law will survive," Professor Gotcher said, referring to the embattled Boston cardinal at the center of the scandal. On the bright side, Professor Gotcher observed, Tom should be happy about this — it looked as if vocations were increasing. At least they were at Sacred Heart. They had a good crop of new seminarians coming in that January. Professor Gotcher thought the rise might be a delayed reaction to 9/11 and the Church crisis — a positive response to bad news.

"I take my hat off to the young guys becoming priests," Tom said.

"Why?" Ron asked.

"Because they're coming in with the nine A.M. shift and we're with the five P.M., and the wages are the same," Tom said.

Ron, low on sleep and beleaguered inside and out, approached Father Brackin after the last rector's conference of the fall.

"What would you say if I wanted to stick here?" Ron asked the rector.

"We'd be happy. You're not out the door yet," Father Brackin said.

"Okay," Ron said, inching toward commitment. "I want to stick here."

Snow began to fall in earnest in early December. The significant accumulations delighted Dean Haley. He was especially tickled when Bob Brooks went into a ditch trying to show Bobby Rodriguez what *not* to do when driving in snow. George, a former airline worker, made fun of the way Dean shoveled. In retaliation, Dean and Bobby buried George's car deep in the snow and poured water on the windshield while George activated the car alarm from his dorm window in a futile attempt to disrupt them. Dean threw a snowball at Philip Kim. The older man had taken it upon himself to clear snow from the area where the men smoked. Philip thanked Dean. It had taken him right back to his childhood in Korea.

Dean felt better than he had since arriving at Sacred Heart. His chiropractor said that his condition was improving and thought that he should stop taking the medication for his ADHD. He went to a tanning salon with Bob Brooks and got burned on his arms and chest, but he was happy to have some color.

Dean had been told many times that he wouldn't last at Sacred Heart. Although he was on a kind of unofficial probation, he felt that the worst had passed. *As long as I never have to live through the first se-mester again, everything's going to be okay,* he thought.

After Mass, Ron made his way to breakfast. The dining room was full. Sun poured in through the tall windows. Father Brackin sat at a table filled with seminarians and seemed to be enjoying himself. Thursday was omelet day, and the men waited in line for Amy's three-egg masterpieces loaded with sausage, cheese, onions, and jalapeños.

Ron felt giddy. "Hey, snookums," he said to one of the men in line.

"This may be a formation issue," the man joked back.

Later that morning, Ron returned to the dining hall for a cup of coffee. It was empty. He sat at a table near the door. To Ron's delight, Don Malin soon sat down next to him. He hadn't had a chance to tell Don the good news.

"You're not going to believe this," Ron began.

He turned toward Don so that he could face the older seminarian.

"See you in January," Ron announced.

Don took Ron's face in both hands. "That's great," Don crowed.

Ron gave him a few of the practical reasons he had decided to stay — the intergenerational program, the difficulty of moving in the winter. "Make sure you have all your qualms settled before you leave," Don advised.

When considering whether to end his marriage, Don had medi-tated on the Gospel passage in which Jesus asks Peter, the future leader of the Church, if Peter loves him. Jesus asks the question three times. Don explained to Ron that the repetition of the question might be because there are four words for love in Greek: *philia, eros, storge,* and *agape.* These mean, respectively, love between friends, ro-mantic and/or sexual love, familial love, and unconditional/sacri-ficial love. But the repetition also serves as a contemplative exercise through which the depth of one's love — especially in the sense of *agape* — is revealed. It is only when the glibness of an easy answer is challenged through repetition that the truth can be discovered. Don wanted Ron to challenge the easy answers that posed as products of discernment. He wanted Ron to find the kind of peace that came from real discernment. It was that peace that had permitted Don to leave a bad marriage — the peace that came from closing one door and knowing that it was shut for good. And it was that peace that would permit Ron to either leave Sacred Heart or stay with genuine freedom.

"I needed that peace that went all the way to the bottom," Don told his friend, and Ron would need time to find that kind of peace.

THE TEMPERATURE IN MILWAUKEE was twelve degrees when Heiser woke up and ate breakfast in the empty dining hall. Sometime that morning, there would be a funeral in the Sacred Heart Chapel for a member of the order who had died in India and been brought back to Milwaukee to be buried. Heiser would be long gone before they laid the SCJ in the mausoleum behind the school. He would be driving north, then west through Madison and points beyond, more or less following the route taken by Lewis and Clark, all the way home to Wyoming. Christmas break had begun.

He had packed his truck with spoils from the seminary kitchen and other sources: turkey and ham sandwiches, bratwurst in a covered Styrofoam cup, a six-pack of Sprecher's root beer, and several boxes of Girl Scout cookies (Thin Mints and Samoas) sent to him by a friend. This and the deer jerky his father had dried and given to him at Thanksgiving were packed in a cooler behind the front seat. He wanted to stop as little as possible. He had a song in him — it was a song that had come to him again and again throughout the semester: when he was sitting in Dr. Gallam's class looking at the trees outside or at his desk glancing at the postcard of the Tetons; when he was driving along the back road to the seminary and saw buck rubs on a tree or a flock of Canada geese settling on the fields. It was a song that led him to finish his breakfast in silence, slip out the back door, scrape the ice off his windshield while the motor ran, and then drive quietly away, letting the other men who still had tests sleep in until exam time.

George Gerdes wrote this song, which had supplied Heiser's dog with a name:

> I been shufflin' a lonesome old trail.
> I'm gonna send a letter to my dog, in the mail.
> Hey Packy, I'm comin' back again!
>
> My legs tired, my feet they're a-draggin'
> but I ain't a-stoppin' till I see his tail waggin'.

Heiser ate his deer jerky and sipped his root beer. Even though the stereo was playing George Harrison as he left Milwaukee's city limits, it was George Gerdes who was drawing him west to Wyoming. The country turned flat as he sped through western Wisconsin, past the occasional farmhouse and billboards promoting the state's cheese industry. Here the earth turned black, signaling the start of the deep, rich topsoil of the Great Plains.

> The clouds drift n' the world is so wide
> that a fella feels lucky with a dog by his side.
> Hey Packy! I'm comin' back again!
>
> A two bit mutt ain't worth a dollar
> but he'll be glad to see ya n' he'll come when you holler
> Hey Packy! I'm comin' back again!

Packy was the best hunting dog Heiser had ever owned. A mutt that was primarily black-and-white Border collie, Packy had grown up with Heiser's son, Eric. Now Packy was old and deaf, and Heiser wondered whether he would recognize his master this time around. He hadn't the last time.

> Some folks work hard, searchin' for somethin'
> they could see so plain in their dog's tail thumpin'
> Hey Packy, I'm comin' back again . . .

Folks wonderin' why they was born
ain't never been a-swimmin' with their dog in the mornin'
Hey Packy, I'm comin' back again.

Hey Packy! I'm comin' home!
I'm gonna scratch yer head n' feed you a bone!
Hey Packy! I'm comin' back again!

Heiser was excited at the prospect of time off, seeing his son and his friends, reading another Stephen Ambrose book, and hunting pheasants. Heiser had 20/15 vision. He saw things most people didn't see. Driving west, he spotted wildlife all the way. It was like a safari at seventy miles an hour. He spied a bald eagle far in the distance and a hawk on a post. Eighty miles west of Milwaukee, he spotted an excellent field for hunting and two dead rooster pheasants on the side of the road a mile apart. He knew they were rooster pheasants because of their conspicuous red plumage. A hen pheasant is plain and camouflaged to blend in with the nesting ground. Hens stay with the nest. It's important to know the difference, because it's illegal to shoot hens. There are more hens than roosters because of the law. One rooster pheasant mates with twenty-five hens.

Halfway through Minnesota, a crescent moon appeared, and Heiser thought, *I'll be following you all the way into South Dakota.* In the light of the moon, he saw another near-perfect pheasant field. Pheasants favor table grasses for cover but need a food source nearby. *There are the table grasses,* Heiser thought. *And there's the adjacent cornfield.*

Mussorgsky's *Pictures at an Exhibition* was playing on the stereo now as the Minnesota flatlands fanned out to the horizon in the moonlight. Heiser passed a series of billboards informing passersby of the Spam Museum, dedicated to the ubiquitous canned meat product: SPAM: THE SUM OF ALL HUMAN KNOWLEDGE and BELIEVE THE HYPE. Heiser had always wanted to stop at the museum but never had. He wouldn't this time either. Spam was a great thing to take camping, he thought. Then he sang the words to a popular

Monty Python skit: "Spam, wonderful Spam." Driving past exit 76 and the Hormel plant was like driving through a tunnel lined with Spam. For a short while, the air was greasy and redolent with an acrid sort of meat smell. But this passed, and outside his window, though Heiser couldn't see it, he knew the soil was getting blacker and deeper. The highway grew more desolate, the air grew richer with the smell of manure, and the sky lit up with shooting stars.

Even though Heiser still had hundreds of miles to go, he had crossed into his country. South Dakota was pregnant with memories. There was the time his ex-wife had stopped there as she sped from Philadelphia west in a nearly nonstop marathon to be with him in Wyoming. He also had come to South Dakota many times to hunt pheasants with Darold, a friend from the USDA whom everyone called "Spud." Heiser remembered the hunting parties with Spud's family at Spud's sister's farm near Platte, South Dakota. They'd play cards until all hours of the night, sleep in the next morning, eat a huge breakfast, and then hunt all day.

Heiser had met Spud in 1982, when Heiser arrived in Riverton to work for the USDA. Spud had taught Heiser almost everything he knew about agriculture in Fremont County. They would hop in the government pickup and drive around as Spud told him about the farms and the people who owned them. It was to Spud that Heiser had confided during his divorce.

Heiser's thoughts returned to Packy. Packy's dad was named Chaz. Chaz also had been a wonderful hunting dog. He would disappear for days at a time on romantic adventures. (Heiser could spot Chaz's probable offspring all over Riverton.) When Chaz ran off, Heiser would always find him at the same place: Spud's house.

The last time Heiser and Spud had gone hunting, Heiser had noticed that his friend seemed short of breath. They took more breaks than usual. On the way back to Wyoming from South Dakota, Heiser stopped to play the slots at a roadside casino. When he was leaving, he ran into Spud in the parking lot, and they made plans to hunt in Wyoming soon. A few weeks later, Spud called to tell

Heiser that he was having open-heart surgery. A little while after that, he was diagnosed with cancer. Spud fought the disease for a year, but then he called Heiser again and said that the doctor had given him two to six weeks to live. Heiser flew to visit Spud in Colorado, where his friend had built a log home after leaving Wyoming. Heiser did not know what to expect, but Spud exuded optimism and inspiration. He had been a convert to Catholicism, and his faith seemed to have swaddled him in a profound peace. Spud died in February; it was hard to lose his friend.

These were the things Heiser remembered as he drove through South Dakota. He also remembered that the closest he had ever come to hitting a deer was in that state, so he stayed alert. When he decided that he had driven far enough for one night, he pulled into the nearly empty parking lot of a small motel off the interstate. The trip odometer read just short of seven hundred miles.

The cinder-block walls of the motel room were painted white. Heiser awoke at 5:55 without an alarm clock. It had always been that way. As a teenager and as a forty-six-year-old seminarian, he never had a problem waking up. He took a shower and read his breviary. All through Advent, the Old Testament readings had been from Isaiah. The second reading today was from a Vatican II document, *Lumen Gentium*.

Heiser was in his truck within an hour. Venus was still bright in the sky, and the air was utterly still. Sunrise would be behind him on the prairie. For breakfast, he ate a muffin and some Tastykakes he had brought from Philadelphia. He stopped at the Kadoka truck stop to eat more Tastykakes and Girl Scout cookies. He set his clock back to Mountain Time.

The land grew rocky and gray as Heiser approached the Badlands. He knew that out west, every square inch of land that could be grazed was grazed. He didn't agree with that practice, but he also knew how farmers struggled and had sympathy for them. Driving south on Route 73, he saw a golden eagle with a six-foot wingspan fly right in front of his truck at windshield level. He spotted a burrowing owl on the side of the road. He had hit one once, and the force of the impact and the dust of the bird's feathers had left an outline on his vehicle that he'd thought of as the owl's spirit. Birds, coyotes, and prairie dogs blended into the landscape, but Heiser saw them. He spotted six prairie chickens in a row of Russian olive trees.

Road hunting is allowed in South Dakota. That means you can stop your truck and hunt the road's margins between the fences on either side. Heiser didn't have his gun with him, but he wouldn't have stopped and hunted even if he did. He knew a guy who kept his gun with him at all times and would take shots with one hand on the wheel and the other on the trigger. That kind of thing was inconceivable in the East. Heiser liked the fact that it wasn't inconceivable in the West.

The cover grew sparse. Patches of yucca appeared, indicating sandier soil. Looked at from the north, the hills appeared to be snow covered, but from the south there was no trace of snow. Now he was heading west again, as he crossed into Wyoming. He had on the slippers given to him by David Placette and broke out a snack of the Hungarian sausage that Deacon Don Wright had sold to some of the seminarians the previous week. It was a vividly clear day with a wide blue sky. When he had left for Wisconsin more than three months before, Laramie Peak, to the southwest, had been shrouded in smoke and haze from wildfires that had burned all summer. Not so today. He crossed the North Platte River, a brilliant blue sliver that flows slowly to the Missouri, then on to the Mississippi, and finally into the Gulf of Mexico. A long freight train carrying citrine and coal rode a track atop a ridge, and the dry, rocky land looked harsh but peaceful. Heiser had his foot to the floor, but a strong headwind kept him from topping sixty. Sometimes the wind and snow got so bad that the highway had to be closed.

When he passed Hell's Half Acre, a desolate moonscape, he knew he was close to home. He tuned in to KTRZ, the radio station where Eric worked as the sports director. He listened to classic rock, hoping to hear his son break in with sports.

Heiser wondered what Riverton would be like. The weather so far had been warm for the season, but Riverton sat in the Wind River valley, and the valley was notorious for getting socked in with cold air. This thick frozen fog ate right through your clothes to your skin. It could stay in place for days, until a good strong wind scoured it out. Once, the people at the weather station had floated a balloon up over Riverton and found a fifty-degree difference between the ground and air temperatures.

Heiser crossed the town limits, driving past the farms he had known so well during his time with the USDA. He saw thick, icy deposits on sagebrush, greasewood, and rabbitbrush. Riverton had frozen fog. He spotted the Trailhead, a family restaurant where all the ranchers congregated. Cows grazed next to the Wal-Mart, and the sheriff drove by in a four-by-four pickup equipped with a powerful winch. Heiser passed Honor Farm, a minimum-security correctional facility, where he used to bring the Eucharist to the inmates. And then he was home, walking in his front door to find Johnny and Judy, his brother and sister-in-law, watching television in his living room. Their little girl, Marianka, was darting about.

Heiser loved his brother, but he knew that Johnny and his family had been driving Eric crazy. He had been listening to Eric's complaints for months, and now he knew why. The kitchen was a disaster: days-old dirty dishes in the sink, cereal boxes strewn about, a stick of deodorant on the counter.

Johnny told Heiser that the financing for the house had fallen through again. Johnny was supposed to be buying the house from his brother. Heiser was upset, and he let it show a little. He had been hoping to finalize the sale before he went back to Sacred Heart. He wanted to be free of this last entanglement, plus he needed the cash to pay for his final years at the seminary. Johnny said that he would take care of it — speak with the bank, do something. Then Heiser noticed that the cuckoo clock on the wall wasn't running. It was a family heirloom. He pulled the center cord a few times to wind it.

"That's how you do it?" Judy asked, not sounding particularly interested.

All the while, Packy had been trying to figure out who Heiser was. Just when it seemed that the old dog wouldn't remember, he followed Heiser into his bedroom, and something clicked. Packy knew his master. He got excited and wouldn't leave Heiser's side from then on.

Heiser received a stream of visitors that night, each one tracking in the cold air with him. Casey, Heiser's next-door neighbor and the local track coach, arrived first. Then JVH, one of Heiser's best friends, came through the door with Heiser's Browning automatic shotgun. He pointed the empty gun at Casey's crotch, then gave the gun to Heiser. Heiser cradled the gun, then propped it against the back of the sofa.

Eric arrived, dressed in business attire, at quarter to six. Heiser and Eric embraced. They talked about Eric's twenty-first birthday, and Casey joked about seeing Eric start the evening at the bar at the local Holiday Inn. Heiser had already heard about the outing. As far as Heiser could tell, Eric had behaved responsibly. Eric disappeared into his room and emerged in a huge Philadelphia Flyers jersey that Heiser had bought him. Eric's friends arrived, hoping to score some of Johnny's famous cheesesteaks. Johnny had owned (and lost) two restaurants. When they heard that there were no sandwiches at the house yet — Johnny had gone to drop off a sandwich for the counterman at Safeway — they left for the Holiday Inn. Sometime later, Heiser's friends also left, and Johnny, Judy, and Marianka went to bed. Heiser felt content and happy. He continued reading about Lewis and Clark's journey west. But before long, he was fast asleep in his own bed.

The next morning, Heiser awoke while it was still dark. He drove down the ice- and snow-covered streets to a small brick church called St. Margaret's for the seven o'clock Mass. The frozen fog had been blown away during the night, and the air was slightly warmer, but Heiser knew that it would not get above freezing that day. Twenty or so parishioners sat scattered among the pews, and Father Duncan officially welcomed Heiser back at the end of Mass. Heiser followed

Father Duncan into the sacristy, saying hello to a few parishioners as he went. Heiser talked with the priest while he put away the chasuble and chalice. Heiser asked Father Duncan if he wanted to go pheasant hunting one of these days. The priest said that he was a terrible pheasant hunter but might go anyway. Then he invited Heiser to the adjacent school's cafeteria for a light breakfast.

Heiser did not know Father Duncan that well. The priest had arrived during the time that Heiser had been busy preparing for the seminary. But as they ate their breakfast of oatmeal and milk, Father Duncan told him how some of the people they both knew were faring. The custodian walked by and gave Heiser a warm welcome, then showed Heiser the roasters he would be using for the Knights of Columbus prime rib fundraiser. His wife arrived and asked Heiser how long he would be staying.

"I'll be back until the third," he replied. He had already said that a lot and would be saying it a lot more over the next few days.

Father Duncan mentioned the controversy over the Harry Potter books, which feature a young wizard who attends Hogwarts, a preparatory school for wizards. Some people saw Satanism in the magical premise, Father Duncan said with a laugh. But anyone who had been to the seminary, he said, could identify with Hogwarts.

Later that day, on his way to meet his friend Craig to go hunting, Heiser stopped by the USDA office where he used to work. The women who had made up the majority of his coworkers gave him hugs, then sent him to the backroom, where a table was spread with food. These women had become close friends of Heiser's over the years. In some cases, he had become a confidant and counselor to them, seeing them through family crises. The office was suffused with light. The Christmas "tree" was made out of a dozen poinsettias.

"Remember the sage tree we did one year?" Kathleen said with a laugh. "Everyone had allergies after that."

Packy was scuttling around the back of Heiser's truck as they bounced and rattled down Burma Road toward Muddy Creek. An orange dog lying in the sun jumped to its feet as the truck passed by and gave chase, but the dog soon fell behind. Heiser used to run Chaz and later Packy behind his truck for a mile or so to give them exercise, but he wouldn't be pushing Packy that way anymore. In fact, he was wondering how well Packy would perform in the hunt. It had been a year since their last one.

There was no sign of Craig or his dog down the long dirt track. But there was a pheasant — a rooster pheasant — just as conspicuous as could be in the tall grass on the road's edge. Only after Heiser brought the truck to a stop did the bird break into its more predictable bob and weave and seek cover. Heiser hoped this was a sign of a healthy pheasant population. There hadn't been many pheasants in this drought-stricken land for several years. He also hoped that it was evidence that no one had been hunting Muddy Creek and its surrounding fields.

He drove a few hundred yards more, and Craig, a spry, white-bearded man in a hunting cap, appeared with his gun held over his head as if he were surrendering to an enemy. His young dog bounded from side to side on the road. Heiser let Packy out of the truck, then turned around and drove back to where he had seen the pheasant. Packy ran after the truck, then dove into the bush, immediately picking up the bird's trail. Craig's dog followed at a run. Craig walked.

Heiser parked the truck, got his gun, and followed the dogs into the short grass. He walked toward the clump of trees where he had last seen the pheasant. The dogs were running in circles, then straight lines, then circles again. Their tails wagged furiously. Heiser and Craig walked, then broke into a little jog, and then walked again. All the while, Heiser knew what the bird was doing, even though he couldn't see it. The pheasant was running and keeping low in the brush. The last thing it wanted to do was fly, and that was what the dogs were trained to make it do. This was no easy job. A good hunting dog would catch the scent and drive the pheasant from one hiding spot to the next, eventually forcing it into the air so that the hunter could shoot it. The problem was, the dog might reach the bird too soon and send it up while the hunter was yards down the field and out of range. Or the dog might lose the scent entirely, especially if the dog was old.

Pheasants are smart, and they are patient. Heiser remembered one hunting party where the dogs lost the scent. Everyone sat down to rest, only to have the pheasant, which had been hiding in a clump of grass right next to them, fly up halfway through their break. This time, the pheasant wasn't so clever. Craig's dog flushed the bird, and it tried to fly away. Heiser lifted his shotgun, calmly took aim, and dropped the pheasant with one shot.

That night, Heiser cleaned the pheasant over the garbage can, efficiently peeling off the skin until all that remained was a shiny, fist-size portion of white meat that he would use to make pheasant salad. Johnny cooked pork tenderloin, and the family gathered for a chaotic dinner. Heiser managed to catch up with Eric a bit, while little Marianka tossed corn kernels on the floor. After dinner, Heiser left for church, where he had offered to help Casey with religious instruction.

At church, Heiser led the rosary. Then the forty high school students in attendance and their parents, each holding a candle, announced their prayer intentions one by one. A woman asked that the community be given the strength to oppose a group of white supremacists who, the news had reported, had chosen Riverton as their headquarters. JVH, who also was helping, prayed for adequate rainfall for the Wind River valley. As each person spoke his or her intention, he or she lit the candle.

When Heiser got home, he found Johnny, under an orange blanket, watching TV alone in the living room. Heiser had given Johnny an ultimatum: he must either buy the house or move out. Heiser asked Johnny if he had gotten rid of the porn channel that had somehow appeared as part of his cable package. Johnny said he didn't know there was a porn channel, but he was wearing a grin.

The next morning, Heiser attended Mass at St. Margaret's. It was the Feast of Our Lady of Guadalupe. JVH arrived after Mass, driving his big orange Suburban and dressed in a blue denim shirt and tan coveralls.

Were they still going hunting? Father Duncan asked.

Yes, they answered.

"Going hunting?" a tall man asked as he passed them in the foyer on his way out of church.

Yes.

Soon the hunting party had acquired two more members. The tall man, named Joe, was a weatherman. He decided to take a half day off from work for the hunt. Father Duncan, who had to get back in time for a funeral at eleven-thirty, thought he would chance it, too. So Heiser and JVH drove to JVH's house to pick up a Remington pump action shotgun and JVH's dog, Minnie. On the way to Heiser's house, they stopped at Daylight Donuts for coffee, hot chocolate, doughnuts, and hot apple fritters. Then they stopped at Heiser's so that he could change out of his church clothes and pick up Packy and his gun.

Driving in Father Duncan's car, the priest and the weatherman followed JVH's clattering Suburban out of town on Burma Road. "We've got the whole thing covered — the spiritual and the atmospheric," Heiser observed.

They picked up Craig at the trailer where he was living out on Missouri Road. He had been busy shooting at foxes with his high-powered rifle that morning.

"I hope Father's laying bread crumbs down," JVH shouted as one serpentine road led onto the next. Heiser, leaning out the window, was busy scraping the frost from the windshield with a plastic card that JVH had given him. "Father's probably wondering where the hell we're going," he said.

Homesteads were far apart now, and the land stretched in all directions to distant mountains and highlands. Most hunters had a standing agreement with the farmers out here about hunting on their land, but it depended on the farmer. Heiser had a good relationship with most of them, but one or two might be moody. One day you were welcome, and the next day you weren't. And sometimes the farmer had a very good reason for that: he might have livestock nearby that he didn't want spooked, or there weren't enough pheasants on his land, and he wanted the population to grow.

"Since there's going to be an army on his land, maybe we'd better check in," Heiser said.

They found the farmer working on his tractor. With a few words and a nod, he granted his permission for them to hunt all the land on the right side of the road. The fields to the left were off-limits.

It was rough going as the men spread out, with the three dogs zig-zagging across uneven, rocky land that was thick with brush. Early in the hunt, a pheasant went up and flew right at JVH, who managed to get off three shots but missed the bird anyway. The pheasant crossed the road and settled in the off-limits field. Heiser moved quickly, stepping high when he needed to, playing limbo with wire fences, and keeping a close eye on Packy. They worked one long ditch, then another. The sun began to warm up the land, and the fields became a brilliant rust-gold.

Jim heard a pop from one of the men's guns and then another soon after. *Maybe they got one,* he thought, but the day wasn't looking too good.

"The pheasant population ain't what it was," JVH had complained earlier in the truck. An hour into the hunt, it looked as if he was right. Heiser thought he would be lucky to get his quota of two that day. He and Packy worked one field and then another. He skirted ditches while Packy dove into thick clumps of reeds embedded in ice, driving his snout into the undergrowth. More pops from distant shotguns.

Packy's tail wagged a bit more, and he darted from one place to another. *It could be an old scent,* Heiser thought. The dog darted about some more and then settled down and jogged a little circle around Heiser. And then all of a sudden Heiser knew that his dog hadn't lost it. Packy was off, tearing through the brush, spinning around clumps of vegetation, rocks, and trees, almost as if his nose was center and the rest of his body the spinning radius of a circle. With Heiser running to keep pace, Packy ran in a straight line right down the middle of the field. Heiser checked his shotgun; he carried it away from his body in his right hand. Heiser gauged every move the dog made, every dip of his head and flick of his tail. The bird was invisible. It was moving, and Packy was moving right behind it. Packy veered right, then went straight at the base of a sapling a few hundred feet from Heiser. His nose was hovering just above the ground, and his legs were moving at a brisk trot.

The bird went up at a sharp angle, perpendicular to Heiser's line of fire. With a fluid and precise motion, he brought the shotgun up, steadied it against his shoulder, and took the bird down with a single shot. There was still some life in the pheasant when Packy picked it up in his teeth. The dog shook his head, and the bird went limp.

That night, Heiser wanted steak for dinner. The two apple fritters from Daylight Donuts had been his only food all day. He rounded up his son and a small group of friends and drove to a steakhouse in the next town. It was good to be back, he told them.

The days that followed were filled with visits and more dinners with friends. He got his two-bird quota on each of seven hunting trips, turning pheasants into salads, giving the salads away, and reading Stephen Ambrose in spare moments. He drove Eric to the airport in Jackson on December 23. Eric was going to spend Christmas with his mother and aunt in Las Vegas. They saw six bald eagles on the way. Heiser told Eric that Danny "O" always said that seeing a bald eagle was good luck, and Eric said that was a nice thought because he would be hitting the gambling tables that night.

Near the end of his stay, Heiser went hunting alone with Packy. It was New Year's Eve, the last day of pheasant season. Heiser thought, *This is going to be my last hunt with Packy for the season, maybe forever.* They worked Muddy Creek. After Heiser shot one bird, there was still some light left. Then Packy drove another bird directly at Heiser. It flew just in front of him. He could see its eyeball. The pheasant knew it was in trouble. It came down with a single shot, and Heiser gave Packy a hug. He got into his truck and opened a beer. The Grateful Dead were playing on the stereo. The sky stretched forever as the day waned. Another year was coming to an end. *Heaven,* Heiser thought. *This is heaven.*

THEY TOOK RON KENDZIERSKI'S nameplate off his door before the other seminarians returned. Ron was not coming back to Sacred Heart, even though his name still appeared on the official spring student list with an asterisk indicating that he was on a leave of absence. In spite of his eleventh-hour reversal, he had decided against heeding Don Malin's advice to give himself a second semester. He was not going to take any more time to go all the way to the bottom and weigh what he found there, at least not at Sacred Heart. Some of the men claimed that they had expected as much. Heiser thought that their words were disingenuous. The news had taken him by surprise.

Ron had returned to collect his things and take them back to Michigan. He chose a day in early January when the men were returning for their annual retreat. Heiser was one of the few who saw him that day. He spotted him down the corridor from the dining hall, went to say hello, and learned that Ron wasn't going to continue. Ron said he was going ahead with Tina and spoke of his hopes for his intergenerational project.

Heiser thought it was strange that Ron had chosen the one day to clear out his room when he was most likely to bump into his classmates. A day earlier, and the seminarians wouldn't have returned yet;

a day later, and they would have been off on their retreat. But Heiser did not ask Ron about this. Perhaps Ron had put off the decision until the last minute. Or perhaps he wanted to run into the people he was leaving. For someone to demand that he reconsider? Or to help shut the door? Who knew?

For the larger-than-life presence that Ron had been at Sacred Heart, there was little talk of his departure. Neither Don Malin nor any of the other seminarians heard from him in the days after he left. As with other men who walked away, the seminary moved on without him. Ron's room went back on the hospitality list as one of the more comfortable spaces for guests to stay. It had its own bathroom and TV.

Dean Haley returned from the Christmas holidays in a spirit of quiet triumph and lighthearted defiance. Dean had earned a 3.3 grade point average for the fall semester. He had counseled a cousin through a personal crisis. Father Krebs now said that Dean was making good progress.

Ron's disappearance presented more pompoms for Dean to shake. He was also relieved that Ron didn't seem inclined to drop in on his old friends at Sacred Heart. Dean didn't want to hear anybody report on how nice it was to be sleeping next to a warm body again. *If you're gonna move on,* Dean thought, *move on.*

"My hope all first semester was to *have* a second semester," Dean told Don Malin. The two men sat at the same table in the dining hall on the second day of classes. They rarely ate together.

"I guess you got your goal," Don replied.

Don had heard enough stories about Dean to know that the man across the table had a long way to go before ordination. Don himself had watched Dean serve on the altar. As Dean missed one cue after another and seemed to do everything in the wrong order, Don thought he might be watching the creation of a new liturgy. But Don knew that anyone could learn how to serve eventually; that was just mechanics. The deeper issue was whether the seminary could help

Dean overcome enough of his internal impediments to create a pastor and whether Dean was even open to the process.

At lunch, Dean was in high gear. He was excited because of what Father Krebs had said and was determined to take the priest's advice to read the Gospels the day before Mass so as to get more out of them. He was excited that he had rearranged his room again and sold the computer desk he had bought at the beginning of the year but never used. Most of all, he was excited about academics. Dean had just received the reading list from Dr. Bruce Malchow that day. It looked insanely hard, he thought, but the feedback from alumni was that Dr. Malchow's Introduction to Scripture course was *the* class they used most when they became priests.

"My first name is Jody," Dean told Don. "Every time I changed schools, I lied. I'd always get the girls' dorm at summer camp. Every time I got a credit card, I'd get female products."

Dean said that by the time he joined the marines, he had changed the Jody to J. His fellow marines would invariably ask him what J stood for.

"Just J," Dean would hedge.

In the marines, "Jody" was a much-despised figure, the eponymous subject of running songs, or "double-time Jodys" as the tunes were called. Jody, Dean told Don, was the name of the guy servicing all the marines' girlfriends and wives while they were on deployment.

"Ain't no sense in lookin' back," Dean sang in cadence as if on a march. "Jody's got your Cadillac. Jody took your girl and *gone*. Jody's got your girl and *gone*."

A few seminarians joined them, and someone mentioned how full their mailboxes had been when they had returned from the break. Don said that he had a huge stack of letters from home and many Christmas cards, although he still hadn't sent out most of his own. Dean said that he had received money. The first envelope he opened was from the Knights of Columbus. It was a check for five hundred dollars.

"There you go," Don said encouragingly.

"Then the next one I opened was a check from the diocese for one hundred dollars. And I said yeah!" Dean started laughing. "And the next one I opened was a bill from the chiropractor for $571."

"So you're ahead by twenty-nine dollars," Don observed.

"Woohoo!" Dean exclaimed.

Outside, Milwaukee was in a deep freeze. The Church had returned to Ordinary Time. In the liturgical year, Ordinary Time falls between the end of the Christmas season and the beginning of Lent and between the end of the Easter season and the beginning of Advent. But it was ordinary time in a more generic way as well. There was no grand "welcome back" for the second semester, only a sense of continuation. This semester was technically shorter than the first. School ended in late April, with two long breaks before then.

That morning, Father Brackin had delivered his first homily of the semester. The purple vestments of Advent were gone. The rector wore a green chasuble, and Don, serving beside him, wore a green stole. Father Brackin's homily could just as easily have been delivered in the middle of a semester. He made no sweeping observations on new beginnings, as he had at the start of the first semester, and instead used something in the news to illustrate the Gospel. The rector referred to the governor of Illinois's recent decision to pardon all of the inmates on death row in his state. The pardon seemed politically expedient, but the rector did not comment on the expediency — only on what he suggested was the world's negative reaction to an idealistic decision. Are we ready, Father Brackin asked the men, for them to say "Crucify him. Crucify him" about us at every step of our journey? Father Brackin said that this call to crucifixion could take many different forms. Don arranged the altar for the consecration with intent, downcast eyes.

As a new deacon, Don was beginning to experience in practice what he had known only in formation theory: once a man is empowered to act, he will be asked to act — again and again. Don had returned to his home diocese of Pueblo, Colorado, to find a Christmas holiday crammed with work. There had been three men studying for the diaconate, but one had recently dropped out. Only Don and Martín Frias, who had been ordained with Don, remained. Directly upon Don's arrival home, he was told that he had a funeral the following day and would be preaching at four of the seven Masses that weekend. His workload remained heavy throughout the holidays. He served at a Mass for high school students after the town's first murder in six years, a particularly brutal one in which a partygoer had had his testicles shot off. Don met with a local charismatic group to help them develop a better relationship with the diocese. There was some talk that Don would be appointed the diocese's director of Charismatic Renewal after his priestly ordination, but he thought it more likely that the bishop would send him to a parish. On Christmas Eve, he did the five P.M. and midnight Masses. There had been an awkward encounter with his ex-wife. She had put in early to help at the midnight Mass, but when the pastor decided to have Don serve, he rescheduled her. He didn't want both of them at the same service. They had crossed paths anyway. Don arrived at the church when she was leaving. "Nice collar," he thought he heard her mutter as she walked past him toward the exit.

Don had managed to fit in lunch with a female friend from his divorce recovery group and later spend time with the Jesuits down in Albuquerque, New Mexico, just before a solitary retreat, but he had been unable to visit either of his parents. It was not only the constant round of Masses and his other regular duties that kept him busy. It was the unexpected things, such as being asked to translate for an old Spanish woman at confession or finding a hotel room for a sick transient who had no shelter for the night. All of this work was so new to Don that he felt as if he were watching himself perform from outside his body.

Don blessed the house of a woman with bipolar disorder who wanted to make sure that the voices she was hearing were inside her head before she went back on her medication. The house was filled with religious icons. Don prayed the general prayer of the Church for house blessings and then prayed a prayer composed by the woman asking that the evil spirits be driven out of the house. Don hoped that he had provided some comfort to the woman but on his way out suggested that she start taking her medication again.

An even stranger episode occurred when Don returned to Sacred Heart. Gary, a new member of his Milwaukee charismatic prayer group, approached him with a request to rid his restaurant of a suspected poltergeist. The Cobblestone Inn is located on the outskirts of Milwaukee, about forty-five minutes from Sacred Heart. It had been a hangout for Chicago gangsters in the 1920s and the scene of at least one murder and a suicide. Don had visited the inn shortly after a heavy cash register had been hurled onto the floor. He saw the cash register, and Gary told him of a series of strange events that had occurred since he had bought the place, including one in which a glass flew off the bar and hit an entryway divider. The incident had emptied the place. It was common knowledge that the Cobblestone Inn had been haunted for as long as anyone could remember. The haunting was even mentioned on the back of the menu. But now Gary wanted it to stop.

Don asked two other Sacred Heart deacons, LeRoy Schik and Dennis Cloonan, to join him. He also asked his friends the Hersils, who had some experience with deliverance prayers — formulations designed to vanquish evil spirits. Don asked Gary to have all the staff present during the ritual and to put out bowls with greenery that could be used to sprinkle holy water. The deacons arrived. Don, Dennis, and LeRoy were dressed in their clerics. They blessed water and salt and then fanned out through the inn. They opened every drawer and cupboard and got into every closet, corner, and crevice. They threw blessed salt and holy water everywhere. All the while, the Hersils murmured their deliverance prayers. No one encountered any supernatural phenomenon. *We're just doing what the Church does*, Don thought. *We're helping restless spirits rest. We're giving peace to those who are disturbed. We're purifying and sanctifying.*

Theologically, the idea of restless spirits speaks to the connections between the dead and the living. The Church has rituals for dealing with how a lack of forgiveness, a broken relationship, a violent death, or the absence of a proper burial can prevent a spirit from resting. Don instructed the staff not to talk about the haunting. Two weeks before, he had told Gary to remove the blurb from the back of the menu. Don also told Gary and the staff that whatever these spirits were, the best thing to do was to ignore them, because to pay them any attention would only pull them back from their rest.

After the deacons had done their work, Gary had the chef make two thick quiches for them. Don ate with gusto. He respected the rituals but also recognized that it was better not to talk too much about them, because they were easily sensationalized. It wouldn't take much for a priest to get a reputation for driving out evil spirits, which might hurt his ability to perform his regular ministry.

This ministry included weekly preaching around the Milwaukee area, some of which was being evaluated for Father Andre Papineau's course. After one homily, Don got another taste of what his new clerical state demanded of him. He had begun the homily at Mary Queen of Heaven with a favorite rhetorical hook: "How many people would believe that before I came to seminary, I was a juvenile delinquent?" Don had gone on to speak of his life story and the notion, central to Catholicism, of personal redemption.

Afterward, he was swamped with requests to follow up his homily with individual conversations. One mother e-mailed him with a request to speak with her teenage son, who she said was troubled. "Does he want to speak with me?" Don asked her. He did not, the mother replied. Don concluded that he'd better not speak with him. He was in the business of dealing with moral and spiritual issues, not psychological problems. *For me to practice psychology would be a travesty,* he thought, *and probably illegal.* Another man phoned Don and told him that he had been moved by Don's reflections on his own divorce. The man's brother was going through a divorce, he said. Could his brother call Don? Don said that of course he could call.

Don was elated at the positive response to his homily. His elation didn't last very long. One of the staff of the parish mentioned that a relative who had attended a Mass at which Don spoke in November had been offended by his upbeat assessment of the priestly life. You've got to understand, the staff member explained, my aunt is an ex-nun, and she has issues with the all-male priesthood. Don mentioned the elation and disappointment to a few priests at lunch one day. "Welcome to parish life," one of them said. "You open your mouth, and you're going to upset someone."

On the Saturday in early February that the space shuttle *Columbia* exploded and sent its wreckage all over the Diocese of Tyler, Texas, Dean made his way to the library to read about the history of Christianity since the Reformation. Not once since he'd arrived at Sacred Heart had he studied in the library. Dean had hardly cracked a book the first semester. Now he decided to change all that. After lunch, he picked up the history book and became enthralled. He wasn't certain why he went to the library. Perhaps it was to avoid the temptation to keep checking the news. He had gone to college in Nacogdoches, Texas, where much of *Columbia* fell to Earth.

The electric clock above the copier occasionally made a sputter and a click as the second hand moved. Dean had just read about Martin Luther when the door at the top of the stairs opened and a second-year seminarian working the front desk came in to ask a favor. Visitors to the seminary always came in past the front desk. It wasn't unusual for strangers to show up looking for the gift shop or the shrine, but the second-year student had found himself facing two teenagers who wanted to talk to him about God. They had a lot of questions, and he had the phones to man. He asked if Dean could take care of their request.

The boys came into the library. One was a Catholic and the other a Lutheran. They seemed to be in the middle of a furious debate about salvation. Dean dove into the fray. The Lutheran was from the Missouri Synod, a conservative branch of Lutheranism that embraces biblical literalism and has 2.5 million adherents. Whenever Dean made a point, the Lutheran would demand that the seminarian show him in the Bible where it said what Dean had maintained. To his surprise, Dean found himself describing Scripture as "documented oral tradition."

"Is this your Bible?" Dean asked the Lutheran. He picked up the book and began to leaf through it until he found what he was looking for. "Who killed Goliath?"

"David," the boy answered confidently.

Dean read from the well-known verses in which David kills Goliath with a sling and presents the giant's severed head to the king. But go back a few chapters, Dean observed, and you have someone else with a long and barely pronounceable name killing the giant Goliath with a spear. Of course, it could have been a different giant named Goliath, but how likely was that? More likely, since Scripture is based on an oral tradition, the telling and retelling of the story resulted in David, who was renowned for his other feats, being credited with the defeat of Goliath as well. After all, Dean said, I just read the passage today, and I've already forgotten the other guy's name. People who are easier to remember often get credit for things they haven't done. True today, true back then.

The Lutheran objected, noting a footnote claiming that a mistranslation from the Hebrew caused the confusion.

"Why are we discussing a footnote that even suggests a mistranslation?" Dean challenged. "How can there be a mistranslation in a Bible that's absolutely perfect?"

"He's got you, dude," the other boy said to his friend.

"If you're going to be a literalist, be a literalist," Dean concluded. "But don't start bringing reason into it if you won't let me."

Dean spoke with the boys for four hours. He saw their desire to learn about God, and it made him think of the needs of the young. He imagined the two teens driving up and down Highway 100 past the strip malls, looking for a foothold in a barren, commercial landscape that was duplicated thousands of times across America. They had told Dean that the night before, they had talked to someone at a Barnes & Noble store but had gotten nowhere. That morning, still restless and deadlocked, they had been driving down the highway and seen Sacred Heart's sign. God was in this moment, they said. Dean agreed. I've been here six months, and I never study in the library, he told them. I never study on a Saturday. I had just read about Luther, so I was ready.

Encounters like this made Dean believe more than ever that there are legions of passionate, high-energy young people who are being missed — being completely left behind — by the Church. He thought back to that turning-point night around Halloween. He had met a woman and her boyfriend. The woman said that she was a cop who arrested pedophile priests and ministers. She said that what was so repugnant to her was when they started saying the Bible this and the Bible that. I book these people, she said, so I know what the perverts in the clergy are like, but I know I can trust you. Sacred Heart believed one thing about what was needed in a priest, Dean mused, but there was also this other reality. Young people needed to hear someone — someone like Dean Haley — tell them, "I get it, dude."

Jim Pemberton's vision of the Church was growing more complex and his desire for ordination more urgent. He had come away from a visit to a synagogue with deep admiration for several Jewish practices, especially carrying the Torah through the pews so that the faithful could reach out and touch the law. He thought Catholic worship could be enriched if the Gospel's centrality were embraced through a ritual like that — that and better preaching, of course. Jim had also become less concerned about the big Church issues and more concerned about what he perceived as the quiet voice of the Holy Spirit. He called this voice "the little voice," and he sought to follow its lead with ever greater awareness.

If he was walking down the hall and the little voice urged him to take a detour into the St. Joseph's Chapel, the seminary's third worship space, he made the detour. At least that was the case one Saturday morning when he found himself engaged in a centering prayer, a kind of meditation, in the chapel. In the midst of his prayers, he heard the little voice again, quite distinctly suggesting that he "invite that man over there out to dinner." "That man over there" was the only other person in the chapel, a fellow seminarian whom Jim held in high regard. Jim did as the voice suggested; they had dinner.

To Jim's astonishment, the seminarian told him that when serving at Mass, he suffered from panic attacks so severe that he was certain his shaking was visible from the pews. The seminarian said that he was losing his courage. *I would have lost every penny had I bet on this guy being as confident as he looked,* Jim thought. *I would never have known what was going on inside him.* Jim had a copy of the book *If You Want to Walk on Water, You've Got to Get Out of the Boat* with him, and he gave it to the seminarian. The man read it soon after and reported that it was just what he needed. Their friendship developed from there.

After the incident, Jim marveled, *The little voice feels like an external thought.* Rather than second-guess or debate it, the best route was to follow it. He knew that he might not always see the immediate benefit. He thought, *I may be the planter of the seed and be gone before the harvest.*

Once a week, Jim attended Parochial Activities, a class that exposed second-year students to parish life through a series of speakers. Often the presentations were heavily practical. One parish priest emphasized keeping a calendar as a way of conserving one's strength and reducing stress.

"Don't ever let the job of running the parish take you away from ministry," the priest said. He told the men how easy it is to get caught up in the bureaucratic hustle and lose sight of a priest's first duty to the people.

"Don't ever choose to finish the budget over going to see someone in the hospital," he urged. He told them to take time for what is important, not for what is merely urgent. He quoted Pope John XXIII, who avoided insomnia with the reflection, "It's your Church, God.

I'm going to bed." This was Jim Pemberton's kind of talk — rolling up your sleeves and addressing the real needs of the flock while maintaining perspective.

When the job becomes too much, the priest said, it's time to do something creative. "Pick up a paintbrush. Take a watercolor class. We need to do this as priests. We have to be the balanced people in the congregations."

He also implored them to eat right, exercise, pray, and continue to learn. "If you don't have good, healthy habits now, you're not going to get them after ordination."

Finally, he said, "Be happy and let it show. Don't let the world take over. I want you all to be priests. And I want you all to be happy priests."

*Patience,* Jim would tell himself. *Patience.* Jim was torn between the desire to be ordained immediately and the reality of the study and preparation that still lay ahead. Then one day, without any attendant fanfare, he received a memo in his mailbox that challenged his patience some more. The memo informed him of an impending rite of passage: "Re: Paperwork for Ministry of Lector."

The next major step had arrived, and he hadn't even been expecting it. Reading the memo, Jim Pemberton began to cry. At one time, seminarians had four ministries conferred upon them prior to ordination: porter, lector, acolyte, and exorcist. Vatican II had eliminated porter and exorcist but had retained lector and acolyte. Jim made twenty copies of the three-paragraph memo and mailed it to family and friends. "God's call just got a little louder!" he wrote on the bottom of the copies he sent to his kids. The memo informed him that the ministry would be conferred on March 26, 2003, at 4:30 P.M. By that date, he and the twelve other men (including Heiser) who would also be receiving the ministry would have attended two workshops with Father Andre Papineau. *He really wants me to be here,* he thought.

Jim felt the eagerness to serve build up inside him. *Patience,* Jim reminded himself. *Patience.* But it was hard to be patient. He always seemed to be being set on fire. The words of a Jesuit during the January retreat returned to him: "If this is not the work I am being called to, then what is the work? If this is not the time, then when is the time? If I am not the one, who is?" He was scheduled to be ordained to the Roman Catholic priesthood in May 2005. That seemed like a very long way off.

Father Jim Brackin began the rector's conference with a prayer: "On this anniversary of *Roe versus Wade,* we pray especially for our nation, for all those people who suffered because of abortion. We ask your guiding spirit upon our nation to transform our hearts and our thinking that we continue to pray for an openness and respect for all life. We pray this in Jesus's name."

"Amen," the men responded.

*Roe v. Wade,* the monumental Supreme Court decision that legalized abortion in the United States, had been handed down thirty years earlier, in 1973. The American bishops had designated January 22 as "A Day of Prayer and Penance," and Sacred Heart was observing it.

Father Jan De Jong, professor of moral theology and a well-respected medical ethicist, celebrated the community Mass at eleven A.M. Dean assisted, serving more adeptly than before. Father De Jong spoke of the late Cardinal Bernardin's description of life. The cardinal had called life one seamless garment that included abortion, euthanasia, the death penalty, and caring for the elderly and others. Pope John Paul II had written "profoundly" of this unity of life, Father De Jong said. A long silence followed his homily, during which people stared down into their laps or straight ahead. Then Don Malin began to play his guitar, a haunting and reflective arrangement of Ravel's *Pavane pour une infante défunte* (a pavane is a slow, stately dance dating back to the Renaissance). Professor Christian Rich accompanied him on the organ. As the Mass concluded, Father De Jong dismissed the congregation by saying that he hoped they would all go forth in a spirit of prayer and penance until life in all its forms was valued. People lingered, staying to kneel or sit silently in prayer.

Wiggy didn't think Father De Jong had gone far enough in his homily. *If I had been speaking,* he thought, *I would have stood up and read the letter I just got.* He had received this letter as a result of a recent inquiry into his biological parents. He had known that he was adopted since he was eight years old, but Catholic Charities in Baltimore had told him more about the adoption than he had known before.

"She called you Christian," the letter stated. *Christian,* Wiggy reflected. *And now I'm on the path to priesthood. How weird.* The letter also told him that his birth mother had been sixteen and his birth father twenty when he was born. He could take the matter further, if he chose. For four hundred dollars, Catholic Charities would try to find his mother. If they found her, they would contact her. It would be up to her whether she wanted to meet her son.

Heiser had never told anyone how fear over Donna's pregnancy had driven him back to God and the Church. He was not prone to anxiety. He was a prudent man, but not the kind of person to see danger around every corner. Twelve years of attending Catholic schools and being altar server had yielded to the preoccupations of his early manhood: partying and the opposite sex. Things changed when he married Donna, but they really changed when she became pregnant with Eric.

Even twenty-one years later, Heiser still said "when we got pregnant." At the time, he had found himself afraid. He was irrationally convinced that something would go wrong with the pregnancy and the baby would be born deformed. He knew that there was little chance of this happening, and he told himself this constantly. But the fear would not go away. He had lost his job, and they were living with his in-laws two blocks from a Catholic church in Philadelphia. It was the church where he and Donna had been married. He started to attend Mass. He would get to church early and pray before the service started. He pleaded with God that the baby be born healthy and whole. He prayed during Mass and stayed afterward to pray some more. Years later, he would say that it was the one-tenth of one percent chance that something would go wrong with the pregnancy that had brought him back to prayer. And once he returned to the Church, he stayed.

Don Malin spent the afternoon of the *Roe v. Wade* anniversary getting artificial nails at First Lady Nails, a small salon a mile down the road from the seminary. The air was heavy with chemicals. Soft jazz played in the background.

"Don't hurt me," he joked with the Asian manicurist across the table. She wore a blue surgical mask and held an electric sander. As a classical guitarist, he had been wearing artificial nails since 1987. The work would last for three weeks or so, until the nail grew out and left a lip at the back that could get caught in the strings. The manicurist sanded down the nails on the thumb and three fingers of his right hand, leaving his pinkie untouched. Then she dabbed the coarse surfaces with glue and attached the nails. She picked and filed around the cuticles but left Don — who was very particular about this process — to shape the ends.

As for the anniversary of *Roe v. Wade,* Don had begun to think of it as he believed a pastor must. His pro-life convictions were not ambiguous, but you had to be aware of the harshness and the intensity you might bring to the question. A harsh approach might turn people off, preventing them from giving the Catholic position a hearing.

After the application of a heavy acrylic that would strengthen his nails, the manicurist continued to buff with a machine before switching to a small, coarse sponge.

Professor Christian Rich had asked Don to arrange the Ravel piece for that morning's performance. As Don had done so, he had not thought about what he himself would like to hear but about what the parishioners would expect. If Ron Kendzierski had been there, Don reflected, it would have been better. He would have doubled his own part and made it an octave higher. Perhaps his guitar and Ron's violin would even have had a "conversation" — played *in concertante* — as they had done many times in the fall.

Don examined his nails, thanked the manicurist, paid with his Visa card, and walked out into the bitter cold. He returned to his office at Sacred Heart. On one corner of his desk sat his *Onion* desk calendar, which still bore the previous day's offering:

OUR DUMB CENTURY (FROM THE *ONION*, JULY 27, 1956) PRESI-
DENT ORDERS BRANDO TO GAIN 250 POUNDS — STAR'S RAW
SEXUALITY TOO DANGEROUS AT PRESENT WEIGHT, IKE SAYS.

A stack of letters congratulating him on his diaconate ordination sat next to the calendar. He still had to write thank-you notes.

Also on his desk was a notepad courtesy of Gerken's Church Supplies. In the coming weeks, Don suspected, he would be inundated with catalogs and solicitations targeted at the soon-to-be-ordained priest. Already a representative of a chalice company had spent two days plying his wares in one corner of the dining hall, leading transitional deacons through full-color catalogs. It was rumored that one of the seminarians had spent more than ten thousand dollars on a custom-made chalice. That wouldn't be Don's style, even if he had the money. The Knights of Columbus had recently sent Don a check for $950, but that money was needed for more practical things, like keeping his Jeep on the road.

On the top shelf of Don's bookcase sat his hospital pyx, a gift from the Essers. It was the deluxe model, capable of carrying seventy-five hosts for Don's visits to hospitalized and homebound Catholics. Beside the pyx stood a shiny chalice borrowed from a local parish. Engraved around its base were the words "Calix Sanguinis Mei," Latin for "The Cup of My Blood." Don was to use the chalice for practice when he began the process of memorizing the Mass later that semester. They called the exercise a "straw Mass," similar to the mock baptism the previous fall. Don would be learning the proper form of the Mass while not yet having the power or authority to make anything happen.

The shelves along one wall bore large red liturgical books, the books every priest needs to say Mass and perform other functions.

The office also contained a large metallic wall calendar plastered with pastel dots that indicated events, deadlines, and other obligations. And on his computer, Outlook Express informed the new deacon when it was time to set up his confession appointments; a new sound card gave him the capability to refine his musical compositions; and a flight simulator helped him blow off steam by bombing the airfields and missile launchers of a virtual enemy.

Ever since his diaconate began, the things that needed to be completed before June 6, the day of his ordination to the priesthood, seemed to be multiplying. Graduation photographs had been taken in one of the basement rooms. Don and the other transitional deacons had worn clerics for the photos. The photographer's assistant had cracked jokes to try to get them to relax. But it wasn't easy to relax. In only a few months, he would have to say farewell to five years of seminary and begin his life as a priest. Don wavered between feeling that he was ready for the challenge and feeling that he would never be ready or worthy at all.

Father Michael McLernon rubbed some of the men the wrong way. The more conservative seminarians saw him as an activist priest with strong left-wing leanings. Others considered him intellectually arrogant. Most, however, recognized that he was a unique resource — a man who had been a priest for forty-five years and could discuss his experience with riveting immediacy. This was evident one morning when he walked into formation class with the second-year students, only to have the conversation suddenly cease around the room. One of the men apologized, assuring the priest that the conversation hadn't stopped because of his entrance. Father McLernon said that after decades as a priest, he had gotten used to the hastily changed subject. Even family members expected that he would want to talk only about God. Sometimes, he said, he felt like exclaiming, "Let's just talk about sex!" That would shake them up. He remembered how, when he was a newly ordained priest in his twenties, his Irish relatives would speak of him in the third person: "How is himself this morning?" or "How is Father?" Reflecting on it later, he concluded that it was a way of distancing the religious from the daily life. It was an understandable, but unfortunate, dichotomy, Father McLernon explained, because the holy was over there somewhere, tucked safely into a collar.

Father McLernon began edging the group of seminarians into the celibacy issue by bringing up the oath of fidelity, in which the person who takes the oath, usually a rector or someone in charge of doctrinal education, swears to "preserve communion with the Catholic Church whether in the words I speak or in the way I act . . . [and] preserve the deposit of faith in its entirety, hand it on faithfully and make it shine forth." Father McLernon wanted the oath to spark a discussion on the nature of commitment, and it did. Oscar, a seminarian from Colombia who had already spent several years at a very conservative seminary in his native country, contended that few people at Sacred Heart had real vocations. The problem was that they were not in love with Jesus. When you were in love with Jesus, he said, you gave up everything. You gave up money and time, and made all kinds of sacrifices for unity and obedience — just as you would if you were truly in love with a man or a woman. He didn't see this kind of sacrifice around him.

Father McLernon agreed. You must decide to love the person or the institution beyond the chemistry. It is a leap of faith, he said, to believe that love is real and will last.

"It is saying yes with fear," Father McLernon insisted.

"I know for me," Wiggy said, "I've been looking for a way out since day one."

He spoke of the Gospel passage in which Christ told Peter that he would one day go where he did not want to go. In both marriage and the priesthood, there would be some days that you had to make the choice to love without the supporting feeling. That was not a problem for Wiggy, nor was swearing obedience to the people or the Church. The problem was in swearing obedience to a particular bishop who might be a nincompoop. Even so, Wiggy said, he appreciated the corporate model of the Church and valued the chain of command that made possible its structural continuity around the world.

Father McLernon bristled at Wiggy's concept of the Church. There had to be more to one's connection to the Church, he warned, than simply a corporate allegiance.

Obedience was a promise, and it was countercultural, Father McLernon reasoned. Obedience was a source of grace. It did not mean that one could not disagree with one's bishop, although he thought the day was coming when disagreement might be equated with disobedience by some in the Church. Even the language of the oath of fidelity had room for disagreement, he pointed out, in its vague language of the relationship between priest and authority. He read from the oath: "With Christian obedience I shall *associate* [emphasis added] myself with what is expressed by the holy shepherds as authentic doctors and teachers of the faith." The word "associate" was meant to be vague, Father McLernon said.

"If you make the Church into IBM," he concluded, "the day will come when you say to hell with this."

One day at breakfast, Father McLernon told Dean Haley a story about a priest he used to work with — a young man for whom gesture and image were more important than spirit and substance. Father McLernon had noticed that the man usually wore violet or black vestments when he performed funerals, but that he wore a white vestment for the funeral of his own grandmother. After the service, Father McLernon asked the priest why he had worn white. "Because I'm sure my grandmother's in heaven," he replied. So, Father McLernon continued, what did purple mean? "Purgatory," the priest replied. And black? "He just smiled," Father McLernon recalled.

"Oh, gosh," Dean said.

"Interesting man," Father McLernon said wryly.

"See," Father Brackin observed, indicating the men in the back rows, "we've made them good Catholics. They used to sit in the front row."

The priest had a lot of ground to cover at this regularly scheduled rector's conference. The focus was academics, but the theme of this meeting would echo the question of obedience that second-year formation had recently explored.

Three days before, on February 2, Punxsutawney Phil, the Pennsylvania groundhog, had seen his shadow, predicting six more weeks of winter. The men at Sacred Heart required no such confirmation. The streak of single-digit weather gave no sign of breaking, and the men were plagued by congestion, fever, and flu. Heiser was unable to shake what he called "the crud" in his sinuses. It had dogged him since October, but he was holding off on a visit to the doctor because of the expense.

On the surface, the rector's conferences had become very predictable in recent weeks. Father Brackin had decided to lead the seminarians through a document titled "Educational Principles," the product of a long and involved process sponsored by the Eli Lilly and Company Foundation a few years earlier. Its introduction read:

> Sacred Heart School of Theology affirms the following education principles. These grounding principles help faculty and administrators preserve the school's theological integrity, promote its service to the Church, and provide for the academic freedom appropriate to a Roman Catholic seminary. They further serve to guide the decisions of academic faculty concerning the pedagogy and content of their courses and assist spiritual formation and field education faculty to appropriately prepare students who exhibit widely different views of the cluster of issues which arise in the context of spiritual and pastoral formation.

The measured language of the introduction and the talking points that followed concealed a war that had been raging since the conclusion of the Second Vatican Council in the mid-1960s. The Church, as Father Brackin often liked to observe, is not a democracy. Its doctrines are not subject to a vote or the embrace of a consensus. Democracy or not, the Church after the Second Vatican Council broke into two distinct camps: those who thought the reforms had gone too far and those who thought they had not gone far enough.

In the years directly following the council, many seminaries became places of tumult and chaos and were transformed — sometimes almost overnight — from the hothouses of scrutiny and micromanagement of Jim Pemberton's memory into freeform institutions where seminarians could come and go as they pleased and where everything from doctrine to formation seemed up for grabs. Father Marty, who had attended the seminary during this period, said that it was like being let out of jail, both heady and disorienting, although other priests reported less of a radical change. Many priests left the Church, and no one could say with certainty what had caused this mass exodus. Conservatives blamed a perceived liberalization of the Church, while liberals blamed things such as Pope Paul VI's reaffirmation of Church positions on human sexuality in *Humanae Vitae*. They insisted that such proclamations showed that Catholicism was hopelessly stuck in the past while the progressive culture leaped healthfully ahead.

"Educational Principles" seemed designed to confirm a truce between left and right (although some might see it as a conservative victory). One concept of Church evolution held that it took decades for a council like Vatican II to be fully implemented, because the generation that had lived through it had to die first. That generation, the theory went, had reactionary expectations based on the past and what it had been through and thus was convinced of certain things, perhaps unalterably. The document suggested that the fullness and clarity of the council's intent and direction were muddied by sentiment, prejudice, and unsupportable enthusiasms or imaginings on both sides.

"Educational Principles" also acknowledged something that everyone already knew: there was a perceived ideological gap between most seminarians and the men and women who instructed them. This was the subject of whispers and conspiratorial musings among the seminarians at Sacred Heart: this professor said there was no original sin; that professor weakened the case for natural family planning. Most often the whispers and rumors were simply misunderstandings of what had been said. Almost always they remained in the domain of student scuttlebutt and never reached the level of an official complaint. "Educational Principles" was a recognition that seminary formation across the board had shifted back toward tradition. It was also a defense of the official position that, perceptions aside, Sacred Heart had already accomplished this shift.

Don Malin walked in late, and Father Brackin handed him a copy of the document. There was some pain associated with this topic for Don, but he saw promise in this attempt to clarify things. A few years before, Don had watched a man graduate who had come from one of the more conservative dioceses. The diocese would occasionally send its vocation director to poke around Sacred Heart, looking for the unorthodox. This man was bright and knew his Saint Thomas Aquinas backward and forward. The problem was, as Don saw it, that Saint Thomas Aquinas was all the man knew and, worse, all he believed he needed to know. As a result, he held the curriculum and the school in thinly veiled disdain. In his final days at Sacred Heart, he participated in the traditional ringing of the bell near the school's entrance. This was an act performed by graduating seminarians and Sacred Heart priests leaving for the missions. The man rang the bell, turned to all present, and announced, "Press the delete button." Don knew that he meant that everything he had learned at the seminary was irrelevant and he would now go about forgetting it. Don thought that "Educational Principles" might help prevent something like that from happening again by setting clear parameters for both students and professors. Dissenting opinions among the academic faculty were to be welcomed, Don thought. What didn't work was when a professor taught a Church position but, out of personal prejudice, either polemicized it or presented it in a weak light.

Don wondered aloud about professors who explained Church teachings to their classes, then said, "But this is what I believe." Don had seen this kind of thing done in the past, but he admitted that he hadn't seen it happen recently. Without hesitation, Father Brackin said that this kind of teaching style was unacceptable. He read, "We create a learning environment based on mutual trust and respect for our theological expertise and the significance of students' individual histories and diverse religious sensibilities."

This had been a challenging concept for some of the faculty, Father Brackin acknowledged. He talked about the expectations many people had had in the 1960s and 1970s about the post–Vatican II unfolding of the Church. There had been a vision of what the Church would be like forty years after the council, he said, but the Church today didn't resemble that vision. And since there had been a strong sense that the Holy Spirit had been driving change then, there was a temptation to reject any retrenchment. Sometimes students would take positions that looked like retrenchment, but the faculty must be willing to accept the possibility that a student's life experiences and long years of living with his faith had cultivated wisdom and that wisdom had informed these opinions.

Brother Raph, a monk who had recently arrived at Sacred Heart, said that he didn't mind learning about the "different colors of the rainbow," but he wanted first and foremost to know where the Church stood on the issues.

Father Brackin agreed. "Academic freedom in a seminary is very different from academic freedom in a secular university," he said.

Pope John Paul II, the rector said by way of example, had brought an end to the discussion of the ordination of women. "Therefore, within a Roman Catholic seminary, it is inappropriate to discuss this issue," he concluded. His hands came together in a gesture of finality. "The debate has ended. At least at this point in history."

Don took issue with Father Brackin's interpretation. He said that, in reality, it had taken some time for the ordination of women issue to work itself out and that prior to the pope's statement, there had been a substantial amount of discussion about it. But in the end, Don continued, the lesson was that it was crucial to follow the bishops' lead in the interpretation of new documents lest chaos reign.

Father Brackin nodded. Just as liberals might struggle with the limitations of doctrine, he observed, conservatives might struggle with perceived intrusions on doctrine. But often these intrusions are not so much intrusions on actual doctrine as on a sentimental attachment to a theology from the era of the *Baltimore Catechism*. This is where obedience is important. Ultimately, a seminarian will become a priest, who will have to minister out of the Church's theology, not a personal theology. The priest is a priest for everyone: the charismatics, the Knights of Columbus, the Blue Army, the liberals, those who say the rosary before Mass. Thus, the rector said, he found it odd that in response to a recently proposed Holy Hour of Praying for Peace, so much controversy had erupted among the students.

"Some members of our community want to bomb the hell out of Iraq," he exclaimed with his hands held in the air in a gesture of incredulity. How could this be? The entire hierarchy of the Church had come out in direct opposition to the brewing war, from the pope to the United States Conference of Catholic Bishops.

"We have to continually call people back to the demands of our faith," Father Brackin insisted. "As priests, we can't pick and choose what we believe." Obedience runs both ways — it is for liberals and conservatives alike. "One is going to do a lot of damage to the Church," he concluded, "if one is not going to be obedient."

Don was sitting alone in the dining hall when Dean Haley approached.

"Were you there at the rector's conference this morning?" Dean asked.

"Yes, I was," Don answered. "Which one did you go to, the first or second one? I was at the first one."

"Ah," Dean said cryptically.

"What happened at the second one?" Don asked.

"Oh, nothing happened," Dean said. "He just went over the education and how basically everything here that will be taught has to be congruent with Catholic theology."

"That's the mission," Don agreed.

"I just wanted to know . . . ," Dean said, his voice lowering and becoming vaguely conspiratorial, "if everything was."

Don thought for a moment before answering. "Well, let's put it this way. As we've gotten the academic statement out, everything is sort of approximating it."

With a laugh, Dean said that meant the curriculum would conform to the policy after the fact.

Don agreed. You could be sure the faculty would be going through their notes to make certain that things matched up with "Educational Principles" and to fix anything that didn't.

A different aspect of the rector's conference was on Dean's mind when he found himself at another dining hall table later that afternoon with Brother Raph and Richard Perko.

"Ron [Kendzierski] had a vocation to the seminary, in my opinion," Dean said. "We talked about that. He'd say, 'I love the seminary. This is the greatest place in the world. I'd hate to leave.' And I'd tell him, 'You're not going to be here forever.'"

Richard nodded. He had been a funeral director for years and had noticed that many of his employees dreamed of being something else. His security guards wanted to be priests. His hearse drivers wanted to be funeral directors.

"There's a charisma about wanting to be," Richard said. But the aura that drew people to the profession couldn't necessarily sustain them through the steps that were required to join it. "That's why people read. They get lost in the illusion of becoming the heroine or the hero. We all have these fantasies. But when push comes to shove, you've got to make the commitment. That's why a lot of marriages fail."

Brother Raph said that in religious communities, they have a term for the charisma Richard was talking about. They call it "first fervor." If you are lucky, maybe it will last a year. First fervor is a wonderful feeling, like puppy love, but it's never enough.

"God uses natural means like feelings to accomplish supernatural things," Brother Raph observed. But you have to be careful. Fervor is a good thing, but it can become a trap if you believe that the feeling is your vocation.

Brother Raph had joined Dean's Caritas group, and Dean had become close to him. He valued the experience Brother Raph brought to the table as a religious brother of twenty-five years and also as a registered nurse and a lawyer. Brother Raph had even been the superior of his order for a while. Dean wanted to talk about obedience.

Brother Raph told Dean and Richard that celibacy had never been as hard a discipline as obedience. Obedience means obeying people even when you are convinced they are wrong. Of course, if something is sinful, you aren't obliged to obey.

Dean wondered whether obedience makes sense when you move up the hierarchy a few notches, look down, and see how things really work. Brother Raph said that it makes more sense.

Dean had read a book called *The Mafia Manager,* which says that a manager should never keep anyone around who has not learned how to obey — especially if the person is talented.

"Absolutely," Brother Raph agreed. Dean related the story of Bishop Fulton Sheen, who was sent to a one-horse town for parish work, despite being an academic standout seemingly destined for loftier heights. He accepted the assignment, but later he asked the archbishop why he had been sent to the town. The archbishop said that he had done so to test Sheen's obedience. If you are not obedient, the archbishop said, you are worthless to me.

Not only worthless, Brother Raph observed, but dangerous. Once a man is ordained, he said, you almost have to hogtie him if he goes bad. Dean laughed. Had Brother Raph heard about the priest on the gay Web site under the "silver fox" section?

"Posted a picture of himself nude in a precarious position," Dean related. "He liked to refer to himself as Papa Bear and gave his contact information, including his e-mail address — the same address that parishioners used to reach him. That's what I woke up to this morning on the news."

"You've got to have a means of getting rid of these people," Brother Raph said with disgust.

"Priest or no priest," Dean said with a laugh, "when you're sixty-three years old, you don't get into that position."

*     *     *

Oscar took Dr. Esther Warren's hand in his and held it for an uncomfortably long time. The basement room was perfectly silent. Dr. Warren blushed.

"This is sex," Oscar observed in his soft voice and thick Spanish accent.

He released her hand. The point had been made. The second-year seminarians could breathe again. Sex meant virtually everything.

By February, Heiser, Jim Pemberton, and the other men in second-year formation were well into the question of celibacy. The topic defied easy approach. Heiser found himself chopping at the table with the blade of his hand and demanding a definition of sex; the discussion had ranged too freely, and the word had come to mean too many things. Was it the sexual act or the sexuality of a person? Father McLernon spoke of how priests and nuns are not considered sexual, and yet sexuality is a profound part of every human being.

Father McLernon had served through the pre–Vatican II days and the tumult of the 1960s and 1970s. Celibacy had gone from being accepted but not discussed to being openly questioned and challenged by both clergy and laity. He had lived through the crazy period of the so-called "third way," in which a priest could not get married but "could" have a committed sexual relationship. At that time, he said, many progressives believed that if a person wasn't having sex, something was wrong with him or her. He remembered attending a seminar in Florida run by a priest and a nun he would later regard as wacky. The priest had rings on all his fingers and earrings up and down his ears. At one point, he broke the participants into small groups to discuss the question "When did you have your first sexual experience?" One of the members of Father McLernon's group was a feisty nun in her seventies. She refused to participate, but she was no prude. Father McLernon and the rest of the group encouraged her to tell the larger audience how she felt.

"This is nonsense," she announced. "Why should I tell you the first time I touched myself?"

Father McLernon believed that the nun was right. Celibacy might be problematic, but the answer was to embrace the challenge, not misconstrue it.

To embrace the challenge, one had to know what was at stake. Dr. Warren passed out a detailed questionnaire that was intended only for each seminarian's own use, although he could share his answers with his spiritual director, if he chose.

"The idea is that knowing yourself will be extremely helpful to you as a priest," Dr. Warren explained. Students in the past, she added, had appreciated the exercise.

The questions covered a range of issues: "Toward whom did you feel attracted as: (a) Pre-Adolescent? (b) Adolescent? (c) Young Adult?" "Were you attracted to persons: (a) Older than you? (b) Peers? (c) Younger than you?" "If you are *heterosexual* and never married, did you engage in sexual activity prior to coming to seminary?" "How long between your last sexual activity and coming to seminary?" "What is your understanding of friendship?" "Do you have friends?" For most of the men, these questions were hardly surprising. They had already endured a barrage of psychological questions just to be considered for candidacy to the seminary.

In Jim Pemberton's section, Father McLernon used an exercise that he warned would make everyone a bit uncomfortable. He wrote the words "vagina," "penis," and "rectum" on the board. The men broke up into groups of two or three and were given the task of listing as many words or associations as possible for each word. After the instructors had left the room, there were a few jokes about "boners," and one man regaled the others with an account of a former girlfriend's remarkable anatomical abilities. When Father McLernon returned, he asked each group for a tally, without asking for the specific words. He wrote each tally on the board. There were dozens of word associations. If you went into a bar, Father McLernon observed, and challenged the crowd to see how many names they could find for penis or vagina, there would be hundreds. He erased the board, then wrote the word "elbow." How many other words for elbow? he asked. No one had any.

"Why are we talking about this?" Father McLernon asked.

"Because you brought it up," Jim Pemberton said. Everyone laughed.

Then Jim tried to be serious. The number of word associations and their harsh and demeaning tenor betrayed the puritanical quality of our culture, Jim offered. Take the f-word, he said. How could such a violent word, which more often than not was used to punish, blame, and curse, be used to refer to the sexual act, which he considered sacred?

"Wherein lies the dynamic of our need to have such a plethora of expressions for that area of our body which is sexuality?" Father McLernon wondered.

"Sexuality is a major dynamic of our lives," Jim said. "It shows up in all areas: culture, art, movies, books, language, cartoons. More and more it seems . . . Twenty years ago, *nada*."

"That raises a question in my mind for you, then," Father McLernon said. "Where are the places you can go that you're not likely to see sexuality? You're suggesting that there's almost an obsession with sexuality — not just an awareness of sexuality, but an obsession with it. In some cultures, they are very aware of sexuality, but they're not obsessed with it. We're obsessed with it."

"We seem to be driven by it," Jim agreed.

"Where are you likely to go in our culture that you're not going to be hit with that?" Father McLernon repeated.

"Religion, church, that whole atmosphere," Jim said. "There seems to be a tendency to leave sexuality at the front door."

"Now if, as you suggest, sexuality is such an important component of our experience — our life experience, of who we are as individuals — that it pervades every aspect of our lives, why is it that you don't deal with it in the Church?" Father McLernon asked.

"Thank you, Saint Augustine," Jim said archly.

Don Wright disagreed. Catholicism deals with sexuality but focuses on the love portion, he said.

"Maybe one answer to your question is that somehow we have

lost the sense of the sacred in conjunction with sexuality. We automatically think of it as something dirty, something not good," Jim advanced.

"I don't think our culture's saying that it's no good or dirty or sinful — not at all. You think our culture's saying that?" Father McLernon countered.

"No, I don't think they give a damn about sin," Jim said.

"The culture is saying that it's okay to do it with anybody and everybody, do it as much as you want," Mike Mallard contended. "Whereas the sacredness of one person, the commitment, they're saying that part's not good."

"In the context of a religious service, you're not going to deal with the issue of sexuality in an inappropriate way," Father McLernon emphasized. "However, it is something that ought to be . . . Just recently, I did a homily in a parish, and it was on the text of Saint Paul. He was talking about 'Don't you know your body is a temple of the Holy Spirit?' and what I talked about in the homily was the difference between puritanism and pornography. I was really surprised at the number of people who came up and thanked me for talking about it."

Time was running out, and Father McLernon had a piece he wanted to read. "Let's end with something about sex," he said. He read from the Song of Songs, as translated in the New American Bible:

> Ah, you are beautiful, my beloved,
> Ah, you are beautiful!
> Your eyes are doves
> Behind your veil,
> Your hair like a flock of goats
> Streaming down the mountains of Gilead . . .
>
> You are all-beautiful, my beloved,
> And there is no blemish in you.
>
> You have ravished my heart, my sister, my bride;
> You have ravished my heart with one glance of your eyes,
> With one bead of your necklace . . .

Your lips drip honey, my bride,
Sweetmeats and milk are under your tongue;
And the fragrance of your garments
Is the fragrance of Lebanon.

"That's very sensual," Father McLernon said after a long silence.

"Are you hearing confessions afterward?" Jim Pemberton joked.

"The spirituality of our sexuality," Father McLernon mused.

"A gift from God," Jim concluded.

"The Hebrew Scriptures are filled with sensual references to human relationships and to our relationship with God," Father McLernon said. "And of course not only this book, but also some of the mystics. Their language is unbelievably erotic. So they're tapping into that energy, but they're doing something very different with it than this culture is."

He paused and looked around the room.

"We're tapping into that energy, and we're using it for destructive purposes or for selfish purposes: to sell things, to seduce, to get our own pleasure. But that energy is there. It's there to be tapped. That energy is in all of us. Sexuality is there. It gets your attention. Where are you gonna go with that energy? That becomes the question for the celibate. You have all that energy, and it ain't ever going anywhere. You're gonna have it when you're seventy as well as when you're seventeen. It's not about denying our sexuality. It's about harnessing it."

After class, Heiser passed a seminarian from the formation class in the hall, and they started talking about celibacy. The seminarian mentioned that three women in their fifties were going after his pastor back home. "They'd leave your ass," he had told the pastor in case the middle-aged priest had any ideas about responding to their advances.

The collar seemed to attract women. Seminarians accepted this as a strange but irrefutable fact. Maybe it was the challenge, getting the attention of someone they weren't supposed to have. The seminarian told Heiser that just before he had left work to come to Sacred Heart, a married female coworker had actually propositioned him.

He recalled her words: "You spend one night with me, and I'll make you forget all that priesthood stuff. I'll turn you every which way but loose."

Jim Pemberton's wife, Joy, had died the morning after Valentine's Day two years before. On that day, just before dawn, Jim woke up his two sons. They had been staying overnight because he had asked for their company.

"Mom's dying," he told them.

Jim had nursed his wife through the long, final illness after the cancer she'd fought off a decade earlier had returned. When it became clear that Joy was not going to make it, Jim's prayer became "Lord, what would you have me do with the rest of my life?" There were options, but none of them were palatable. His job as a successful fundraiser with the State Fair of Texas had positioned him to become a consultant, but his enthusiasm for that kind of work was gone. From time to time, the possibility of the priesthood broke the surface, but Jim would usually push it away. The diocese would never take someone his age, he thought. But the idea kept coming back, until the priesthood seemed to be the only option.

Later, his brother, Joe, would say that he didn't think Jim had ever really lost his vocation, even after he married and had kids. It had been there since 1948, when he had first entered the seminary. Joe observed that anytime the subject of seminary or priesthood came up, even in jest, Jim seemed to come alive. Joe also said that he noticed that Joy seemed to resent this a little bit.

Jim never told his wife that he was thinking about returning to the seminary. Jim knew that Joy would feel guilty, and he didn't want to saddle her with that guilt as she died. He knew that his wife would feel as if she had stood in the way of his becoming a priest the first time. Jim did not believe that she had had any part in his decision to leave the seminary. If he hadn't met her, there would have been another reason to leave. He had fought the idea of celibacy for three years and finally decided that maybe the Lord was telling him something. With Joy, of course, there had been proximity and familiarity. She was the sister of his best friend. Jim liked her family, and they seemed to like him. There was a lot of positive chemistry, but it wasn't as though he had been seeking her. He had been struggling with leaving the seminary, and then she had come into his life.

Joy had been private in her spiritual life, Jim the opposite. For a while, he had fallen away from religion, but his faith had been reinvigorated in the early seventies by Cursillo, a retreat movement that had originated in Spain. After his Cursillo experience, he became much more active in the Church, which caused some tension between him and Joy for a short time.

Two years after her death, he would agree that he had been faking his corporate life but not his marriage or fatherhood. Throughout his career, Jim had never had the sense of fulfillment that he felt even just training for the priesthood.

In the weeks and months after Joy's death, three friends asked Jim when he was going back to the seminary. He was taken aback, because he had told no one about this possibility. Why had they asked this question? They all said that they knew he had been in the seminary once and they thought he'd make a good priest. Jim took this as a sign. Many people told him that he would run into problems with the bishop in Fort Worth because of the bishop's policy against ordaining men over age sixty-five. Jim called the chancellor of the diocese, whom he knew personally and who reiterated the policy. The bishop was in South America, the chancellor told Jim. The chancellor would talk with him about it when he got back. A few days later, Jim got a call. The bishop wanted to see him. Jim immediately thought that they were bringing him in out of courtesy and respect for his brother and brother-in-law, both priests of the diocese. He arrived at the meeting convinced that his hopes would be dashed.

The bishop came around from behind his desk and sat with Jim face-to-face. "I understand you want to go to seminary," the bishop said.

"Yeah, for the second time," Jim replied with a smile.

"Well, there are two seminaries which specialize in second-career men," the bishop said. One was in Massachusetts and the other in Wisconsin. As a native of Massachusetts, the bishop said that he could assure Jim that the seminary in Boston was French cuffs and stiff white shirts — and they didn't need that in Texas.

Jim was stunned. They were actually going to send him to seminary.

It was clear to Jim that the bishop had already done a lot of thinking about his case. They had tried to get Jim into Wisconsin for the fall semester, the bishop continued, but there was too much paperwork, so he would start in January.

What about the bishop's policy? Jim asked.

"I don't have a policy," the bishop replied. "I have a practice." Jim was a known entity in Fort Worth, the bishop explained. Other men of the same age who had been rejected for the seminary were not.

Instead of twiddling his thumbs that fall, the bishop added, how would Jim like to go to Mexico for Spanish-language immersion? Jim agreed on the spot.

After the meeting, Jim called his daughters to tell them the news. They didn't seem surprised at all.

Apart from mealtime and short bursts of camaraderie around class time, Sacred Heart could seem as lonely as a hotel. Its hallways had that sweet, vaguely musty dormitory smell, especially on the two upper floors, which housed the seminarians. The hallways were chilly and particularly uninviting in the winter, although they were brightened by doors bearing flags, bumper stickers, and the occasional poster. During the day, these doors were mostly shut. Dean Haley spent a lot of time in his room in front of his computer or on the phone. He often got restless and looked for reasons to leave the seminary grounds.

Dean talked to almost everyone at Sacred Heart, but his closest friend was Bob Brooks. Apart from his regular visits to the chiropractor, Dean also escaped the seminary by taking advantage of Bob's free tanning sessions. Bob had earned the sessions because of his own frequent use of the salon. Bob seemed to be very concerned about his appearance. He kept an enormous container of protein powder underneath one of the counters in the dining hall so that he could make low-carb shakes instead of eating the seminary's food.

One day Bob arrived to pick Dean up for tanning. They were going to use Bob's truck because Dean's BMW had a dead battery. He hadn't driven it in weeks.

Bob talked about a facial defect he said came from trying to remove a cyst himself. Did Dean see it? Hardly at all, Dean said. Then he told Bob that he had basically "lost" his own face in a car accident when he was eight years old. He'd had to wear a special mask for his face to heal.

"I don't want to change my face," Bob said. "I want to get rid of the scar."

"I'm trying to understand," Dean replied. "But to be honest, I really don't understand because I don't see it. But like you said, you see it."

"It's all I see," Bob said.

"You've got a lot of face there," Dean observed. "You sure that's all you see?"

"Absolutely. But it's okay. I'm a guy. You know what I mean?"

"It adds character?"

"No, I don't mean that. It's just that you can only be so good-looking if you're a guy. You're still ugly."

"No clue what you're talking about," Dean said. "I saw Leonardo DiCaprio and watched women watch him — they don't get tired of that."

Bob tried again. "You go to the movie theater, where the screen is so big, and they do a close-up of Mel Gibson. Don't you feel like you want to throw up?"

"No, not at all," Dean replied.

Bob switched the topic to women. "Pamela Anderson, she's almost like a cartoon figure to me . . ."

"Liv Tyler," Dean said. "I don't think I could ever get tired of Liv Tyler."

"Don't get me wrong," Bob said. "The girl on the cover of the swimsuit issue, she is an eleven."

"Isabella Rossellini," Dean mused. "Never get tired of looking at her."

Dean and Don Malin had loftier exchanges. One afternoon in the dining hall, they wrestled with the idea of dogma and Scripture.

"Dogma is something explicitly stated," Don said. "It is an infallible teaching. We don't have many of them."

Dean didn't respond.

"So anytime the Church in council proclaims something to be true, that's a dogma," Don continued. "Or if the Holy Father does it ex cathedra. So *Humanae Vitae,* whether we like it or not, is a dogma."

Don said that every encyclical of Pope John Paul II was not dogma, although it could be confirmed later in a council. "The Dogmatic Constitutions of Vatican II is dogma," Don said. "*Lumen Gentium* — that's dogma . . ."

Dogma had to be definitely adhered to by all the faithful. Don defended Cardinal Ratzinger, the controversial head of the Sacred Congregation for the Propagation of the Faith, who had confirmed *Humanae Vitae* as infallible teaching. *Humanae Vitae,* an encyclical written by Pope Paul VI in the late 1960s, had reasserted the prohibition of birth control and was seen by many both within and outside the Church as a major mistake.

"Let me ask you a trick question," Dean asked, turning toward his ongoing struggle with Scripture. "In Matthew, Christ says any man who divorces a woman — then he has that comma — except for infidelity . . . Do you think that Christ said that?"

"Exegetically, first of all, the commas were added by an editor," Don said. "They didn't do that sort of thing back then."

"I mean, specifically that exception," Dean clarified.

"That exception was put in by the writer, because it doesn't exist in Mark's version," Don said. "So what's up with that? Why did Mark think that and the other one thought something else? Probably because he was carrying it forward from the Law of Moses. Matthew was so rooted in Moses. Moses's main rule was the question of *porneia,* a Greek word, which doesn't necessarily mean only infidelity. It means lewdness, whatever that is. So you've got to look at what the meaning of *porneia* is and specifically what its sense is in this text. Also, the Matthean document was written in a different context than the Markan document. Because it wasn't all one Church then, it was lots of little churches."

Don returned to Dean's question. "I don't know if Jesus said that directly. I don't think anybody can really say whether Jesus actually said that or not. But the Scriptures are in conflict about it."

Don paused and looked at Dean. "So how's that for carefully negotiating your question?"

"Thank you, I really wanted to hear something thorough," Dean said gratefully. He had had problems with that passage since he was a kid. His mom and dad had divorced, and the seeming sternness of Christ's words had terrified him.

One night in February, Heiser had a phone conversation with Eric about the prospect of war in Iraq. He learned to his dismay that his son was in favor of military action.

"You could be drafted," Heiser cautioned. So be it, Eric said, something had to be done over there. If he was called, he would do his duty.

Heiser remembered the night before the Persian Gulf War began. Eric was ten years old. They had prayed the rosary together for peace.

"I don't want to have anything to do with the death of anyone," Heiser insisted.

"It requires lives, Dad," Eric said. "This guy needs to go down."

Eric had gotten a bonus of twelve hundred dollars that Christmas for selling advertising spots at the radio station. He used the money to buy a flat-screen TV. Heiser couldn't believe it — he wouldn't have spent his money that way — but he kept his mouth shut. His son was twenty-one and free to make his own decisions. Eric's grades at college were good, and father and son were competing to see who would have the higher grade point average at year's end. Eric hoped to get a scholarship to the University of Wyoming at Laramie.

As student council president, Heiser was busy overseeing the vote for the ratification of a new constitution and the faculty appreciation dinner slated for February 12. This year, the dinner would feature Native American dancers from Milwaukee's Congregation of the Great Spirit, carved buffalo steamship roast, Chippewa trout, and corn bread. Heiser found time to attend one of Barb Haag's seafood cooking seminars. The seminars were offered on the assumption that unlike priests of the past, who had cooks on staff, new priests would have to fend for themselves. Heiser learned how to make coconut shrimp.

Heiser was also waiting to hear about whether Sacred Heart would be cosponsoring a semester abroad in Dublin, Ireland, for two of its seminarians. If the school went ahead with the sponsorship, he would have to scramble to put together an application. Like Jim Pemberton, Heiser was facing the ministry of lector in a month. A little over a week before, he had found himself writing a letter to his bishop requesting that he be considered for this ministry. Like Don's letter for the diaconate, it was pro forma and had to be copied in longhand. It read in part:

In accordance and compliance with Canon 1035 #1, of the 1983 *Code of Canon Law*, I am petitioning to be installed in the Ministry of Lector by Most Reverend Paul A. Zipfel, D.D., Bishop of the Diocese of Bismarck, North Dakota, on March 26, 2003, here at Sacred Heart School of Theology . . .

I am aware of the ministry I am undertaking and I shall make every effort and employ suitable means to acquire that love and knowledge of the Scripture that will make me more of a disciple of the Lord. I also realize that the conferral of this ministry does not imply the right to sustenance or salary from the Church . . .

Don Malin had written another letter as well. This one would be his last as a seminarian: requesting permission to pursue his ordination to the priesthood. One afternoon, Don brought out his brushed stainless steel Scheaffer fountain pen with a brass point. He had bought the pen upon his arrival at Sacred Heart with the idea of using it for such letters. He had used it for other letters to his bishop, including the one petitioning for the diaconate. He began, "I believe and feel that I have a call . . ."

The previous Wednesday, Don had been summoned to the rector's office by a brief memo. The rector was holding a folder when Don arrived and told him that the faculty had voted. Don had just been passed onto the priesthood unanimously, 26 to 0. The rector would be wholeheartedly recommending him to his bishop for ordination.

Father Hugh Birdsall stood before the seminarians at the early-morning Mass and asked them to revisit their pasts. The professor of interpersonal communications spoke in a studied and soothing tone. Reflect, he said, on those good and happy relationships. After a pause, he also asked the men to reflect on those relationships that had been shattered.

Heiser was serving that day and sat on the dais dressed in a long alb. The shapeless garment had a way of making everyone look the same. Heiser thought briefly of high school friends. He still had many strong relationships there that had evolved from hard-living young adulthood to family life. He would be seeing most of these men when he returned to Philadelphia for spring break, now only a few weeks away. But soon Heiser's thoughts turned to his ex-wife, Donna, for both the happy and the shattered. Over Christmas, he had given a backgammon board to one of Eric's friends. The board had sat in a closet since his divorce. A wedding present, it had been a staple of their early marriage. He and Donna had played the game all the time. Backgammon for blood, they called it. He hadn't played a single game since she left.

The years they spent together had been beyond any friendship

Heiser had ever known. The divorce was the worst experience he had ever had. During the consecration, as Father Birdsall said the transformative words over the bread and wine, Heiser thought of a terrible car accident that he had had in New Zealand just before entering the seminary. Donna had been the first one to call him in the hospital. No, Heiser reflected, nothing compared to the pain of his divorce.

Jim Pemberton also followed Father Birdsall's instructions. He thought of Joy, but then the image of an old acquaintance came to mind. Jim had fired the man; he hadn't handled it well and had let his anger get the better of him. He had been merciless and unkind. Jim prayed for the man and his family frequently and asked for forgiveness. The memory was always colored with guilt and regret.

Jim Pemberton moved from the man to the cause of the breach: his temper. He used to have a bad one. He had been one of those exacting men who was quick to anger, but just as quickly, the storm would yield to calm. Age had gradually softened his edges, and he recognized the futility of such outbursts. He used to have football tantrums when he watched the Dallas Cowboys. Everyone, even the dog, would steer clear while he watched *his* Cowboys, as he called them. He finally realized that he wasn't mature enough to watch the games, and he stopped.

Then there was the moment when Jim saw his temper for what it was — a destructive force. Their oldest son, Michael, never gave them any problems until one day in his first year of college. He was attending the University of Texas at Arlington. Michael had wanted to go to Notre Dame, but Jim was concerned about being able to afford college for his other three children, and Notre Dame was too expensive. One day Jim got a call from security at the university. They had found Michael's books abandoned on campus. Jim didn't think it was a big deal until Michael didn't come home. The first time he ran away, Michael was gone for three or four days. The next time, he was gone for weeks. A pattern began to develop, with Michael disappearing for longer and longer periods of time. Jim and Joy felt as if they were on a roller coaster. Michael would disappear and then resurface, asking for their help. He would frequently be gone for months at a time. The pattern was always the same: "I'm on my own, leave me alone" became "I need to be rescued." Michael had become a street person.

After several years of this behavior, Jim had had enough. Michael had been gone for months when he called the house on a Sunday afternoon. He needed to be picked up again. Jim was livid. He felt fury spilling out of him.

"I'm gonna pick him up, and I'm gonna give him one hundred dollars and tell him to get the hell out of our lives and stay out of our lives," Jim told Joy.

Jim stormed out to the car, so angry that he was throbbing with the pain of it. But as he slid into the driver's seat, the anger entirely disappeared. He had taken no deliberate action to calm himself. He had said no prayers, nor had he tried to bring his anger under control. If anything, he had fanned his rage. But the anger was gone, and in its place was compassion. Jim knew immediately that God had changed him. He picked up Michael and brought him home.

Jim would have loved to have been able to say that Michael never ran away again. But he did, and Jim and Joy took him back. But Jim believed that the moment his anger disappeared was the moment the healing began. Michael was eventually diagnosed with a treatable disorder. He married and had two children. He was an active member of the Unitarian Church and raised his children with a sense of the importance of spirituality in one's life. Jim was proud of him. The thought of what would have happened had he followed through on his anger that day was both a dark reminder and a sign of hope.

After Don Malin's divorce, he bought a convertible. Don had always thought it would be fun to own one, and for the first time in his life, he felt as if he actually could. As he was driving the convertible from Colorado to Santa Clara, California, to begin work on his master's degree in liturgy, he crested a hill in Nevada and was surprised to see a shepherd with a large flock of sheep. He pulled over and watched as the man and his dogs moved hundreds of animals across the desert. Something about the sight moved Don deeply. He reflected on the fact that Christ had been called the "Good Shepherd" and that priests were often considered shepherds of their people. He watched for a long time.

Music, always a constant in Don's life, had become even more important during the final stages of his marriage. Even if he had a horrible day, he would get excited about choir practice, which he saw as a sort of ninety-minute oasis before he went home. He hid the pain of the last year of his marriage from his friends and family. He and his wife were in therapy together, but by the end of October 1992, Don realized that there was no way that he could make her happy. He would weep for himself, for what he had lost and what he had been unable to do. He knew it was over and began reorganizing his life, but he took no other action because he wanted to give the marriage one last chance. By the middle of February 1993, though, he had had enough. The tension was too great, and his wife's hostility had become debilitating. He packed up all his things and moved them into storage and then moved out of the house. His wife was devastated, and his therapist advised him to stay. We're still going through the process, the therapist told him. Don moved back into the house but kept some of his things in storage. Finally, in June, Don told his therapist that it wasn't working; he needed to get out. The therapist suggested a trial separation.

Years of spiritual direction and therapy had convinced Don that he needed some objective standard by which to judge this separation. He developed a statistical measurement that assessed how he felt about staying or going over the ninety-day period: $0 =$ the desire to stay; $2.5 =$ ambivalence; $5 =$ the desire to leave. He skewed it to staying. Don was well over 3 for the period. When the three months were over, Don met his wife after work. "I'm tired," he told her. "I can't work on this anymore."

Then he made an appointment to go to the courthouse and file for divorce. She seemed to be holding up well. She said she was okay. *We tried,* Don would think. *We really tried.*

They had been married for twelve years. She had converted to Catholicism and gotten an annulment from her first marriage to marry Don. He had just finished his master's degree in sacred music when they got married. After their wedding, they moved to Boulder, Colorado, so that he could begin working on a doctorate. She had a doctorate in American literature and found work at a junior college. He became deeply involved in running two choirs. Over time, he found himself working three jobs so that he could afford to meet his wife's needs. His health began to suffer; he had stress-related heart palpitations.

It seemed to Don that his wife was angry with him all the time. He remembered her telling him that she hated that he was a church musician and working for the Catholic Church. This was more than he could bear; the Church and his music were nonnegotiable.

Many people in unbearable situations dream of flying. The dream gives them a feeling of peace amid otherwise discouraging surroundings. Other people derive comfort from other kinds of dreams. While still married to his wife, Don had a very vivid dream of celebrating Mass in green vestments. When he woke up, he felt momentary peace — the peace of a shepherd crossing a desert with a flock of sheep or of a man taking flight.

He didn't put much stock in the dream. It was just his brain trying to cope with a difficult situation. He had been in therapy long enough to know that stress made the brain do funny things.

"I'm convinced that each of us somehow lives the history of the whole human race in our own lives," Father McLernon had mused to his Medieval Philosophy class on the first day of the semester. Statements like that and his growing affection for his professors, even when he disagreed with them, kept Dean Haley going. His second semester had a fraction of the pressure of his first, and by the last two weeks of February, he found every class he was taking riveting. In Medieval Philosophy, he sparred with Bob Brooks and Father McLernon. He seemed to be heading toward his contracted grade of an A. (Students contracted for a grade at the beginning of a course by agreeing to complete a certain number of assignments at a certain level of proficiency. For instance, a contract for a B might entail one term paper, a contract for an A a term paper and an oral presentation.) But more than the grade, Dean seemed to be inspired by Father McLernon's mandate: "I want you to be philosophers and love it." Every time he thought he got an answer to one of the big questions, it just spawned more questioning.

Introduction to Scripture with Dr. Malchow also was challenging Dean, sometimes painfully so. The challenges served as good examples of Don Malin's "growing edges," the shucking off of old beliefs for new. Dean had avidly read the Bible as a boy. This had been of questionable value. It had won him prizes at a Bible study summer camp, but his literal interpretation of what he read had caused him trauma as he watched his mom go through her third divorce and he struggled to find a glimmer of mercy in Jesus's harsh words on the subject of marriage.

Dr. Malchow dispensed with literalism. He insisted that to understand Scripture, the reader must discover how the authors and the original audience understood storytelling. In the ancient world, people saw time as circular, beginning and ending with the new year, not linear, as modern people do. Theirs was an agrarian understanding, a concept of time based on sowing and harvesting. Thus, the idea of historical fact was not the same. Objective fact and the symbolic value of fact were often conflated, and the ancients did not worry if the symbolic was woven into an objective narrative. If it served a writer's purpose to change the depiction of actual events to tie a story or person to a larger biblical or religious tradition, he would do so, and his readers would understand that he had done so. For instance, in the New Testament, Jesus is often compared with the Old Testament prophet Elijah. In areas where it might have served writers to depict events or recount statements in such a way as to evoke this comparison, they did.

One day around midsemester, Dr. Malchow, working from Daniel Harrington's *Interpreting the New Testament,* outlined conditions that could help in determining the authenticity of a particular Scriptural passage. Up until that point, the class had worked on the Old Testament. The professor warned that they were now turning to the more controversial part of the course, because the subject matter was closest to their hearts. Dean had already told the class that he no longer enjoyed reading the Bible because he needed five books around him for reference just to understand what he was reading. Most of his classmates had agreed, and Dr. Malchow had said that virtually everyone who pursued Scriptural studies faced a similar crisis. If one persevered in one's faith, the professor had insisted, in the end one's appreciation of Scripture would be stronger.

At one point, Dr. Malchow discussed the Ascension of Jesus. This event is often understood by Catholics to mean an actual physical ascension up through the sky into heaven. The professor said that although such an understanding was possible, it was not necessarily central to one's belief. After all, only one of the four Gospel writers made reference to the Ascension.

"In fact, Matthew kind of says the opposite," Dr. Malchow said. "At the end of Matthew, Jesus says, 'Lo, I am with you always until the end of the world.' He doesn't leave in Matthew's Gospel. So it's kind of hard to know what to make of the Ascension. It's pretty hard to believe that Jesus's body went up into the sky. In their world, by going up into the sky, he went up to heaven, up to where God was. In our world, where are you going, past Jupiter? Out of this galaxy? Into the next galaxy? I mean, it doesn't make a whole lot of sense in our world. To us, I think, what the Ascension means is that Jesus's physical presence with his disciples ended at a certain point, and only his spiritual presence continued."

"We can think that?" Bob asked.

"I would think so," Dr. Malchow said to a wave of uncertain

laughter. Dean frowned, winced, sighed, and stretched. He didn't know what to make of this.

"And maybe, even, the way he accomplished it was by going up in the sky. Maybe the body did rise," Dr. Malchow offered.

"But that would be contrary to the laws of nature," Bob said.

"Yeah, it could have been contrary to the laws of nature," Dr. Malchow said. "I'm not saying it couldn't happen . . ."

"Because God can pretty much will what he wants," Bob observed.

"But I'm saying it didn't *necessarily* happen, and I don't think you're denying any essential article of faith if you didn't think it happened that way."

"Makes the rosary a little challenging," Dean muttered. (Part of the rosary is dedicated to the Ascension.)

"Except the point is never history," Dr. Malchow said, his voice rising emphatically. "It doesn't really matter whether the physical body of Jesus rose. It does really matter that Jesus is present among us today as he always was. He was there, you know, during his earthly ministry in his physical form, and he continues to be present among us spiritually today. And that's what really matters."

"But doesn't Paul kind of disagree with that, or am I just interpreting it wrong?" Bob said, sounding concerned. "Because he's, like, if it didn't happen, then we're the biggest fools of all."

"We could almost be pitied," Dr. Malchow agreed. "But that's the Resurrection."

"Yeah, the Resurrection," Bob said.

"Oh, and I agree with you," Dr. Malchow said. "If the Resurrection didn't happen, I don't think we have any basis for faith."

"I don't understand what you meant when you said it doesn't really matter if Christ's body rose again," Dean said. He was seeing red, and when he saw red, he didn't listen as closely as he should.

"I didn't say that," Dr. Malchow said with a hint of annoyance.

"I said I didn't understand," Dean said defensively.

"I was talking about the Ascension. I was *not* talking about the

Resurrection," Dr. Malchow said. "But I *am* trying to tell you that not every Christian is going to agree with that, and they're gonna still be Christians. Some Christians don't believe in a physical Resurrection, and they're still Christians and they still believe that Jesus is alive and continues to live, which is the most important thing. From my perspective, I think his body rose."

Another student made the point that Scripture scholarship should be viewed as tentative, just as science had once arrived at conclusions based on incomplete evidence that were later proven incorrect.

"Could be," Dr. Malchow allowed. He then took up the subject of miracles, whose authenticity Church scholars now doubted. "When Harrington's talking about the nature miracles, he's not talking about the Resurrection and the Ascension. What's he talking about?"

"People running out on the water to meet Jesus?" Mike Mallard ventured.

"Jesus walking on the water, and Peter walking on the water, calming the storm," Dr. Malchow clarified.

"Multiplication of the loaves and fishes?" someone offered.

"Fig tree?" another student said.

"The cursing of the fig tree so that it died," Dr. Malchow explained. "And turning water into wine . . . That's it. All right, so he's saying it's likely that those five events did not take place — that they're stories to show the power of Jesus and the status of Jesus in our lives, and that the early Church made up those stories in order to teach about Jesus . . ."

"So that's another reason — not just because they're contrary to the laws of nature. It's because there are not a whole lot of them," Bob said.

"In fact, he doesn't say that the problem is that they're against the laws of nature. He's got four reasons, and one is what you said," Dr. Malchow said. "That there are so few of them. What we're basically saying is that while the Gospels tell dozens and dozens of stories about Jesus's miracles, the only ones we're questioning are five. All those healings did happen."

He paused and looked around the room. "That's one reason," Dr. Malchow continued. "What are his other reasons?"

"They usually only occur in the presence of the disciples," Bob Brooks said.

"So they're not as provable as the other miracles — the healings," Dr. Malchow said. "The healings often happened before crowds of people and could be authenticated. And the fourth reason is one of the best reasons, and no one has mentioned it yet."

"There's an allusion to the Old Testament," Bob answered.

"Yeah. Many of them are like stories in the Old Testament and maybe a retelling of the Old Testament stories. The best example is the multiplication of the loaves and fishes. That is *exactly* what the prophet Elijah does in the Book of Kings. He multiplies food for a crowd. But, of course, in making up the Jesus story, it's made a much bigger miracle. Elijah starts with more food, and he has a smaller crowd. So Jesus is a greater prophet than Elijah because he does a greater miracle."

"Like any good sequel," Dean advanced. "Like an action film. Monster's got to be twice as big."

Dr. Malchow moved on to things that were likely to have been said by Jesus. "These are the criteria that scholars use to figure out which of the sayings of Jesus in the Gospel are genuine — that come from him — and which, perhaps, were created by the later Church. Now, these are not final conclusions for everybody. These are the criteria we start with."

If something is original, it has a good chance of being from Jesus. That means that it is not like something the Church held later or Judaism held before Jesus. The second criterion is "multiple attestation," which means that the saying comes up again and again in independent sources. The third is "Palestinian coloring," which means that the saying fits Jesus's own environment and made sense where he lived. If the saying would make more sense in the Greek world, to which the Church later spread, Jesus likely did not say it. The fourth criterion is "coherence," meaning the saying fits with other things Jesus said.

"So you can't use this one until you've used the other criteria, and once you've used other criteria to figure out the basic message of Jesus, then you look at an individual saying to see whether it fits with his general message," Dr. Malchow said.

There is a fifth criterion that is also commonly used, the professor continued, and he didn't know why Harrington hadn't offered it. "It is the criterion of 'embarrassment.' If the Church could well have been embarrassed by something in the Gospels, it's probably true; otherwise, they probably would have eliminated it. Now your best example is that Jesus died on a cross — that the founder of your religion was killed as a common criminal with a common criminal's death. That's very likely true, because of the criterion of embarrassment."

"Would Peter's denials of Christ fit this category?" Bob asked.

"That would be one, too," Dr. Malchow said. "Or the time that someone said to Jesus, 'Good teacher,' and he said, 'Why do you call me good? Only God's good.' The Church never would have kept that one if it weren't true."

But these criteria aren't foolproof. Something could pass all five criteria and not be from Jesus, Dr. Malchow said, and vice versa. Dissimilarity, for example, is a flawed criterion because Jesus certainly said some things that were in keeping with the Jewish tradition because he was a Jew, and some things in keeping with the later Church because he was its source.

"Okay, back to the literalists and fundamentalists," Bob said. "Do they think somebody was following him around, writing everything down as this was happening?"

"Well, they kinda do," Dr. Malchow said. Although the Church later identified the Gospel writers, he added, literalists "still contend that Matthew really wrote Matthew and John really wrote John and they were writing down what they heard Jesus say. Did you ever read *The Last Temptation of Christ*?"

"Yeah, I love it. It's a good book," Bob said.

"Well, I think what he does with this idea is hysterical," Dr. Malchow said. "He has Matthew sitting down every night writing down what he heard, but the Holy Spirit keeps perching on his shoulder and whispering in his ear and telling him to write down different things than he saw."

Dean, feeling a bit more in tune with the direction of the discussion, jumped in with an observation about the Sermon on the Mount.

"I've never imagined some mountain or hilltop and he got up and said all of those things at once," Dean said.

"That's correct," Dr. Malchow agreed. "The Sermon on the Mount is a constructed sermon out of sayings that came from different times of Jesus's ministry and some sayings that didn't come from Jesus but came from the early Church. One thing that substantiates that is that Luke has got large parts of the same sermon, but it's at a different location."

Dr. Malchow summarized the most challenging class of the year. "Why do the Gospels cause historical problems? Because they wrote things differently than we do — that's one good reason. That they have a different way of writing history than we've got today. Our modern way is to emphasize the facts, be sure you've got everything right. *No one* in the ancient world did that. The thing in the ancient world was you told stories of your community, and you were allowed to change the stories."

Then there was the problem of no eyewitnesses for the Gospel accounts. And even if there had been eyewitnesses, that also would be problematic. "Who shot John Kennedy?" Dr. Malchow asked. "Everyone's got a different theory. We saw this thing on television, while it was happening, and we still don't know who did it. All I have to do is tell something to one of you and let it pass around the room, and we'll see what we get at the other end of the room."

He paused to let this sink in.

"So what are the Gospels? The Gospels are the proclamation of who Jesus is. The Gospels are the Gospels. They are the Good News about Jesus and how important he is for our lives. Certainly, there is a lot of true historical material in the Gospels."

One question still dogged Dean. He knew how prevalent doubt was in the world outside the seminary. How was he to answer doubt if we were left with a historical, but not a divine, personage? How could he respond to the common anti-Christian position that held that Christ never intended to be the center of a religion.

"The great atrocity," said Dean, paraphrasing the anti-Christian argument, "is that Jesus was trying to bring people closer to God. He pointed to God, and people didn't get the message. Instead, what they've done is based a new religion on him when he was simply a finger pointing to God. So at the time, people were saying, 'Well, what proofs do you have?' And they start coming up with these nature miracles to show signs — for them signs were proofs. And now we're looking at Scripture as proofs which are recordings of the signs of proofs."

Dean looked up at Dr. Malchow. "How do you respond to that?"

"Miracles only go so far," Dr. Malchow said. "Miracles aren't the center of my faith. Well, one miracle is — the Resurrection — but not much else. My faith is that Jesus is the Savior, who died on the cross for my sins and rose from the dead, and my faith is continued because I've had experiences in my life where I have known the presence of God. I could tell some really shocking stories about things that have happened to me. I'm not going to tell you the whole story now, but I'm at Sacred Heart School of Theology because of an experience of the presence of God in my life, and when I retire in two years, I will have been here thirty years. So these things happen in our lives, and that is what we believe. We believe that Jesus had direct contact with God, that Jesus was divine, and through Jesus we are connected to God and God keeps influencing our lives. If faith healers heal people — I don't know whether they're genuine or not genuine — but they aren't going to be the reason I believe, any more than the fact that Jesus did healing is the principal reason I believe."

"I'm in dire need of ketchup," Dean announced to the men at his table during lunch. Then he asked everyone about the rector's conference that day. Father Brackin was still using the weekly sessions to talk about academic standards, and Dean was still preoccupied with the thought that wrong doctrine was being taught.

Jim Pemberton tried to assure him that the rector's point could be summed up easily: "You come here with a lot of preconceived notions. You need not be shocked when those are challenged."

Mike Mallard observed that Jim was correct, but that the real problem was when people count only on their gut instincts and those instincts are wrong.

"I'm banking on that I've got it wrong," Dean said, referring to Dr. Malchow's statements on the Ascension. "I'm banking on that I didn't hear it right."

"I disagree with you there," Brother Raph countered. "Perhaps you heard what you think you heard. What he's teaching you is what Scripture is telling us. You can fight some of these things. Genesis might not have happened a certain way, but it doesn't take away from its reality."

Dean said that he was having trouble with the historical versus the theological, especially with respect to the nature miracles.

"What did you hear?" Brother Raph asked Dean.

Dean had heard that perhaps the Ascension didn't happen. "All I said was that should make the rosary more interesting," he said.

Jim Pemberton stepped in. "In Malchow's discussions, he's always quoting other Scripture scholars. These Scripture scholars are in effect theorists. This is their theory. What I have going for me is that I have something concrete before me that supports my belief. Now, the theorists are certainly scholars — they are far more educated than I will ever be — but it's still a lot of theory."

Dean said that from what he could tell, Dr. Malchow didn't go as far as other Scripture scholars who dispute all the nature miracles.

"It's a little like the medical profession," Jim continued. "The practicing doctor is following procedures that not only are accepted but have been proven time and time again to work. Now, there are scientists who are researching new procedures, and maybe some of them will work and be an improvement and maybe some will not. But there is no practicing doctor who is willing to jump on that new bandwagon until there are ten thousand cases."

It's experimental, Mike summarized.

"We're back here where the rubber meets the road," Jim concluded. "As a priest, I'm not about to stand in a pulpit and say, 'Guess what? These miracles didn't happen.'"

Academically, Heiser's spring couldn't have been better. His course load was so light that he found himself reading all his assignments twice.

On a personal front, things weren't as trouble free. The 102-year-old trucker he had visited since the fall as part of his fieldwork died after a rapid deterioration. The sale of his house to his brother, Johnny, finally went through. Heiser had lived in the house with Donna, and Eric had grown up there. But the thing he was most upset about was Packy. The dog had always lived in the backyard, and now he had moved with Eric to the house of a divorced friend and was living in the garage. Heiser checked up on Riverton daily via the Internet, keeping an eye on the weather and the local news, but he wouldn't be going back until the end of the semester. He had decided to visit Philadelphia over spring break and had already bought his ticket.

One rainy Sunday, the topic of the break came up when Heiser was driving Bill Hill, a seminarian from Wyoming, to see his first Ukrainian Mass. Hill attended Mundelein, a seminary outside Chicago, but was visiting Heiser at Sacred Heart for the weekend.

"So how long is your break?" Heiser asked.

"Two weeks," Hill replied with a wide grin. He knew Heiser's was only one week.

"You dog, you," Heiser said as he struggled to see the road through sheets of rain.

"Just remember how long you had to go hunting over Christmas," Bill reminded Heiser.

"What gets me," Heiser continued, "Bishop Ricken's coming when we're on spring break." Bishop David Ricken was in charge of Heiser's sponsoring diocese, and a seminarian was expected to be on hand for such a visit. Heiser had tried to change his plane reservations, but he couldn't. He and the bishop would see each other for only a couple of hours.

Having Bill in the truck presented Heiser with the rare opportunity to learn how the rest of Wyoming's seminarians were faring. Wyoming had a robust seminary program relative to its sparse Catholic population. The state had roughly 400,000 people, 50,000 of whom were Catholics. The diocese sponsored three men at Hill's school, Mundelein, three at Sacred Heart, and six at a minor seminary.

"I don't know if you know this or not," Bill began, "but Dan's not going on."

"No kidding," Heiser responded. "Do you know any more about that?"

"He's gonna go out and try to find himself a job and see what life is like."

Bill said that they were losing another seminarian to a monastery. He was a straight-A student. Heiser pondered the idea of leaving a seminary to go to a monastery.

Being on a mailing list can be an annoyance, but it can also be evidence that one has arrived. For Don Malin, it was a bit of both. One afternoon just before the Midwinter Follies, Don shuffled down the hall to his mailbox and found a priority mail pouch. *The graduation photographs,* he guessed. But the package was too heavy. He opened it to find catalog after catalog advertising every possible priestly accouterment he could imagine.

There was a cover letter congratulating him on his coming ordination. It offered him a 20 percent discount on his first purchase of one hundred dollars or more and told him about the gift registry option. Gift registry made it easier for "family and friends to share in your joy and celebrate your ordination." *How did they get our names?* Don wondered. Then he remembered that he had filled out a survey for the United States Conference of Catholic Bishops. Every graduating seminarian in the United States had been asked to do so, and Don had done it on-line.

Don leafed through the offerings. The catalogs were printed in full color on thick, glossy paper. There were items for Mass and liturgical celebrations: "memorial chalices," a Mass kit (including a chalice, host box, two glass cruets, and a candleholder-cross combination, all in an ABS carrying case) for $495, a Paschal candlestick, a censer stand, and a set of stacking ciboria. Then there were the clothes, so many clothes, some of them modeled by a range of clean-cut, religious-looking men, a few of whom seemed to be caught in the midst of profound contemplation: cleric cassocks ("Summertime Roman and also Summertime Semi-Jesuit with Cincture"), a cassock rabat ("with two special 'comfort' collars"), and a sports cleric ("100% Polyester Comfort Knit and pulls on like a golf shirt"). And then there was the "Jim Brackin collar" (Don's impromptu coinage), a detachable collar that went with a collarless black shirt. One gray-haired, second-career-looking model (clothed in #6025 "All Saints" Chasuble) had an almost pugnacious look on his face, as if he couldn't wait to come out of his corner fighting for Christ. Under "My Funeral Appointments" ("complements for this solemn liturgical rite"), a young cleric sprinkled a coffin with holy water, and an interesting historical note explained why one might need an urn for ashes: "In 1997 permission was granted for Catholic parishes to celebrate the funeral liturgy with cremated remains present. While a white pall is not used in the funeral liturgy with cremated remains, the MV Ossuary may be used."

The catalogs catered to almost every possible aesthetic, sentimental, and theological taste. An entertaining and overwhelming variety, Don concluded. These catalogs would help someone, he supposed, but he would never need this stuff. Besides, most of his vestments and clerical needs had already been taken care of by generous friends.

Don had been bedridden for almost a week with the flu. The

Follies were upon him, midterms had already begun, and he had papers to write. He turned to his work and dropped the catalogs in the trash.

Don Malin, Jim Pemberton, Wiggy, Chris McClellan, and Father Marty sought late-night food and drink at the Genesis Family Restaurant a few miles down Highway 100. The 2003 Midwinter Follies were over, and all that remained were faint traces of greasepaint on their faces and the slightly giddy theatrical afterglow of spent adrenaline. Wiggy, the codirector, went tropical, ordering a strawberry daiquiri. Jim asked for his usual Jameson's but in the end had to settle for Scotch. Save for Wiggy's consumption of "dog food" (Braunschweiger liverwurst) during one skit and the "God Bless My Underwear" routine of a first-year student that almost ended in an inadvertent *Full Monty* striptease, this year's Follies had been tame. Father Hugh Birdsall had impersonated Lawrence Welk and led a middle-aged kazoo band through the theme songs to *Green Acres, Hawaii Five-O,* and *The Addams Family.* Father Brackin and other administrators had played schoolchildren in trouble in the principal's office. And the ESL students had stomped about the stage dressed as giant papier-mâché top hats and sung "I want to be in America" from *West Side Story.*

Wiggy and Chris, the other codirector, were just happy that nothing had gone seriously wrong. Chris, a former professional bowler and social worker, had helped temper Wiggy's directorial anxiety. During rehearsals, Wiggy had gotten into the habit of stepping into the freezing cold outside the backstage door, dragging on a cigarette, stamping his feet, and talking a mile a minute into a cell phone as if he were a big-time Broadway director.

Wiggy soon turned the conversation to classes. He said that in Father De Jong's Human Life class, which he had nicknamed "De Jong and De Restless," the moral theologian had brought up cloning. Wiggy wondered what would happen if the pope were cloned. Would the clone also be infallible?

Father Marty, who had played Johnny Carson in the Follies and was only now easing out of the role, thought the clone might have to be baptized. Maybe yes, maybe no, Don contended. It was an ontological question.

Don and Jim's flaming cheese dish arrived. Jim decided to bring up something that had been bothering him. The previous week, a female pastoral assistant had lectured to his Parochial Activities class. In outlining her responsibilities as an aide to the parish priest, she told them that the priest for whom she worked didn't do funeral vigils — she did them. This upset Jim. Some jobs should be done only by a priest, and funeral vigils was one of them.

"But the priest just doesn't do them," Jim repeated, his voice pitched somewhere between disgust and amusement.

"You mean wakes?" Father Marty asked.

Jim nodded. What message did this send to his parishioners? His brother-in-law, Father Joseph Scantlin, had told him how difficult it was for people to accept a deacon at such times, and a deacon was an ordained member of the clergy. How much harder must it be for them to accept a pastoral assistant?

Father Marty agreed — it was not the right thing to do. But sometimes a priest might have no choice if he had to perform 150 funerals a year.

Wiggy put his strawberry daiquiri down. "I'm more like Reagan — I delegate," he joked. "You guys can handle it? I'm going to take a nap."

Jim said this was serious. He detected in the no-wake policy a dereliction of duty. The men at the table were skirting along the edges of an enormous issue in the Catholic Church: the increasing role of the non-ordained, especially women, in the day-to-day functioning of parishes and general ministry. As the number of priests declined, choices were being made — sometimes actively but more often by default — to turn power over to the laity in ways that many suspected would challenge the role of priests in the future. Jim believed that the pastoral assistant was quite happy because the priest's negligence gave her more authority. He also noted that she was preaching, even though only priests and deacons were technically permitted to deliver the homily. This practice had crept into some Catholic churches. Jim didn't think that Archbishop Dolan of Milwaukee would permit her to preach for much longer. But Don said that the word was that the archbishop knew about her role but would be passing on the question for the moment. He had already ruled against a similar question of allowing seminarians who were not yet deacons to preach. But as for this question, well, Don said, it was very delicate.

"Nurse?" Chris said, holding up his empty glass to an imaginary waitress and jangling the ice.

Heiser and the student council had added something to the Follies weekend festivities. They billed it as "Sacred Heart's First Annual Sports Tournament," and it would occupy most of Saturday. Actually, there was really only one legitimate sport, volleyball. The rest of the offerings were barely athletic: foosball (on the new table that Heiser had bought for the fourth-floor lounge), pool, Ping-Pong, and chess.

The morning of the tournament, Father Brackin led Mass in the intimate confines of the downstairs IHM Chapel. With a mischievous expression on his face, he prayed for the "athletes."

At breakfast, a Styrofoam cup of coffee and a small plate with a single healthy-looking muffin sat in front of the rector. Bring a cell phone to courtside, he advised Heiser, just in case you have a medical emergency. He reminded him of the seminarian who had broken his arm twice in two years playing basketball in the gym. Then there was the annual Christmas animal show when the camel lunged at a little boy and sent him to the emergency room.

The volleyball tournament was furious, but there were no injuries. Despite grunting, spiking, and trying to psych out the other players — some of whom were female ESL students and elderly nuns — Dean Haley's team lost. Even so, by the end of the day, Dean was happy. "The whole thing is a great idea," he said, congratulating

Heiser in the fourth-floor lounge. With so many new men milling about (eight more had entered at the beginning of the semester), Dean relaxed. He wasn't the new guy anymore.

Stevie Nicks was on the radio singing, "Women . . . they will come and they will go . . ." The foosball doubles final was being played in the corner: handles spun, the ball banged, and the electronic crowd cheered each goal. On the other side of the room, Heiser was cleaning up at the pool table, one studied shot after another. A new man, an ex–navy officer named Robert, started talking to Dean at a rapid-fire pace that made Dean's own speed-talking seem lethargic.

"He's a seminarian-slash-lawyer," the man said of one of the eight seminarians who had arrived in January. "He still hasn't sold his firm yet. Won't sell it till June. Still practicing."

Heiser won his pool game. Dean played the seminarian-slash-lawyer in chess. Robert was still talking. "What's wrong with this picture?" he asked, surveying the room. "It's a Saturday night, and here I am with a bunch of seminarians. I'm talking about the old days. I'd be out clubbing . . ."

Dean sized up the chessboard. The seminarian-slash-lawyer was proving to be a tough competitor.

"You'd be out working the beat?" Dean asked Robert.

"Yep."

"Most of us finished the beat *prior* to coming here," Dean said.

Robert said he had, too. "No fräuleins," he concluded.

"You're still in transition," Dean observed in a heavier drawl than usual. "You've got a whole semester before I take you serious."

"I've got my parachute packed already," Robert said. "I'm ready to jump."

"You're still in transition," Dean repeated, slowly shaking his head.

Robert bounced around the room. The Who were on the radio now. Robert attacked the end of the song with a performance on his air guitar. "I get on my knees and pray," he belted out.

Don Malin grew up in a house that looked a lot like a flying saucer. In fact, it was the house that had helped inspire *The Jetsons*, the classic cartoon about a space age family. It was called Chemosphere and could be found poised, as if in midflight, near the top of a narrow road on a steep hill above Hollywood, rising above palm trees and passionflowers. To get from the garage below, they boarded an electric platform that ran on a rail up and down the hill. His father, an engineer in California's aerospace industry, built the house with sponsorship from various companies in the mid-1960s. From its windows, with their 230-degree view of the San Fernando Valley, Don, as a young boy, watched a power substation's arc and gas mains erupt into flames during an earthquake. In its single-level interior, he and his three siblings, a brother and two sisters, were raised by their mother and father.

As the number of days to his ordination diminished, Don examined this past as a necessary part of who he had been and who he would soon become. He was a happy child, with an abundance of energy — so much energy, in fact, that he was asked to leave his first school because they thought he was hyperactive. (There were fifty kids in a classroom, and the school didn't have the resources to handle him.) He made his First Communion later than the other kids at a grand old, wood-darkened church near Universal Studios. The experience made him want to be "holy." Later, Don would think of it as his first holy moment.

After leaving his first school, he attended a school with more resources and a psychologist. The school did wonders for him. His second holy moment occurred when he was thirteen, on the occasion of his confirmation. He never forgot the palpable sense he had of the presence of God and the inflow of God's grace.

Then things changed. Don was molested by the husband of a youth worker. Later, a worker at the YMCA also abused him. The abuse continued into high school, at which time Don spiraled downward into delinquency. He displayed all the symptoms of a victim of child abuse, but the situation went undetected. His parents were at their wits' end. Although the local pastor tried to get him involved in teen religious activities, Don was unmoved until he attended a charismatic gathering at Loyola University in Los Angeles.

There, among four hundred people, Don experienced what he would later consider his third holy moment — the moment of his conversion and the turning point in his life. He saw what these people had and desperately wanted the same kind of relationship with God. After the Mass, he prayed, "I screwed my life up, God. You fix it." The moment he said that prayer, it felt as if a high-pressure hose had begun to wash out of him all the shame and darkness of the past several years. A sense of acceptance swept over him. He began to sob. Someone watching him might have thought he was having a breakdown, but instead he was bursting with love.

He had the same feeling when he woke up the next morning. "Thank you, God, I'm alive," he prayed. "I love you." He began to read Scripture and any other book that might help him make sense of what had happened. Only much later did Don come to understand that when you made the fundamental choice to stop living for yourself and start living for God, you would spend the rest of your life trying to figure out how to pay God back.

It had been a great night, but not for sleeping. On the surface, it resembled one of Dean Haley's bouts with insomnia from the fall semester. Sleep had been elusive until close to dawn. But such a night felt healthy and inspiring. Instead of fretting about the passing hours, Dean had felt composed. The black light on the wall cast a strange glow over everything in his room, making some objects invisible and others catch a silky, purplish fire. The screen saver on his computer was a Yule log, its flames flickering madly to the techno beat pouring from his speakers. The halls were empty but for the occasional late-night foray to the bathroom or the dining hall, where the previous day's desserts were probably still out for the taking.

Lying flat on his back, staring at the ceiling, Dean felt as if he was in a trance. Thoughts drifted in and out of his mind. His ex-girlfriend had sent him her summer plans via e-mail. She planned on working as a counselor at a camp. Would Dean like to visit? she wondered. He felt vaguely jealous, but he was not sure of what. She did not mention that she was seeing anyone. Was he jealous merely because he could not have a romantic relationship with her or anyone else?

He would never be one of those priests with something on the side. He knew men like that. You could tell the ones who really struggled with celibacy: they were hostile and uncomfortable around women. Dean tried not to judge them, but he knew that for himself, the walk down the aisle to the altar would be too long and all those eyes looking out from the pews too forbidding.

Dean also knew that his own struggle with celibacy wasn't over. In fact, he felt as if he was walking around with a box of Band-Aids, ready to patch things up, constantly aware of what his eyes were watching. *I have no idea how to do this yet,* he thought. He knew one thing, and that was that the whole celibacy proposition was absolutely impossible without God's help.

The night moved slowly on. *What if we have the whole thing wrong?* he thought. What if the Ten Commandments weren't rules but rather evidence of an abiding relationship with God? Was God really saying, "Because you know me, you won't commit adultery, murder, steal, etc."? This thought led to a recent memory of receiving the sacrament of the sick at a local parish after Mass. It was the first time Dean had ever done so, and he'd received it even though it had been more than a week since he'd recovered from a bad sore throat. (Ironically, the sore throat had developed soon after the Feast of Saint Blaise, the patron saint of throat ailments, when two candles were pressed against the sides of his throat to prevent such an illness.) The highlight of the Mass that day had been the celebration of a couple who had been married for fifty-five years and had ten children, twenty-two grandchildren, and four great-grandchildren. Over and over, as Dean had surveyed the church, he'd thought, *Community . . . Community . . . Community . . .*

Now, as he lay alone in his room unable to sleep, that word circled around him again. *I've got to learn how to love God,* he thought. What he thought had been love in his personal relationships had — he saw this clearly now — been a way of not getting hurt. It hadn't been love at all. He wanted to return to that five-year-old inside himself, the one he knew was still there, the one who had not been permanently lost. He suddenly wanted to send out letters to the parishioners back home. He needed to learn how to love God through loving other people.

Celibacy could be liberation, he thought, because it gave you the opportunity for many relationships and freed you from romantic exclusivity. Dean remembered a young priest who had told him that one of the greatest things about ministry was being "adopted" by a family. The freedom of committed religious life seemed heady. Every woman, he thought, had a right to have a relationship with at least one man whose interest in her was strictly spiritual. Dean thought of Jesus at the well with the woman who had had a series of failed affairs and his complete freedom to minister to her.

Dean wanted to grow that instant, to evolve into something better, a man closer to God. Not long before, he had gone to Father Charlie Bisgrove for confession. *What a priest — a real priest — a man in the trenches who told it like it was,* Dean thought. When it was over, Father Charlie had told Dean that he would pray for him in the hope that he would find a new spiritual director, someone who would push him and challenge him to grow.

It was almost prophetic. Dean would be meeting with his new spiritual director, Father Michael van der Peet, for the first time the following week. It felt like name-dropping (even to himself), but he couldn't help it: Father van der Peet had been Mother Teresa of Calcutta's spiritual director for more than two decades. Father van der Peet knew firsthand of the years of spiritual darkness and trial that Mother Teresa had suffered, years during which, in the absence of spiritual consolation and perhaps even belief, the nun had behaved as if she believed.

Somewhere near dawn, Dean finally fell asleep. He felt wonderful the next day. There was no past. There was no future. There was only the present. *Dean Haley is exactly where he is supposed to be at this moment,* the seminarian marveled. Suddenly, it seemed quite possible that he could keep up this schedule forever.

Ash Wednesday arrived, and Lent with it. Forty days of fasting and prayer had begun. The whole Church had suddenly disappeared into the wilderness and begun the dark and reflective journey that led to the Last Supper and Golgotha. Ash Wednesday is one of the more curious observances in the liturgical calendar. Priests know that crowds materialize for this day, not to return until the following year. Churches are filled with people kneeling when they're supposed to stand and vice versa. For a religion that prizes the preeminence of conscience and the confidentiality of the confessional, the large black cruciform smudge on one's forehead is an extraordinary public display of repentance.

It is not as if the ashes are sacramental. Perhaps it is their communal quality, the prominent mark of belonging, that makes the ritual so compelling. "He got you good," one Catholic might say to another who has a large blotch of ashes on his forehead. Jim Pemberton liked to tell the story of sitting in a restaurant on Ash Wednesday with a particularly prominent mark and having a man stop at his table, reach over, and "borrow" some ashes, explaining that he hadn't been able to get to church that day. Priests in the Southwest tell stories of driving out to parishioners working in the fields to distribute ashes and of the workers' gratitude.

"Remember that you are dust and unto dust you shall return," the priest says, dipping his thumb in the ashes and tracing the sign of the cross on a forehead. Why this ritual has such a powerful pull is a mystery that most priests don't even bother trying to figure out.

At Sacred Heart, Ash Wednesday had been designated a day of recollection. This meant a morning lecture followed by silence for most of the day. Prayer was deeply personal. It could be shared in the way that Mass and daily prayer might be shared, chanted or sung, but inevitably each seminarian would have to find his way on the wings of his own idiom. A pink handout that suggested several approaches to prayer began with these words from Pope John Paul II: "How to pray? This is a simple matter. I would say: Pray any way you like; so long as you do pray." The guidelines that followed recognized that Catholic prayer can often seem Byzantine and overly formulaic, even idolatrous.

The saints warranted a section: "We do not pray to the saints in the sense that they have any power of their own. We ask them to pray with us to God, just as I can ask you to pray with me to God . . . However, we do venerate saints, which is not to say that we give them adoration or honor due to God alone. It means we honor them as people who successfully cooperated with God's grace in this life and are among the great cloud of witnesses in heaven."

Mindfulness earned a section as well: "From the Buddhist tradition, the art of focused breathing and meditation through mindfulness can be very useful as a prelude to more traditional Catholic prayer by getting rid of distractions, removing tension, and focusing our attention on God." The handout also attempted to clear up confusion arising from the concepts of meditation and contemplation: "Meditation is mental prayer rather than vocal; it is thought rather than ritual . . . Meditation is the way we analyze something spiritual. It is not something that is merely study, which helps inform the mind, but it is something that leads to prayer." Contemplation, as outlined by the *Catechism of the Catholic Church* and summarized by the pink sheets, goes further than meditation because it does not stop at the cerebral but ventures on to the ineffable experience of being in the presence of Jesus. The *Catechism* quotes Saint Teresa of Ávila and defines contemplative prayer as "nothing else than a close sharing between friends." The contemplative says to Christ: "This little bit of time is my gift to you. I will simply sit here in your presence, focus my attention on you, and direct my love toward you. I will not allow anything to distract me, not anxiety about my future, not worry for the sick, not even a vision of angels. This time in silence is my gift to you."

Sometimes Jim Pemberton thought his prayer life was suffering as a result of too much activity — classwork, community obligations, outreach, and so on. But he remembered how his spiritual director, Father Charlie Bisgrove, had once leaned toward Jim and said, referring to all his activity, "Guess what? That's prayer, too."

But activity, even selfless activity, needed to be bolstered by contemplation. Jim watched how Father Charlie would gather himself in a corner of the sacristy before celebrating Mass: no chatting or light conversation before the procession to the altar began. The only things Father Charlie believed could get a priest through the inevitable trials of his priesthood were prayer and holiness. "Prayer and holiness," he would say, "are the mainstays of a successful priesthood. Prayer and holiness." After the parish politics and the interminable budget meetings, the Masses and baptisms, the almost insatiable needs of the people — no matter how wonderful — each priest returned to the rectory worn-out and alone. Only prayer and holiness would enable him to remain a good priest.

Holiness was not a platitude for Father Charlie. It was a demand for a radical, life-changing honesty. Father Charlie had been in religious life for almost thirty years, first as an SCJ brother and later as a priest. He had a soft, doughy face and spoke with a faint lisp that could be disarming. But these traits belied the force of his convictions and the sharpness of his insight.

Spiritual direction wasn't rocket science, Father Charlie would say. The men who couldn't talk openly about themselves or were capable only of niceties and Pollyannaish assessments of their progress were usually in deep trouble. It wasn't a question of sociability. Many of the problem priests were winningly sociable — just look at the news reports. He couldn't always put his finger on the exact reason, Father Charlie reflected, but he usually knew that this seminarian who seemed to be pleasant and playing by all the rules would self-destruct somewhere down the road. He would get involved with some woman or man or proposition a police officer. Something bad would happen. You were as sick as your sickest secrets, and if you didn't want to be honest, well, then you were just blowing smoke or tap dancing — Father Charlie's favorite reprimands.

If a man didn't want to be honest with Father Charlie, the spiritual director didn't have much leverage. A spiritual director was prohibited from voting on the formation process. Nor could he share what he learned with anyone unless it fell under a very narrow category of reportable matters (such as the threat to do violence to oneself or someone else or the threat to harm a child). A future spouse, making a confession to the priest preparing the couple for marriage, could admit to an ongoing homosexual relationship, and the priest could do nothing about it. The confidentiality of spiritual direction was almost as extreme. Nevertheless, Father Charlie believed, the direction process wouldn't be as effective if it were public. The spiritual director might not be able to use the things he learned to judge the man's fitness for the priesthood, but if the sessions weren't confidential, he never would have been given that insight. The most a spiritual director could do in the face of an unfit candidate was to urge the man to consider that perhaps he didn't have a vocation to the priesthood.

It could be hard to break down the walls of his seminarians. Many men are simply unused to speaking about personal things. They are taught to be self-reliant. But men aren't as strong as they like to think, Father Charlie believed. Men want to be the ones to tame everything, rule everything, control everything — but most are still little boys. They feel afraid, overwhelmed, unappreciated. In his experience, men are affected by a lack of appreciation much more than women. It is also telling to watch men show other men appreciation. How many men, Father Charlie liked to ask, would go up to another man and say, "I really appreciate you; I love you"? Instead, men punch each other in the arm or slap each other around to show their affection.

A spiritual director ran into these walls often as he sought to make the seminarian more aware of his internal life. If the man was struggling with pornography or masturbation, it was the director's job to break down the walls and try to get at the source of the problem. Father Charlie had gotten better at this over the years. He would pepper a seminarian with questions — Is this it? Is that it? — and then judge from the man's expression or voice what direction to go in next. If something was there, it would usually come out.

Father Charlie recognized that he wasn't a psychologist and that occasionally a man required professional help. But he also believed that the importance of the Holy Spirit is often downplayed in the modern world. The Holy Spirit can be very powerful. Healing is indeed possible, but each man must confront his secrets. Father Charlie saw a parallel in the American bishops' failure to address the sexual abuse scandal. The truth may hurt us. It may be painful. But you cannot start healing until you have spoken the truth. As long as there are lies, healing is not possible. Jesus always spoke the truth about a condition before he healed it. For instance, he didn't deny that the woman at the well had been caught in adultery. He acknowledged the fact, forgave her, and told her to go on with her life.

Father Charlie insisted that his seminarians understand that as priests, they would be called upon to help people in their lives. If they had not examined their own, they would be poorly prepared for this task. He felt badly when seminarians didn't use spiritual direction frequently, because it could only make them better priests.

It was a gift to see and hear things that no one else would ever hear, but it was also a huge responsibility. He had had men in direction for three years who only began to reveal their secrets in their final session. It was sad, Father Charlie would think in these cases, but at least they had that one moment.

The certainty caused by Dean Haley's inspiring night and the progress he'd made in the first half of the semester was shattered by a simple oversight. At least it seemed that way to Dean. He had contracted for an A in Father McLernon's Medieval Philosophy course. The grade wasn't supposed to be too hard to get, but Father McLernon had warned at the beginning that there would be no handholding. One of the requirements for attaining the contracted grade was to take an oral midterm exam. When midterms rolled around, Dean scheduled his exam with Father McLernon but somehow missed the appointment. Father McLernon gave him a talking-to but agreed to reschedule.

They rescheduled for Friday morning at eleven. But Dean had agreed too hastily, forgetting he had class until noon on Friday. When he told Father McLernon, the priest informed him that they would simply skip the midterm. Dean was stunned. *How do you skip a midterm?* he thought. *That means a zero. Average a zero with any other grade, no matter how high, and it's still really bad news.* Father McLernon told him that he wasn't so focused on grades. Dean should maintain A-level work. Even though at this point he could not possibly get an A, something might be worked out at the end of the semester.

But if Father McLernon was trying to telegraph a positive message, Dean was not receiving it. Soon everything was tainted by this problem. He had received high midterm marks in all his other classes: one point away from an A in Dr. Malchow's class; an A in Dr. Shippee's with a note that Dean's was one of the finest exams in the class; Professor Gotcher had labeled one of his answers "excellent." The philosophy mix-up was like being thrown back into the mire of the first semester. In an angry and confused moment, he told Father Krebs that he was ready to pack and leave.

Dean's sleep patterns suffered. He began to medicate himself erratically, even though his mentor, Father Tom Latham, insisted that he keep taking his drugs. He started missing classes, meetings, and Mass. And when a seminarian started missing things often enough, it got noticed. Especially if that seminarian was Dean Haley.

Heiser needn't have worried about any repercussions for leaving Sacred Heart during his bishop's visit. When Bishop Ricken heard the news, he immediately changed the time of their meeting to accommodate Heiser's flight. At age fifty, the bishop was only two years older than Heiser, even though Heiser perceived him as being much older. The bishop told Heiser that he had been selected to spend the fall semester at Trinity College in Dublin, Ireland. He also told him that he couldn't wait for Heiser to return to Wyoming as a priest. Heiser, Bishop Ricken observed, was one of those men he could put in a parish and not worry about — an administrator's dream. The comment reminded Heiser of what his old boss at the USDA used to say: "We never have to worry about your office."

Heiser arrived in Philadelphia the next day, after an early morning flight, for what he hoped would be a relaxing visit. He had vague plans to visit an exhibition on Lewis and Clark at the Academy of Natural Sciences and to meet his high school friends for a beer.

The first night back, he had a major shock. All his friends could talk about was Doug, who had been a member of Heiser's group of friends since they were teenagers. There was always a sense that no matter what life delivered, this group of guys was stable and dependable. That sense of stability was shattered that night for Heiser. His friends told him that Doug was having a sex change operation: he had decided that he wanted to live the rest of his life as a woman.

Heiser learned that three years earlier, Doug had had his testicles surgically removed. In high school, Doug had played guitar in a rock 'n' roll band and driven a hot rod. He had been married for fifteen years. When his marriage had broken up, Heiser had always assumed that it was his wife's fault; Heiser had never liked her. His opinion changed when he learned that Doug had wanted to be a woman since he was twelve and had been cross-dressing throughout his marriage.

Doug had taken each friend out individually to share the news. He'd had a brochure of pictures made up. Doug said that he wanted to be called Denise. Tom, Heiser's closest friend in high school, said that his wife had taken photographs of Doug dressed as a woman and he/she was actually very good-looking — six feet tall in a miniskirt and heels.

For the next day and a half, Heiser couldn't get the news out of his mind: *This guy I went to high school with — he's gonna be a woman. He's taking voice lessons. He's had his Adam's apple shaved because wom-*

en's Adam's apples are invisible. *He's having electrolysis: the hair on his hands has been removed. He's growing his hair long. His testicles were cut off because they were counteracting the female hormones that he had been taking.*

Heiser called Eric. "Remember the guy and his son you and I shot pool with over Thanksgiving?" he said. "He's having a sex change operation."

Heiser's friends said that once Doug got interested in the idea of a sex change, he began reading magazines that recommended which psychologists to see and which doctors could perform the procedures. Heiser couldn't help wondering: *Why didn't Doug go to a professional who might have told him to stop dwelling on this thing that had been bothering him since he was twelve? Instead he went to a psychologist who told him he had to get his dick chopped off.*

"So you want to have sex with guys?" one of Heiser's friends had asked Doug. No, he wanted to be a woman because he loved women.

"Then you're going to be a lesbian?"

"Yeah."

Heiser had asked the guys whether Doug would get any physical pleasure from sex after the operation. No one could answer the question.

Doug had told Tom that he couldn't wait until summer, when he could come over to Tom's pool in his bikini. "Don't invite me over for that one," Heiser said adamantly. "If I come over and Doug is in a bikini, I'm leaving."

Tom asked Heiser what the Church's position would be on Doug's decision.

"It's probably one of those things where you hate the sin but love the sinner," Heiser replied. The Church teaches that you need to accept your sexuality; you are blessed with it and need to embrace it.

But when he was alone, Heiser gave a lot of thought to how he should approach Doug. He realized that he was wrong to have said that he would leave if Doug showed up in a bikini. That wasn't a

Christian response. He knew that if he went back east for his CPE (clinical pastoral experience) he would be swimming in Tom's pool three times a week and the chances of running into Doug would be high. He would just have to accept Doug as a child of God, and that was going to take a lot of guts.

Heiser was trying to absorb Doug's news when he got another shock. He answered an urgent call from someone looking for his brother Johnny in order to locate another man, Joe, who was a friend of Johnny's and an acquaintance of Heiser's. Heiser managed to get hold of Joe, whom he had last seen two years earlier at a softball game. It turned out that Joe's only daughter and only granddaughter had been strangled to death by the daughter's jealous boyfriend. The boyfriend had put the woman's body in a cedar box and the baby in a garbage bag and slept near them that night. The next morning, he called his dad and said that he thought he had done something wrong.

Heiser tried to inject some normalcy into his visit by making a trip into the city with Tom to see the Lewis and Clark exhibit. But when they got to the museum, they found out the exhibit didn't open until June. While in the city, they walked past an antiwar protest. Heiser saw a younger man rush up to an old man with a peace banner and scream, "Let's bomb the shit out of them!" Heiser wondered how much abuse the old man had taken that day.

The night after Heiser learned of the murders, he went to bed to read the *Catechism*. He had gotten over the shock of the sex change operation, but the murders were a different story. He kept putting himself in Joe's shoes: *Your only daughter and granddaughter strangled to death by a maniac over sexual jealousy.*

Doug had said something that Heiser found both comical and sad: He wanted to be a beautiful woman. He wanted to turn men's heads.

*I could have easily lived a full life,* Heiser thought, *without having had those two things happen so close to me.*

*       *       *

Jim Pemberton returned from spring break convinced of one thing: silverheads needed to fill the gaps in the priesthood — not laypeople, not even permanent deacons. Silverheads were older men like himself, Philip Kim, and Daniel Cisneros, the deacon from San Antonio who brought decades of work and family experience to the ministry. Jim returned to the news that Daniel was going to be given his own parish straight out of the seminary. The intermediate step of associate pastor would be skipped, a move that would have been unthinkable just five years earlier.

Many new policies that would have been unthinkable in the past were being put into action in priest-starved dioceses. One of these was the "cluster system," in which two priests lived in the same rectory and between them ran five parishes. The cluster system was supposed to address the growing problem of isolation that was often cited when a priest went bad. It would also cut down on housing costs and overhead for the five parishes. In Jim's case, he was pretty certain that the diocese would keep him in his own house in Fort Worth and use him as a "roaming priest" to fill in for other priests who were on vacation or leave.

During the break, Jim had dinner with his brother-in-law, Father Joseph Scantlin, and his brother, Joe. The diocese was having a hard time with the priest shortage. Currently, one parish of four thousand families had no priest. Forty-nine priests served the diocese's eighty-eight parishes. Among those priests, the average age was fifty-five. Deacons and/or nuns currently ran the show at many parishes during the week, and a priest would come to say Mass on the weekend. In the face of the shortage, Father Scantlin wasn't seriously considering retirement. Silverheads, Jim concluded, had become very important if for no other reason than to fill in until some practical, long-term decisions could be made. These decisions might include merging parishes or actively recruiting priests from the Third World, where vocations to the priesthood were often on the rise. Jim thought that if the Church in the Southwest had taken a hard look at the problem ten years earlier, there wouldn't be this panic and lack of preparation. Father Scantlin thought it likely that most parishes might be priestless soon.

Jim also believed that silverheads were part of the long-term solution. He suspected that some priests used the shortage as an excuse to cancel Masses and curtail other activities. Many silverheads had come from careers in the corporate world and would be less likely to use the priest shortage as an excuse. In the corporate world, Jim had observed, there was an ongoing struggle between the constants and the variables. The only way that one could win the battle was to get up early and take care of the constants, such as correspondence and other paperwork. Having dispensed with them, one could face the variables — the fires that had to be put out — throughout the rest of the day.

The first thing this approach required was a willingness to get out of bed. Unfortunately, some priests were lazy, the kind of people who would be fired in the corporate world. Jim also encountered too many priests who seemed to duck involvement with the people by claiming they were busy. During Lent, a layman instead of a priest often led the Stations of the Cross. This was within the rules but unsatisfactory to Jim. His brother, Joe, ran the Stations at his church, and the service was packed. Jim concluded that parishioners just felt more comfortable with a priest as the presider.

Whenever Jim went home, he felt Joy's presence strongly. The one-level house on the edge of the golf course was the last house they shared together. His younger son was living there while Jim was at the seminary, but it still carried evidence of Joy's touch, such as mementos of the family's past arranged delicately in a curio cabinet. The couple's best friends lived across the street. Jim visited them, and they would talk about the trips they had taken when Joy was alive. Jim also spent time with his family. He planned to tour college campuses with his grandson during the summer.

"Spring break's over, kids," Don Malin announced to Jim Pemberton and Brother Raph at the breakfast table their first day back.

Jim told Don that the way things were going in the western dioceses, Don would be an associate for only six months before he took over a parish. Don replied that the diocese had told him to bring his track shoes; there would be a lot of work to do.

"There is a God, though," Jim remarked. "I picked up my mail when I got back here, and there was an envelope from a Texas oncology group." He had thought it was another bill, but it was a check for overpayment. "Joy died over two years ago," Jim observed. "You're so inundated with bills, you'd have to be a CPA to keep up with it."

Time was passing, but not fast enough for Jim. He would have loved to find a way to shorten his stay at the seminary. *Guys like me,* he thought, *want to get in the saddle as quickly as possible because we don't have a lot of time left in the saddle and the need is so great.* He added a prayer for longevity to his daily prayer for patience.

Dean Haley would have thrown out all his gadgets just to be on time. He hated being late and had no idea why he always was. During the first semester, he would sometimes skip a class entirely rather than walk in the door five minutes late.

Dean kept thinking about a series of books on productivity that he had read some time back. The author of the series ran a janitorial service but managed to crank out fifty-five books on the side. The janitor-author wrote that he had 6,500 items on his "to do" list. When his wife asked him what shirt he wanted to wear, he would reply, "The productive one" — by which he meant the shirt with the fewest buttons. Doing up buttons took valuable time. The man's mantra was "Be early."

Dean was enamored of these concepts but couldn't seem to apply them to his own life. After his confrontation with Father McLernon over the missed midterm, he got so upset that he forgot to pick up his laundry for more than a week.

He was taking his medication again after a brief lapse, but his sleep still suffered. He had begun to think the problem was more than medication. Once, he had visited a doctor back in Texas who believed that ADHD was caused by metal toxicity. She said that Dean was toxic with six different metals, so she started him on a cleansing regimen using DHEA, a synthetic hormone. She instructed him to take the DHEA every three days because a more frequent dosage would compromise his immune system. Dean followed the instructions for the first few dosages but then decided that if three pills every three days was good, three pills every day for five days was even better. He discontinued his self-prescribed regimen after a severe allergic reaction to his girlfriend's quiche sent him to bed.

Dean had heard that there were new nonstimulant drugs on the market to treat ADHD. He planned to switch to them when he ran out of his Adderall. (Had he been taking the medication regularly, his supply would have been exhausted the previous month.)

Despite the lack of sleep and the struggle with medication, Dean seemed to be putting the pieces back together with Father McLernon and Medieval Philosophy. One day after class, he sat down with the professor, JJ, and Bob Brooks to discuss a project the three seminarians had agreed to do together several weeks earlier.

Dean asked Father McLernon whether it was still possible to get an A in the course. The priest again gave him no guarantees but suggested that he continue working at an A level, particularly with respect to the commitment he had made to the oral presentation.

Dean worried aloud that they wouldn't be able to pull it off. If they didn't do it, Father McLernon reminded them, all of their grades would suffer.

"We can do it, but . . . ," Bob began.

"The question is time," JJ said.

They asked Father McLernon what they were supposed to make of the topic: "What exactly are the different qualities of person, personhood, and personality from a philosophical perspective?" Should they bring in the abortion issue and the moment of conception and somehow tie that in with the meaning of personhood?

As usual, Father McLernon wasn't going to hold their hands. "I would suggest, gentlemen, to do the reading over the weekend, come up with something, and keep it within certain parameters," Father McLernon advised. "If you go too big, it will be too much."

"Are we doing a presentation or a paper?" JJ asked.

"You're doing a presentation."

The three seminarians were silent.

"Are we together on this?" Father McLernon asked.

The men said that they were. Dean left the classroom determined to do well. He wasn't going to let the other men down.

Looking back on his last five years as a seminarian, Don Malin realized that an important part of formation is a loss of equilibrium. Some men make it past the loss; others don't.

One part of this loss of equilibrium has to do with celibacy. Don had experienced the embrace of celibacy as the death of sexuality. The process didn't make him question his own sexual identity, but he saw how it had made others question theirs.

When he was a second-year student in celibacy formation, Dr. Esther Warren set up a hypothetical pastoral situation for his class: What would the seminarian do as a priest if a gay man approached him seeking spiritual help?

One seminarian was especially harsh. The man was a pervert, he pronounced. He would tell him that if he persisted in a homosexual lifestyle, he would burn in hell.

Don slammed his hand down on the table.

"I'm sick and tired of picking up the dead bodies that lead away from rectories where there are priests like you," Don shouted. He told the man that charity demanded that you meet people where they are. A priest should help people see the error of their ways if they were persisting in sin but must do so gently. Jesus, he reminded, did everything with charity. What about the woman caught in adultery?

The seminarian turned red and left the room. Don thought he had delivered an inspired retort. Dr. Warren thought that the hand slamming down on the table was a bit much. The man didn't last more than a year at Sacred Heart. His diocese dropped him.

Don believed that the man's position on gays was a result of his losing a sense of his own sexual identity in formation. The death of sexuality put some men in an ambiguous state in which they experienced the fear that they were "going over to the other side."

The old system of formation hadn't adequately prepared men for the question of celibacy. The consequence was that many priests were arrested in their development. The sexual abuse scandal had revealed this. Second-career men face a different problem. When they enter formation, their sexual identities are already formed around problematic cultural values that equate sexual prowess with healthy sexuality. To attain a workable celibacy, the men have to go through a period of questioning and re-forming this sexual identity.

A week before Don's outburst, the formation class had watched a video on celibacy. The video featured a series of interviews with priests and religious talking candidly about sexual affairs. The men were repentant about breaking their vows. Don thought their insights were invaluable for anyone contemplating a life of celibacy. But he noticed another seminarian, a man who would also end up leaving Sacred Heart, furiously praying the rosary. He reminded Don of a young kid, hands over his ears, screaming so he couldn't hear what his mother was telling him.

Late one night, while Don was working in his office, he heard loud footsteps in the hallway. A little while later, Don saw Bob Brooks, stark naked, enter Don's bedroom across the hall and close the door. Don crossed the hall and knocked on the door.

"I'm sorry, man," Bob said sheepishly after opening the door a crack. "I'm locked out of the third floor. Could you let me in?"

Don had chucked his laundry down the chute that day, so he didn't have anything for Bob to wear. Don walked him down the stairs and used his sixteen key to let Bob into his own floor. Don noticed that Bob had no tan line.

The incident presented Don with a problem. Bob was obviously ashamed of his predicament. Don had heard that Bob had a problem with sleepwalking. Some of the other men had had similar encounters, and Bob's flip-flops had been found as far away as the dining hall. But Don believed that he had a responsibility to report the incident. *You couldn't have your pastor walking down the street without a stitch on,* Don reasoned. *And if he's sleepwalking and can't walk a straight line, he'll appear drunk.* He also knew that Bob had tried to wear something that might wake him up and had put obstacles in the way of his door, but these measures had obviously not worked.

After thinking it over for half an hour, Don fired off an e-mail message to Father Brackin and copied Father Marty. The next morning, he ran into Father Brackin, who said he was aware of the situation. Don knew Sacred Heart must be working on more than just sleepwalking with Bob. There were the protein shakes, the constant exercise, and the tanning, too. You couldn't have a priest obsessed with his appearance, no matter how smart he was.

Bishop Paul Zipfel of North Dakota stood at the lectern before a congregation swelled by faculty and the friends and families of the candidates. This night late in March, a small group of men were going to receive the ministry of lector. It was a steppingstone to priestly ordination, and afterward there was to be a big dinner. Jim Pemberton had been deeply moved by the symbolic importance of the ministry, but this was not the case for most. What, after all, was the point of making official what most of them were already doing? Why did they need a ministry to read Scripture at Mass? Bishop Zipfel's homily answered this question.

"The ministry of reader," he said, "is about words. It's about *the* Word."

He paused for a long time and gathered himself.

"Words can be weapons. Words can be healing. Words can unite in friendship or sever in enmity. Words can unlock who I am or mask me from others. Words have made slaves. Words have *freed* slaves. They have declared war and imposed peace. Words sentence to death — 'You shall be hanged by the neck' — and words restore to life — 'Your sins are forgiven you.' Words can declare a marriage dead, and words bind a life together in love. Words charm and repel, amuse and anger, reveal and conceal, chill and warm. Words clarify, and words obscure."

He took a breath. His voice snapped with a sudden severity. "A word from Washington can rain down bombs on Iraq."

And then another pause and his voice became soft. "Words from an altar can change bread and wine into the body and blood of Jesus Christ."

His voice became an awed whisper. "Words are charged with *power*."

God had spoken in fragments through the prophets, but he had spoken fully and completely in the person of Jesus Christ, the bishop proclaimed.

"My sisters and brothers, we gather here this evening to recognize your call — all of us really — but in a very special way you fourteen ... recognize your call to carry on the ministry of Jesus Christ. Not only to proclaim the Word of God but to become the Word. The message of the Father. That's your call. And in that way, it is really your call for everyone here. You who are chosen to be readers have a special responsibility in the service of the faith. You who proclaim the Word of God. To proclaim the Word in a liturgical assembly, to instruct children and adults in faith, and to prepare them to receive the sacraments.

"In this way, you will be a minister of the Holy Spirit in bringing Jesus Christ to others. What a marvelous thing to do. And I would want to say you become that message only if you are dedicated to the Word in such a way that it forms you. You have to be molded in your being and your feeling, and in your thinking and in your speaking, by the inspired pages of God's holy Word. Proclaiming the Word, dear friends, is not in the first instance a matter of assonance and resonance, of posture and gesture primarily."

Father Andre Papineau, who had prepared the men in a special session on being a lector, was amazed at the quality and delivery of the homily. He might end a class singing "There's no business like show business/Like no business I know . . . ," but homiletics was a serious matter to him, and this bishop was in the process of delivering the best homily he had ever heard from a bishop in his many decades as a priest.

"John Wesley was asked why people travel so far to hear him preach. He said, 'I set myself on fire, and people come from all around to watch me burn,'" the bishop boomed to the laughter of people coming out of a trance. "Shaped by the Word, you are a different person. How does that happen? Basically, the Word you study has to be the Word you pray, and the Word you pray, the Word you live."

To burn, one must prepare, the bishop insisted. Jim Pemberton thought of those priests who expected that they could get away without doing so.

"I don't minimize divine inspiration. I just suggest that it is rarely allotted to those who are lazy."

The bishop offered a story about the famed Baptist preacher Dale Moody to make his point.

"A student in Dr. Moody's Spirit course at the Louisville seminary wasn't meeting the professor's expectations. So Dr. Moody called him in and said this: 'Son, you're not doin' all that well in my course on the Holy Spirit. You been studyin'?' 'Dr. Moody,' the young man replied, 'I don't have to study about the Spirit; I'm led by the Spirit.' 'Son,' Moody asked, 'that Spirit ever lead you to the library?'"

The Sacred Heart audience dissolved into laughter.

"You must pray the Word," the bishop said vehemently. "If the Word is poorly proclaimed, the liturgy will be less effective in making God's works effectively present. They need to see that you have experienced what you are proclaiming. It can't be forced or faked — people spot it a mile away. It comes from prayer and sweat. You will set hearts on fire only if it comes through to them that you are in love with Jesus — that you have been fired by his presence."

Words matter. And words like the bishop's, delivered as the bishop delivered them, could turn a seminarian's outlook around — renew, energize, and even salvage his vocational commitment. If there is one constant of formation, it is that the seminarian needs to be revived and to hear his call afresh. A few days before the Mass, Heiser had retired to his room with a booklet after evening prayer. The prayer that evening had been a special tribute to Archbishop Oscar Romero. He had been murdered while saying Mass in his native El Salvador, presumably by forces that resented his antiestablishment views. Heiser had sat in his room in silence to read Romero's prayer. He had been transfixed and renewed:

> It helps now and then, to step back and take the long view. The kingdom is not only beyond our efforts, it is even beyond our vision. We accomplish in our lifetime only a tiny fraction of the magnificent enterprise that is God's work. Nothing we do is complete, which is another way of saying that the kingdom always lies beyond us. No statement says all that could be said. No prayer fully expresses our faith. No confession brings perfection, no pastoral visit brings wholeness. No program accomplishes the church's mission. No set of goals and objectives includes everything . . .
>
> We cannot do everything, and there is a sense of liberation in realizing that. This enables us to do something, and to do it very well. It may be incomplete, but it is a beginning, a step along the way, an opportunity for the Lord's grace to enter and do the rest . . .

The Word was taking root in Heiser and Jim Pemberton in ways that neither man could have anticipated. One by one the men proceeded to the altar and knelt before Bishop Zipfel to receive the ministry of lector.

Without Caritas, Dean Haley's life at Sacred Heart would have been almost unbearable. The men in his Caritas group were like his uncles. They were his biggest supporters and also his most outspoken critics. The bullshit ended when the men sat down around a table for a meal. Dean continually broke the older men's hearts in small ways with his inconsistencies and oversights. But what a priest he would be, they thought, when — not if — he managed to get it all together. He would be just what the people needed: invigorating, earnest, energizing, and powerfully evangelical — a handsome young man with a sharp intelligence and a strong faith.

But they also knew that the inconsistencies and oversights were dangerous in the context of Catholic religious life. It wasn't that a Roman Catholic priest should not be creative or should lack dynamism. It was just that creativity and dynamism must adhere to form, structure, and tradition. A priest's relationship with his parishioners is one of the last truly delicate social relationships. So much must be considered — not only punctuality but also the devotional, ideological, and temperamental leanings of his flock — and before all of that is the obligatory service as functionary and officiator of rituals that allow little room for personal interpretation.

But Dean often went his own way. He had squatted that extra room in the first semester. When he learned how to tap the soda machine a certain way and make ice fall into his drink, he was briefly nicknamed "the Fonz," after the character from *Happy Days* whose utter coolness made machines respond with alacrity. So far in the second semester, he had displayed the craftiness of a Tom Sawyer by managing to get designated as the note taker for Steven, the only blind student at the school since Ron Kendzierski's departure. Now Dean was taking notes for courses in which he was already enrolled and getting paid ten dollars a class for the service. The same sort of job had helped him pay his way through college.

Almost every week, the men of Caritas met at St. Martin's Inn.

"We still have some of that Oktoberfest left," the waitress reported after the men had settled down at their places. Spring break was just finished, and Dean had returned to Sacred Heart feeling renewed and optimistic.

"One Oktoberfest and five waters," Tom Mescall said. "It's Lent."

He was only joking. Three Oktoberfests, one brandy, one coffee, and one water swiftly arrived. Dean had ordered the water.

Then Tom, at moments like this still very much the judge, wasted no time in beginning the meeting. He led everyone in the sign of the cross in Spanish. He came from a southwestern state where all the priests were bilingual, and he liked to keep his Spanish at the ready.

"*En el nombre del Padre, del Hijo, y del Espíritu Santo. Amen.*"

"Amen."

Joe McDonald began the Angelus, and everyone at the table joined in response. Their voices rose against the din of the adjoining diners.

"The angel of the Lord declared unto Mary," Joe said.

"And she conceived of the Holy Spirit," the men responded in unison.

After the Angelus, Joe, Patrick Smith, Tom, Brother Raph, and Dean raised their glasses in a toast.

"Mud in your eye," Dean said. He addressed Tom and Joe. "I've got a CD I think you two guys would really enjoy called Irish beer-drinking songs. The first song is called 'Seven Drunken Nights.'"

"Maybe you could burn us a copy," Joe suggested.

Tom mentioned that he was missing a double cassette of the life of Saint Thérèse of Lisieux that he had bought while on retreat. He recounted that Saint Thérèse, though cloistered, had counseled two seminarians by letter on the spiritual life.

"One guy was straight as an arrow," Tom said. "But Maurice was much more human."

The waitress arrived.

"Like many of the saints," he said, before turning to place his order. "What soup of the day is it?"

"Cream of broccoli with cheddar," the waitress replied.

"I don't know about that," he said. "Broccoli? I don't know; that just doesn't do it for me. I'm gonna stick with my salad."

The waitress departed, and as was their custom, the men went around the table bringing one another up to date. Brother Raph said that he was chafing against some parts of the academic program and spoke of his trip back home for spring break.

Joe went next. He had some tax problems caused by a friend, but there was positive news as well. "My daughter's going to be there at Mass for the diaconate, and that's pretty neat — my youngest daughter," he said.

The soup and salads arrived.

Joe also was trying to find a cloistered religious sister to pray for him and his vocation, a so-called prayer partner.

The waitress ground pepper over the salads.

"You're still a little pregnant," Dean said to her.

"You think I'm pregnant?" she said, smiling. "I took a six-mile walk last week."

"Aren't there ultrasound pictures, too?" Joe asked.

"Oh, quick, I'll show ya," the waitress said. She pulled the photographs from her apron pocket. She pointed at bright blotches in a photograph, then pointed out her baby's anatomy. He was three months old.

"There's his head, and those are his eyes and his foot," she said.

Tom shared next. During the break, he had been worried about flying from Chicago to his home in New Mexico because Saddam Hussein had been given an ultimatum — step down from power, or the United States would attack Iraq.

"We have to pray very hard for peace in the world," he said gravely. "I'm particularly disturbed by the Holy Father's strong statements that the United States has no legal or moral right to be in this position of conflict — that we have put all of humanity at risk. Gentlemen, we are in dangerous and serious and troublesome times."

He cleared his throat.

"As far as my personal life," he continued. "I went home. I just felt *Oh, my gosh, three days is not enough*, but you'd be amazed how much good can come in three days.

"As our rector told us," he reminded the men, "when we are in troubled times, we need to have a prayer life, a systematic rhythm of prayer that we can fall back on. We need relationships that we can go to, people who understand us and comfort us, and we need places . . . I felt I got energized and rested, inspired, a little bit centered there."

"Stereo going out on the porch?" Dean asked.

"I did," Tom said. "A glass of wine, sittin' on the porch and looking over the Rio Grande, having dinner with my kids and friends. It was everything that our rector's homily said. I have relationships there. I had a place to go to, and I had my systematic rhythm of prayer. And I feel like I healed myself a little bit over that week, returning back, you know, to Chicago. It's been extremely challenging taking care of my aged mother, and I read an article in the newspaper just before I left. It's now the baby boomers' time to deal with the issues of old age, because they are starting to take care of aged parents, and they are not psychologically, sometimes physically, sometimes financially, able to deal with these challenges. And there *are* challenges!"

But Tom was inspired by the change in the weather and what it meant for the remainder of the semester. "I feel like I have enough energy," he said. "And I'm sorry to say but we only have . . ."

"Twenty-two days," Joe said.

"And then there's about ten days after Easter, and that's it," Tom said.

"Fifteen days to the last day of class," Joe said.

"I felt like I made it to the bell," Tom said. "Ding. I'm back in the corner. I've got somebody spilling water in my face. I've got somebody else slapping me across the face, saying, 'Kid, you know, c'mon. You've just got three minutes to box around.'"

Joe reminded the table that he had met Tom's mother once, and although she was infirm, she was still a sharp woman. Tom's mother had even told Joe that her son had always been interested in the priesthood. Joe probably intended the comment to remind his friend why he was in the boxing ring in the first place, but Tom bristled a little at his mother's recollection. It was not as if there hadn't been life before seminary. "What's also true is that I was a married man and that I had two children, a son and a daughter, who are now adults," he asserted.

This reminded him of something else that had been bothering him lately: the three hours a week spent in his canon law class, during which the seminarians focused on what could be done to help people in troubled marriages.

"This has been very painful for me," he said with a frown. "I'm sitting in there, and day by day I have to remember how I felt when I was married. What was going through my mind at that particular time; what happened during the course of the marriage that caused it to fail; what I did and what I was perhaps the recipient of. It's like everything today, you know. It's like going into very deep therapy for three solid hours, and these are things maybe other people here don't think about. Since I'm in that particular class, I *have* to think about it, because in many respects what went on in my life is happening in some form or another in the lives of other people."

He looked wistful, then continued. "Very painful. But it's ground that — yes, we covered. Perhaps there will be some good that will come from the sorrows that were suffered there. Perhaps being able to understand the troubles of other people, the sorrows of other people, the broken dreams of other people, I might be able to be more pastoral and minister to them."

"I was reading a book by — I can never say his name right — Pope John Paul's name," Dean said.

"Karol Wojtyla," Tom interjected.

"And he said that in his experience, the number one criticism of priests was newness," Dean continued. "How are you gonna be advising anything about marriage never having been married, because as a priest, all of the information is secondhand? My reason for telling you that is that you're not going to have to deal with the number one criticism."

"In addition to the canon law class," Tom continued, "I'm taking Advanced Pastoral Counseling. I'm getting a double whammy, twice a week."

They had watched a videotape about a troubled couple in the class, and everyone seemed to think the couple was beyond help. Tom had objected.

"You know, let me tell you something," he said. "I'm the only one in this class who's a divorced man. We've got three widowers in this class who enjoyed very happy, successful marriages, and we've got three other guys in the class who have never been married. But I was married and I was divorced, and marriage is a tough thing. In spite of all the problems that they had on the tape, as long as they're motivated to get together to solve things, they might be able to put it back together."

The waitress and the hostess arrived with a birthday cake for Brother Raph.

Then it was Dean's turn. Dean mentioned that he was finally going to install the powerful speakers sitting in his closet in the BMW. Tom had some stern but fatherly advice. "In the name of God," he said emphatically, "do *not* jeopardize your hearing. When that goes, you might as well jump in the box. If you fail to communicate with people, they will shy away from you. Pro-tect your hearing."

"The magic number is eighty-five decibels or higher for eight hours a day," Dean said. He insisted his speakers were in the safe range.

The check arrived, but Dean wasn't quite ready to leave. He spoke about his trip to Indiana over the break. He had gone there to get away from the seminary, only to have his BMW break down and have to be hauled back to Wisconsin on a flatbed driven by a biblical literalist who gave him an anti-Catholic tract to read. Dean had called Father Tom Latham back home for some guidance, and Father Tom had talked him through. The trip might have been a fiasco, but now Dean declared that he was on a "super high" after figuring out how to fix his car's engine himself. As the men settled the check, Dean also mentioned that his ex-girlfriend seemed annoyed that he was at last happy in the seminary. She probably felt rejected, Brother Raph suggested.

None of that had dampened Dean's spirits, he said. "I'm on such a high. If someone asked me, 'What did you give up for Lent?' I gave up *can't* for Lent. That's what I feel like right now. Bring it on."

"Well, gentlemen, you want to shut 'er down here, or what?" Tom said.

Joe led the closing prayer.

"Praise be Jesus Christ," they all repeated. "Now and forever. All for the honor and glory of God. To the Immaculate Heart of Mary, Our Lady Queen of Peace . . . and the intercession of Saint Michael, the archangel. Amen."

The men got up from the table, bid their waitress goodbye, and walked out through the bar. They passed the NASCAR photos and memorabilia, then the inn's pièce de résistance, the glass-enshrined NASCAR jumpsuit in the foyer. The big-screen TV played news about Iraq, and the talking heads sounded convinced that the advance to Baghdad would not be easy. When Dean finally pushed through the outside doors, the air smelled faintly of spring.

The march to the end of the year was getting more urgent. The men talked about it around the dining table, before classes, late at night — something to be relished. Summer plans took shape. The second-year students had CPE to arrange, and most had their assignments in place after midterms. CPE comprised ten to twelve weeks of pastoral ministry in a hospital, and it was said to be life-changing, as it spanned intense encounters with birth, death, and illness. The men came back from these summers with tales of white-knuckle counseling, the techniques of Father Hugh Birdsall employed at the eleventh hour, or just muteness before the messy brokenness of human beings at a horrible time — no high-toned religion then, just the ministry of being a physical presence for someone in need. Heiser had hoped to go to Pennsylvania to be near his parents over the summer, but because he was only on the waiting list for a hospital there, he'd decided to work at a medical center in Wyoming instead. Jim Pemberton was going to a hospital in Fort Worth and would be able to live in his own home for the summer.

Don Malin made a trip down the road to Minuteman Press — almost every trip these last days seemed significant. He reviewed the proof of the invitation to his ordination. The invitations would be printed on heavy, ivory-colored card stock and include a photograph of Don in clerics and a prayer from Saint Ignatius: "Take, Lord, and receive all my liberty, my memory, my understanding and my entire will." He had ordered 250.

People back home could see the changes in Don, and other seminarians turned to him when they had doubts or problems. Dean's behavior seemed to be disturbing some of the men. One seminarian had told Don that he wouldn't be returning to Sacred Heart because he resented the way the staff coddled Dean. Don tried to convince the seminarian that the way Sacred Heart handled Dean had nothing to do with his own formation, but Don couldn't get the point across. He could tell the man had made up his mind. Don believed that Dean was an excuse for this man to look at something other than himself.

Saint Thomas Aquinas, the legendary theologian, maintained that "grace builds on nature." A complex Catholic theology had long ago developed concerning grace. According to this theology, grace is not to be mistaken for a feeling, although it could be accompanied by a feeling. Don had learned from his spiritual director that feelings of grace are what are called consolations and that they are given by God. You cannot attain to them by yourself. Trusting your feelings or making your feelings a barometer of your faith life leads to a roller coaster ride. You can feel good because you had some wine. You can feel good because somebody loves you. You can feel good because you've made love. You can feel good because you've taken a drug. You can feel good because you've awakened from a wonderful dream. You can feel good because you've accomplished something. And you can feel bad for all the same reasons. You can also feel nothing — just bland — even though things are going wonderfully.

Don was not becoming a priest because of a feeling or because he had always been certain that he had a calling. He was becoming a priest because the choice to enter the seminary had been the right thing to do at a particular moment in time, and the seminary process that followed had evoked the calling, tested it (manhandled it, really), and finally proven its existence.

But in these last days before his departure from Sacred Heart and his ordination, he was, in spite of himself, waiting for a confirming feeling, a sense that this next step was inevitable. At lunch one day, there were fortune cookies. Don's read, "Somebody's hoping you're not in trouble."

The missed midterm in Medieval Philosophy still irked Dean, but spring break and the approach of the warm weather had cheered him. Although he still didn't know how the mistake would play out in the end, he wasn't as worried as he had been. He kept up his chiropractic visits, tried to stabilize his sleeping habits, and tried to remain open to the formation process. In an exuberant mood, he took advantage of a particularly warm day to test-drive BMW's new models at a local dealership. The first car, a convertible, handled like a dream. The second one ran out of gas, and Dean had to help the dealer push it off the road.

And then, just as his semester seemed to be improving, things got bad again: Father Tom Latham died. Father Tom, Dean's mentor, father figure, and housemate, had succumbed to heart failure. Father Tom had buried Dean's great-grandmother, and Dean retained a vivid childhood memory of the priest locking the tabernacle door and securing the chalice in the sacristy, leading the young Dean to think that something very valuable must be locked behind those doors.

Father Tom had been sick for some time. He had a bad heart and had been in and out of the hospital for close to a year. In his convalescence, he had been confined to the first floor of the rectory because he could no longer climb the stairs. But his death was sudden.

When Dean heard the news, he knew that he had to get back to Texas as soon as possible. Father Tom's death came at a particularly awkward time. The director of seminaries for Dean's diocese was visiting Sacred Heart. Dean knew that his record had some obvious weak spots and that the director would probably want these explained. Dean left the day after the director arrived and was gone for a week. He returned to accusations that he hadn't informed anybody, including the director, of where he had gone. Dean maintained that this wasn't true, although he admitted that he had left abruptly. At the time, the only thing that had mattered to Dean was getting back to Texas. To hell with the consequences; he owed Father Tom so much. Many people at Sacred Heart saw it as a serious lapse of judgment.

No man could go to seminary in the year 2003 without a profound awareness of the fallibility, even the perversity, that might be found among Catholic priests. One's ideals about the clergy were tempered by the reality that there were deeply troubled, profoundly wounded, even evil clerics — just look at the news. But a medical student did not desist from his or her chosen career because there have been doctors who have murdered their patients.

When Dean had arrived at Father Tom's rectory to spend the year with him before shipping out to Sacred Heart, he had learned that his new housemate considered himself bisexual. The frank admission had been followed by another: Father Tom was still involved with a man. He told Dean that he would never give the future seminarian a holier-than-thou image to follow.

"This is Broken Me," Dean remembered Father Tom saying.

Father Tom was not the priest who had inspired Dean to go to the seminary, but he was the man who in many ways had made the journey possible. It was Father Tom who had gotten Dean to focus on the application process and forced him to begin the necessary work of eliminating his personal debt. Ultimately, Father Tom had consolidated some of Dean's credit card debt himself, with instructions to pay him back after Dean was finished with the seminary. He didn't want Dean burdened with debt through the process, he said. Father Tom was like a second father to Dean. He was the only male figure with an active spirituality whom Dean really knew.

Even knowing the priest well, Dean was only partly prepared for what he discovered among Father Tom's personal items when he arrived at the rectory a few days before the priest's funeral. Dean found pornography in a strongbox in Father Tom's bedroom. *Are all fucking priests fucked-up?* Dean thought. He found sex toys and letters from his lover. Father Tom had given Dean a book about priestly celibacy called *The Unhealed Wound*. *So this was the unhealed wound, and that was why Father Tom had an industrial-strength paper shredder in his bedroom,* Dean mused. Dean scanned the video pornography. *Please don't let there be kids,* he thought. There were no children, just gay adult porn that looked very old. *God,* Dean continued, *I don't want to go out that way. Father-walking-scandal-any-minute-now. There but for the grace of God go I . . .*

Dean reflected on what he knew of the priest's life. Father Tom had in many ways been forced into the priesthood. His was a classic story of a son who became a priest because his mother had the vocation. When he'd wavered about leaving the seminary, his mother had told him that he was free to leave if he wanted, but she would never live down the shame if he did. In some ways, Father Tom bore the mark of that pressure for the rest of his life. He seemed to have been frozen into sexual immaturity by it. Some of the questions he had asked Dean during the seminarian's stay at the rectory were so naive, as if he were a child puzzling out the birds and the bees. Dean remembered Father Tom telling him that his sexual compulsion had been evidenced as far back as seminary with habitual masturbation. He had finally been sent to a psychiatrist who, dismissive of Catholic teaching on the matter, seemed to condone the behavior. It was a response that in Dean's experience would have been inconceivable at Sacred Heart in 2003. In those days, though, Father Tom had told Dean, the first time celibacy was addressed was three weeks before his ordination to the diaconate, when he was instructed to sign some paper from Rome.

Despite the shock of his discovery, Dean could not overlook a certain irony. Father Tom was an enormously obese man — so obese that Dean used to be embarrassed to eat out at a restaurant with him. Dean was sure that people would look at them together and think, *Well, we don't have to worry about celibacy with the fat one, do we? That's all straightened out. But dammit, Dean, you're gonna cause problems because of your looks.* In his mind, Dean would counter, *The guys who are gonna cause problems are the ones who've never had people hit on them. Because they're wearing a collar, they're suddenly gonna have people hittin' on them, and they won't know what to do.*

Only God knew where Father Tom stood in the eyes of God, but Dean didn't know how a priest could live with himself if he wasn't true to the promise. He thought, *I have two years, maybe two and a half, before I profess my promises. I'm going to do everything I can to get ready between now and then.* The key seemed to be to remember that you were human and that celibacy wouldn't be under control until you were six feet under. There hadn't been much in the way of formal instruction yet, but in the fall Dean had been enraptured by a lecture given by a visiting monk named Brother Zullo. The monk had outlined practical measures one must take to avoid burnout and the risk of inappropriate behavior. A network of people seemed to be crucial to avoiding burnout — that and, Dean added to himself, God's grace.

Dean disposed of the strongbox and shredded the letters. He called Father Tom's lover on the phone after he puzzled out the number. The lover didn't know that Father Tom had died. He told Dean that he was shocked, but he didn't cry. Dean said that it would be fine for him to call if he needed to talk — the seminarian didn't know what else to say. He kept thinking that he should be in shock himself about Father Tom's activities, but he wasn't.

When Father Tom had told Dean a few months into his stay at the rectory that he had a lover, Dean had informed the priest that he could no longer be Dean's spiritual director. Father Tom had been hurt, but Dean was resolute. Dean knew that his mentor had in many ways been a very good priest — even a great priest. As a pastor, he reached out to people in their need, in their frailness and brokenness, and he had so endeared himself to his parishioners that when he was transferred, they campaigned to get him back — and did. Father Tom had failed at a very high bar, Dean thought, and others struggled with it, too. Many priests had come from beginnings that had stacked the odds against them. This was a human story, as Dean, the child of multiple divorces, knew well.

The Knights of Columbus stood guard over Father Tom's open casket during an overnight vigil. The bishop attended the funeral Mass, as did many of the diocese's priests. The church was filled to overflowing, and Dean helped set up chairs outside for the crowd. During the Mass, Dean sat on the dais and looked at the parishioners over the coffin. Perhaps they were looking at him and thinking, *There's someone from this community. There's someone who's at least looking into the priesthood. Someone to serve us.* Dean knew just how badly they needed a priest to serve them.

He had been thinking lately of Archbishop Dolan's book *Priests for the Third Millennium* and his reference to other pitfalls of priesthood, such as bitterness and reliance on material comfort. Dean wanted to avoid those, too. He wanted to be a priest in whom God could vibrantly dwell and act, and not be hindered by a crippled nature or a double life. But looking at Father Tom's casket, he knew that he must honor this man as well. Perhaps the strongbox was just a reminder to Father Tom of a problem over which he had triumphed. Wasn't Christ the Shepherd-Redeemer searching the shadows and ravines for his lost sheep? So great was his love for each person and his desire that none should be lost, he searched with passion and a fierce, never-resting intensity. Perhaps Father Tom had wanted to get rid of the box himself but couldn't because he was physically unable to climb the stairs to the second floor. *Six months of knowing that the box was upstairs,* Dean imagined, *and not being able to reach it. Maybe that was it, or maybe not.*

Among the things that Dean brought back from Father Tom's rectory was the dart set that he had given the priest for Christmas and a few pages from a journal that in the end Dean found he couldn't shred. The journal was from Father Tom's days in the seminary — when the specter of sexual compulsion first arose. If Father Tom had been told not to feel guilty about his masturbation, was that enough to purge him of the feeling of guilt? *But is it only the feeling of guilt that separates you from God?* Dean wondered. And if you got rid of the feeling? *Guilt is a funny thing,* Dean thought. *If you push it down, it will come out in some other way and wreck your life.*

Sacred Heart's final day of recollection fell on April 9, two days after Dean's return from Texas. There was still snow on the ground, but it began to melt during the bright and cloudless day. After Mass and breakfast, a visiting nun named Sister Pat Kieler gave a lecture on prayer. "When I have changed, the whole world has changed," she said. "Every atom of hate that we add to this world makes it more inhospitable."

Dean was one of the few men who did not attend the lecture and meals that day. He kept to himself. Father Tom was still very much on his mind. He did not hear the nun speak of original sin: "This is the world we inherited and were born into. A world of original sin, where our very genes seem to carry a deep-seated self-centeredness and selfishness."

As usual, the seminary community was instructed to observe silence for the day. Everyone, including the maintenance and administrative staffs, participated and were encouraged to reflect and pray. Many attended confession in the Sacred Heart Chapel. Don Malin did not. He sat alone at a corner table in the dining hall. Two small American flags stuck out at angles from the metal stand near the salad bar that was always stocked with nuts and sunflower seeds. Apart from the flags, there were no other decorations.

That morning, Don hadn't played with the Spanish choir in chapel. He had told them that he would be stepping back from his duties. But he watched and cautioned himself, *You know they're not going to do it the way you do it. They're going to make mistakes, and you won't be there to correct them.* Sister Lucille was still being mastered by her instrument, Don observed, instead of mastering it. Don saw Martín Frias roll his eyes at one mistake, but he let it go.

In the dining hall, Don read from a yellow sheet Sister Kieler had passed out. It was "The Prayer of the Empty Water Jar" by Macrina Wiederkehr, and it spoke of a vessel too full of inessential things, worldly things and illusions — so full that grace could not enter:

> I don't need more
> I need less
> I am too full.

The dining hall was quiet except for the hum of the drink machines and the occasional wanderer's footsteps. The sun filtered through the tall windows. Recently, Don had been practicing saying Mass, speaking the words of the consecration in both English and Spanish. Gary Rottman, who was graduating with Don, had already logged a hundred practice Masses that semester. During practice, Don would lift the chalice with reverence and the paten with delicate awareness of the placement of his fingers, then speak the words slowly and with love. Each man had a different manner during consecration. The Mass, Don's bishop liked to say, was a priest's marriage act, as intimate an expression of his love, fidelity, and utter giving of self to God as a husband and wife making love.

Easter, a final break for the men, had passed, but most had stayed at Sacred Heart to prepare for finals. In some of the classrooms, the windows had been thrown open in anticipation of spring, but this being Wisconsin, there was still a chill in the air. The Sacred Heart Chapel still bore the mark of the holiday, with the altar spilling over with Mary Anne's bright lilies. The Wednesday community Mass after the break served a dual purpose, as both a celebration of the Resurrection of Christ and a recognition of Father Otto Bucher's three decades of service as an administrator and professor as he retired. The lunch that followed was abundant and festive: tablecloths and silver on the tables, two giant rectangular cakes, and a spread including fried shrimp, baked beans, and a dish bearing the label FATHER OTTO'S HOT BEANS. During the meal, Father Brackin rose to present Father Otto with a framed watercolor of the seminary. He also announced that Sacred Heart would be giving the priest a monetary gift for postretirement travel.

After lunch, Heiser met with Father Donald Krebs and his Theological Reflection (TR) group for the last time that year. They talked about the virtues of the group, and then Father Krebs left them with evaluations to fill out. The last man to complete the form was to bring them all down the hall to an administrator's office.

The fall would bring a semester in Dublin for Heiser. Wiggy also had been selected for the program. Heiser hoped they wouldn't be sharing a room — he didn't think he would survive if they did. Wiggy had a way of getting under Heiser's skin. In his first year, Heiser had gone so far as to draft a strategy for handling him. By the second year, things had become much more manageable, but Wiggy still drove Heiser a little crazy.

Eric and JVH had recently flown in to visit Heiser for the weekend. He brought them with him to homiletics class, where they had a chance to critique his sermon. Then he took them to a Wisconsin fish fry at St. Martin's Inn, to Kopp's Frozen Custard, and to a Milwaukee Brewers game. They saw the basilica, drove along the lakeshore, went to three breweries, and gambled at the Potawatomi casino. When Eric got home to Wyoming, he sent Heiser an e-mail message telling his father how proud he was that Heiser was becoming a priest.

Making his way to the last student council meeting right after TR, Heiser spied Don Malin getting ready to go for a stroll. Heiser reminded Don of the meeting, and they went in together. A new council had already been elected, and the members applauded them when they arrived. Don, looking boyish, gave a little salute, then both men left.

Jim Pemberton spent the afternoon and evening guiding a prospective seminarian named Bernie around the school. A lawyer, a widower, and the father of seven children, Bernie wasn't much younger than Jim. He was worried, just as Jim had once been, that his bishop wouldn't accept him because of his age. Jim related his own experience and his conviction that the benefits of an energetic older vocation far outweighed the risks. More and more dioceses would soon understand this, Jim said. Showing someone like Bernie around enlivened Jim. It was another opportunity to spread the good news about Sacred Heart and silverheads.

After dinner, Jim, Bernie, and Mike Mallard delivered Sacred Heart's leftovers to Elena's House, the AIDS residence on the other side of Milwaukee. The deliveries had begun the previous fall after Heiser had become disturbed by the amount of food that was being thrown out at the seminary. With relative ease, he'd arranged for Sacred Heart's excess to go to the home. The food service was more than willing to donate the food as long as Heiser could put together a roster of seminarians to deliver it. He did.

The drive usually took twenty minutes and gave Jim and Mike a short break from studying. As Jim rounded a corner, the aluminum trays shifted heavily in the trunk, and Mike worried that the contents would be scrambled. Jim said he didn't think the people at Elena's House would mind.

Bernie whistled from the back seat. "I knew that this seminary was in Main Street America when I saw McDonald's, a Subway, and Culver's ButterBurgers — they've got those in Nebraska," he said.

Jim nodded and pointed out the Pick 'n Save and the place where he had his laundry done instead of paying for the service at the seminary.

"Bernie, Highway 100 has everything you need," Jim observed proudly. "It's got it all."

"Even a Dairy Queen and a bagel shop," Bernie noted.

"John the barber," Jim announced, pointing at a row of nondescript storefronts that quickly disappeared in the rearview mirror. John cut the rector's hair, Jim related.

"Taco Bell," Bernie said.

"Car wash," Jim indicated.

"You've even got a Wal-Mart," Bernie exclaimed. "You know, Wal-Mart has become the number one grocer in America."

Bernie would fit right in if he came to Sacred Heart, Jim observed. He told Bernie about the widowers' group, which had recently received a sacramentary in memory of their wives. (A sacramentary is a book used to direct a priest during the celebration of Mass and other rituals.) A typed sheet bearing their names had been pasted inside the cover. The book was to be used in the newly renovated St. Joseph's Chapel. In a sense, Jim noted, their wives would now be at every Mass said there.

"What do you think of Sacred Heart so far?" Jim asked Bernie.

"I think it's great," Bernie exclaimed. "I've got to watch the food, though. I don't eat this way at home. I'm kind of a nibbler. My kids are always saying, 'Dad, you don't eat enough.'"

The three men began talking about their families. Jim remembered when his dad had moved into an assisted living residence. His father, a delivery man for Mrs. Baird's, America's largest independent bakery, was in his mid-nineties and had been at the residence for only a few days when Jim received a call from the director telling him that his father would have to find somewhere else to live. It seemed that his dad had coldcocked a nurse and then caused an eighty-year-old resident to faint after driving her Pekinese into a frenzy. Bernie asked Jim if his father had Alzheimer's.

"No, not exactly," Jim replied. "He was ninety-five years old, and he was pissed off."

They started talking about their grandchildren. Mike said that something funny had happened to him over Easter break. After he scolded his five-year-old grandson for calling his little brother a butthead, his grandson had turned to him and said, "Asshole." Mike told the boy that his own mother would have washed his mouth out with soap if he had ever spoken that way. "That won't do any good," his grandson replied, following the statement with more foul language. Mike's daughter arrived, saw what was happening, took her son upstairs, and washed his mouth out with soap. His grandson reappeared, much chastened. "I think she got 'em all," he informed Mike.

They passed a Walgreens pharmacy. "Walgreens is building them all across the country," Bernie marveled.

"Here's the deal in Texas," Jim explained. "Every time a competitor opens a unit, Walgreens opens one right across the street. Because?"

"They already did their research?" Mike ventured.

"They know that eventually the other guy can't keep up with them on price," Jim replied.

"But they've already got the right location," Mike added.

"Exactly," Jim said.

"Isn't that somethin'?" Bernie put in.

"So what Christianity should do," Mike advanced jokingly, "wherever a mosque opens up, build a church right across the street."

"Man, I don't look forward to the Scripture exam," Jim said. The mention of religion had suddenly reminded him of all the work he had to do. Jim and Mike told Bernie that when they'd arrived at Sacred Heart, they had thought that Scripture scholarship would be like Bible study. Instead, they had learned things such as how the concept of angels and devils had come into Judaism through its early encounter with another Near Eastern religion, Zoroastrianism, and that scholars considered many of Jesus's miracles questionable.

"I'll hold on to them anyway," Jim commented.

Bernie wondered how Sacred Heart compared to Pope John XXIII National Seminary in Massachusetts, the other major second-career seminary in the United States.

"They still wear caskets," Mike said.

"Cassocks," Jim corrected.

"You don't see too many cassocks out there anymore," Bernie observed. "They probably do the liturgy in Latin, too."

When they returned to Sacred Heart, Bernie said that he wanted to go to bed early. He was training for a marathon. By nine o'clock, the dormitory was quiet. The silence was broken briefly when Philip Kim returned from a shopping trip with David Placette to find the door to his room festooned with balloons, streamers, and a Miller beer poster of a busty, swimsuit-clad model with the handwritten words I LOVE . . . OLDER MEN coming out of her mouth. Jim and Mike emerged from their rooms to greet Philip and razz him. It was Philip's seventy-second birthday.

"She mean you, too," he told the men, pointing his finger at them. After a while, the group dispersed, disappearing into their rooms to resume the work of the final week and a half.

Like most of the men, Heiser had received many gifts from people and groups supportive of vocations. For instance, a group of women called the New Home on the Range Homemakers had sent "a note of encouragement and appreciation for your service to God and Wyoming." And over Easter, he had received phone cards with a total of 150 minutes of talk time. Heiser was grateful for these gestures. It had been more than two years since he had had a steady income, and he had become acutely aware of how he spent his money — a strange feeling for a forty-eight-year-old man who had worked his whole life. People might be spiritually dependent on him as a priest, but he would definitely be financially dependent on them.

Heiser was not the kind of man to turn his back on his past, professional or personal. As a result, gestures of support often came from people he had known previously. Sometimes this support made him feel uncomfortable. Near the end of the spring semester, he received an e-mail message from a woman named Janet whom he had dated for a number of years. She had been married for more than ten years by the time Heiser had arrived at Sacred Heart. Even so, this message had a funny tone. It began, "You showed up in my dreams last night," and was signed "Love." But she also said that she valued Heiser as a friend. After thinking about it, he concluded that he was probably being a bit too sensitive and the best thing to do was take the words at face value.

Like Heiser, Janet had been divorced and raising a son on her own when they had met. Once, Heiser had tried to tell her that he loved her, but she'd stopped him. "Don't say that," she had warned. He had never said it again. Near the end of their relationship, Janet had asked him whether he was ever going to marry her. At the time, he'd thought she was just covering all the bases before moving on. And besides, marriage had been the farthest thing from his mind. Looking back, Heiser realized that God had had a plan for him since his divorce: raise Eric, then become a priest. Perhaps Janet had sensed this, even though he wasn't aware of it yet.

This was not true of another woman he had dated named Anne. His relationship with Anne also had lasted for several years. When he'd finally told her that he was going to the seminary, she had taken it badly. To say "I'm sorry," he'd sent her a bouquet of flowers, which she returned in a fury, leaving them and a note on his front porch. The note told him to stick the flowers and his rosary up his ass.

Heiser knew that he had let Anne's expectations grow unchecked,

and he regretted it. He had taken the easy road and should have known better. He knew better now.

Downstairs, in one of the basement conference rooms, Dean Haley, Bob Brooks, and JJ were working into the night on the PowerPoint presentation for Father McLernon. Dean had received very bad news that day, but he had other people depending on him, so he kept on working.

One of them mentioned that there was an open casket upstairs in the Sacred Heart Chapel. There was a wake for a priest of the SCJs. JJ said that the same casket was used again and again for burials. "A common grave," he observed wryly. "They dump them in there. Brothers for eternity."

He asked Bob and Dean if they knew how the brothers used to greet one another in the hallway. "Remember death," JJ informed them.

"How cheerful," Bob said.

"Kind of focuses you," JJ said, then turned his attention back to the presentation.

The three men were clustered around Dean's laptop at one end of the table, with empty Mountain Dew and Pepsi cans scattered about. Dean stayed in good form, amenable to the other seminarians' suggestions. He had remained committed to the project since Father McLernon's intervention a few weeks earlier.

Bob, though, was a bit on edge. And when he was a bit on edge, he told jokes. One was about a Trappist monk under a vow of silence. Every seven years, the monk could speak two words to his superiors.

"Bed hard," said the monk after his first seven years at the monastery.

"Food bad," he said seven years later.

"Room cold," he said after another seven years.

Finally, seven more years passed, and the monk was once again at liberty to speak to his superior.

"I quit," he said.

"It's no surprise," his superior snapped. "Bitch, bitch, bitch — that's all you've done since you got here."

A little while later, JJ worried that they wouldn't have time to edit the presentation. Dean reassured him, saying that he would handle the adjustments to titles and all the other elements himself.

They worked until the battery in Dean's laptop died. It would be a late night for Dean if he was to get the presentation just right. But the meeting had gone well, Dean thought, except that he was concerned about Bob.

As they left the room, Dean joked that at least the heavy workload kept their sexuality at bay.

He made his way to the second floor, climbing the hollow, echoing stone stairs he had traveled countless times over the past year and coming out on the floor where so much of a seminarian's life took place at Sacred Heart. The sun had gone down a long time before.

The bad news had come in the form of a phone call that day. Dean had told no one about the call except Bob. It seemed that Dean should cry, but he couldn't. Instead, he felt defiance well up inside him, and also, perhaps strangely, hope.

There was also shame at the thought of his words at the going-away party in his home diocese the previous August. Had Dean really said that this place was his last hope, that if he couldn't make it at Sacred Heart, he couldn't make it anywhere?

Well, the fact was that he hadn't made it at Sacred Heart. The call from the diocese's director of seminarians had made that brutally clear. It was well understood around the seminary that a diocese was never under any obligation to ordain a man. It could support a candidate for as long as it wanted and then stop supporting him for any reason it deemed appropriate. Nevertheless, dropping a man usually occurred only in extreme cases.

*Why hadn't they told him they would stop sponsoring him in person?* Dean wondered. Of the ten peer assessments he had received, all had come back with positive comments. Understandably, however, the seminarians didn't consider the peer assessments too reliable. The men were reluctant to be seen as spies, and no one in the fishbowl wanted to be cited as part of the official record of a man's dismissal. Predictably, Bob had been very positive, calling Dean "a bridge to God, a healer of souls." But even those who didn't know Dean very well had weighed in favorably. "Dean appears to be adjusted and comfortable with his seminary environment," wrote one. "Helpful, thoughtful," wrote another, who, curiously, also checked the box "I do not know him." Even if the assessments were skewed in his favor, Dean believed that they said one important thing about him: he should be given a chance.

But the only opinion that mattered was that of his diocese. "At least I called," Dean remembered the director of seminarians saying. *Yeah, at least he called,* Dean thought bitterly. A letter confirming the decision would arrive soon.

Father Brackin had called Dean a few minutes later to see how he was doing. Dean learned that the seminary had been prepared to invite him to return. The faculty vote had been 1 vote to promote, 23 votes to promote with condition, 7 votes to promote with probation, and 1 vote to dismiss. The condition had been that Dean seek counseling so that he could properly manage his ADHD and smooth out some of his rough edges.

Now the future had been ripped wide open for Dean. He had been geared up for sacrifice, growth, and a deepening commitment. Why had the diocese dropped him? Tardiness? *Is tardiness what the director of the seminarians said?* he thought. What did it mean when the diocese badly needed priests but would get rid of Dean for tardiness? *Tardiness couldn't be the real reason.* Even Father Krebs had recently conceded that the lateness problem had begun to improve. Unfortunately, while the director had been busy discussing Dean's record with the faculty of Sacred Heart, Dean had been back in Texas, with no opportunity to defend himself.

There were no easy answers and no consolation. It would be one thing if he could just drop the whole idea of a vocation. But he wasn't done with it yet — or it wasn't done with him. He wanted to become a priest, dammit. He tried to see things in a less self-absorbed way. It could be worse. Imagine being older, leaving a job with a pension and a home, and then being dropped. But Dean couldn't stop wondering why they had dropped him in his first year. Everyone knew that it was the second year — not the first — that was crucial for determining whether a seminarian should continue on in the process. The first year was turbulent. It was a time for readjustment, not for a permanent verdict of unfitness.

Sometime that evening, a tan hearse had parked outside the smokers' door beside the dining hall. A little while later, the gray casket with shiny chrome handles that JJ had mentioned had appeared in the central aisle of the Sacred Heart Chapel, near the steps to the altar. Sometime after that, a group of SCJs had gathered to pay respects to one of their own. The dead man was a priest who had served and died in India just short of his seventy-fourth birthday.

After the SCJs departed, the casket was left behind, its lid open and the dead priest, wan and pale, floating upon the frilly white fabric that spilled over the sides of the coffin like a bride's trousseau. It was an all-night vigil, but the chapel was empty when Dean entered and approached the casket. The air in the chapel was heavy with the scent of flowers. Dean was lost in thought. He knew that he had made mistakes, but they should have given him another year at least. Dean stood at the foot of the casket and looked down at the dead man, scrutinizing his face. *That's where I want to end up,* he thought, *after a long life of service as a priest.*

No way was his vocation over and done with. No way. There were other dioceses and other options. But anything he did tonight or in the next few days would be reactionary. He would try to be patient, try to have faith and do everything as if he would be returning to Sacred Heart in the fall.

Dean left the casket and the chapel and ran into Father Charlie Bisgrove in the dining hall. He asked the priest if he had time to talk. They found a table in the dark. Dean spoke, and Father Charlie listened. Then the priest asked whether Dean had other dioceses that he could contact.

The next day, Dean sat at seven-thirty Mass, to which he had arrived just slightly late, and listened to the homily. It was delivered by an alumnus of the school, a recently ordained priest.

"Gentlemen," the speaker urged, "you are a needed commodity, needed for the harvest. Rest assured, you will be welcomed when you get home."

He told the seminarians to use their time as the Apostles had and to be at peace with their vocations. When the bishop placed his hands on their heads and they were made priests, they would receive the strength they would need. The priesthood wasn't just a job. "The people love us almost to a fault," the man insisted. "I guess I can't tell you how happy I am to be a priest."

Dean hunched all the way forward, with his chin resting on his palm. Every word seemed spoken directly to him.

"Most of us have quite a past," the priest continued. "Quite a life."

The chapel resonated with agreement.

"The people realize that," he assured them, "and they *love* it."

Don Malin had injured himself again. He sat in the dining hall with his immobilized leg up on a chair and a pair of crutches propped beside him.

"What's going on, my brother?" Dennis Cloonan asked as he passed Don with his lunch tray on his way to another table.

Don had been rehearsing with Voices of Praise, his Charismatic Renewal music group, when he looked around and was overcome by a sense of sadness. The careful words he might use to describe the emotion of these final days to other people — he was "invested in the community" or "experiencing loss" — were not enough to contain the strong feelings that had spilled over and made him throw his leg up onto the stage with foolish abandon rather than take the stairs. Nothing was broken. The bruise was painful and incapacitating, but not nearly as serious as the health emergencies of previous years.

"How you doin', buddy?" Tom Mescall asked.

"Doin' all right," Don answered. "It hurts."

"I bet it does," Tom said. "As long as it's okay for your big day."

Jim Pemberton appeared and asked the same question.

Don already had a number of suitcases packed. He was busy saying farewell all over Milwaukee. The week before, two of his friends, Patty and Mike, a couple who shared his love of music, had taken him out to dinner. Mike had the biggest collection of vinyl records Don had ever seen and an extraordinary sound system. Whenever Don bought a new CD, he would bring it over to their house for a listen. At dinner, they had given him a set of top-of-the-line headphones that could pick up frequencies his current speakers missed.

Patty was one of his "reflectors." Mary Anne, a friend from Charismatic Renewal, was another. Don recognized the need to have women friends whom he could trust to advise him on what he called his "priestly personality." Beyond matters of personal hygiene and table manners, he was concerned about appearing flirtatious to women. He knew that he had always relied on flirtation in his relationships with the opposite sex. Although the tendency was mostly subconscious, and many people did the same thing, it was inappropriate for a priest. He had worked hard to change it.

Don left the lunch table to prepare for Father Marty's class on confession. He had memorized the prayer of absolution in English, but he still needed to learn the Spanish version.

Brother Raph, Dean, and some others sat down at the table. Someone asked whether anyone had heard a bell, a veiled reference to the mission bell that would be rung again and again during the last days of the semester by departing seminarians. Heiser said that he had heard it ring in the middle of the night.

"You're not hearing bells, are you?" Dean asked. "You know that's a sign of fatigue."

The news of Dean's loss of support had spread rapidly through the seminary. He spoke about it at nearly every meal and had solicited collective brainstorming. He had been told to forget getting into another seminary that fall, and some people had even warned that there was a two-year automatic freeze when a seminarian was dropped by his diocese. One priest had advised Dean against moving too quickly. Think about where you want to live for the rest of your life, he had told Dean. Dean could not get over how the diocese had hurried to get him into the seminary, shoving papers at him and telling him to get things done, and now he faced an uncertain future with delay written all over it. Texas had fourteen other dioceses. Maybe Texas was still the place. They said San Antonio was beautiful. Someone at the lunch table mentioned Las Vegas as a possible destination.

"Yeah, they're really pushing for vocations," Dean countered. "But it's hard enough for me to walk down Main Street Milwaukee."

Dean wanted to get back to Texas and meet with some of the administrators from his old diocese. He was still too upset to call his vocation director, but he wanted to meet with him soon. At least he didn't owe them any money. From the beginning, they had told him, "If you leave, you pay us back. If we drop you, you don't."

The idea of leaving Sacred Heart was disconcerting. Bob Brooks had come up with an interesting solution: Dean could stay at Sacred Heart as a nonseminarian master's student. He would be like a shadow seminarian, and when vocation directors visited, he could set up interviews with them. Dean liked the idea. Actions spoke louder than words, and there was no way he was going to move to some other diocese and hang around for a year on the chance that it might take him.

There was also the possibility that he could land a job at Elena's House. He had arranged an interview, and his chances seemed promising. He was getting counseling to address the issues that had arisen during his time at Sacred Heart. After all, the faculty had voted in support of his return on the condition that he attend counseling. He thought that following up on their recommendation would show his good faith, even though he didn't technically have to anymore.

But Dean was still struggling with his sleep patterns. One night that week, he had gone to bed at six P.M. and slept for almost fourteen hours, missing Mass and arriving at class looking as if he had just gotten out of bed, which he had. In a faculty meeting, Father Krebs had apparently defended Dean's erratic habits by using Dean's own words: "You have to admit one thing, I'm consistent about being inconsistent." In light of the news from his diocese, his behavior also was being scrutinized by his fellow seminarians. Some of the men were even more puzzled and frustrated with Dean now than they had been before he had been dropped.

Jim Pemberton couldn't understand why a seminarian would not go to daily Mass when the Mass was so foundational for a priest. The administration should never have to talk to a seminarian about not being at Mass, he thought. That behavior reflected a piss-poor attitude. Perhaps Dean wouldn't have stood out so much among a group of college-age men, who might be wrestling with many of the same issues. But at Sacred Heart, Dean had always been a black sock in a white-sock drawer. He was really his own worst enemy, Jim concluded, a smart guy who had made a lot of dumb decisions.

There was a strong spirit of helpfulness at Sacred Heart, but Dean's actions had tested that spirit. He would be told, "You need to be doing this," but he wouldn't do it. Heiser wondered where the love of the Eucharist was. Don Malin saw Dean as always churning, churning, churning. The most obvious problem that needed fixing: sleeping through things. Just imagine Dean in a parish, Don thought, missing two Masses on Sunday because he had screwed up his sleep cycle.

One day near the end of the semester, after a quick glance at his planner, Dean raced down to an oral exam in Father McLernon's class. He arrived out of breath at 11:05. *Great, I'm ten minutes early,* he thought. Father McLernon poked his head out of the door.

"Dean, it's eleven-fifteen *tomorrow*," Father McLernon said.

Dean looked abashed.

"But I understand why you'd check in today."

*　　*　　*

"It is finished," Gary Rottman called out to Heiser after his last exam. A grin stretched from ear to ear.

But in some respects, it wasn't finished. The line between end and beginning would never be that clear. The Don Malin who would pack a U-Haul trailer at the end of the semester and drive to Pueblo, Colorado, to become a priest was in many ways already a priest. Formation — that multitude of things — had reshaped him, reconfigured him, even renamed him.

The power, authority, and responsibility of the clerical state was already partially Don's in his capacity as a deacon. His Charismatic Renewal group was actually disappointed when he went off alone to turn some tap water into holy water. They told him that they had wanted to see him do it. Don could also baptize and marry now. And there had been that matter of ridding the historic Cobblestone Inn of the suspected poltergeist. Whatever the reality of the haunting, the cleansing ritual had calmed nerves, ended reports of flying glasses, and, more important, made a distinct statement of before and after — the kind of statement that eluded Don in his final days at Sacred Heart.

Right up until the end, in fact, the pace of seminary life remained frenetic. There was the overlay of final exams and the countless loose ends of his activities in Milwaukee to be tied up. And behind all of that was the reality of the role he was about to assume and his basic unpreparedness for what he would encounter.

Nothing exemplified the sense of unpreparedness better than the day, only a week before graduation and a few hours after the Rite of Sending (a brief service during which each man bids his own goodbye before the gathered community), that Father Marty had the men take turns confessing one another in his Liturgical Presiding class. Saint Alphonsus Liguori, the founder of the Redemptorists, famously said, "Be a lion in the pulpit and a lamb in the confessional." When asked why he had become a Roman Catholic, Gilbert K. Chesterton, the early-twentieth-century writer and journalist, replied because only Catholicism had confession. Most of the men knew and embraced the high bar demanded of a priest toward this sacrament. A venerable seminary hypothetical suggested just how high a bar it was: If you as a priest are told that there is poison in the chalice under the seal of confession, can you act on that information even though not acting on it will mean your death and the deaths of others? Answer: No.

Father Marty ran the class with gentleness toward his fledgling confessors.

"What's the right thing to ask about someone's background?" one man asked. "How's your sex life?"

"No, don't ask that," Father Marty said with a comic wince. With the scrupulous — those who come up with minutiae to confess — he advised that the men just listen and absolve. The rest was God's job.

There wasn't enough time for every man to practice confessing, so Father Marty chose Carlos to play confessor while he played penitent. In Father Marty's scenario, the penitent confessed that he was a married man wrestling with his use of birth control, something against the teaching of the Church. At first, Father Marty as penitent did not admit that what he was doing was wrong; he seemed to be hovering over the issue, waiting for direction. Carlos nudged and prodded him in the direction of contrition. Contrition, the expression of regret, was necessary for absolution, or the forgiveness of sins, to be granted. When the would-be confessor finally granted absolution in the face of a rather murky contrition, there was palpable discomfort in the room. The words of the Act of Contrition (a prayer often spoken by the penitent as the priest says the formula of absolution) — "to sin no more and to avoid the near occasion of sin" — defined a high bar that this particular penitent did not seem to reach. The penitent agreed to encourage his wife to speak to someone about their use of birth control, but he did not explicitly say that he would stop using birth control.

Reaction varied. Some saw the confessor as taking the birth control issue too seriously. Others thought that he hadn't taken it seriously enough. One man chided the confessor. He thought that if the position were to become known among other parishioners, which it certainly would, it might discourage them from even bringing up the matter with him. Martín Frías took the opposite tack and said that absolution should not be granted unless the penitent explicitly said that he would be open to the idea of stopping the use of birth control. Father Marty kept repeating that it was a sticky situation. Then another man spoke. This man had raised eight children and had been shifting in his chair, crossing and uncrossing his legs, throughout the discussion. He said that absolution should not have been given and that the priest had an obligation — as uncomfortable as it might be — not to blindly support the penitent in the ongoing commission of a mortal sin. Father Marty bristled at the man's suggestion that the penitent's contrition was not authentic. How could he possibly know? If the penitent said he was sorry and then recited the Act of Contrition, that was enough. Going beyond that would be presumptuous and judgmental. But the man insisted that more questions were in order before absolution could be granted. How else would the priest clarify exactly where the penitent stood?

Birth control was a good choice for the exercise because it was a pastoral briar patch. Father Marty told the men that they would get a lot of people confessing birth control under the category of "I know it's a sin, but . . ." Someone said that the reality was that most Catholic couples practiced it. Another seminarian jumped in with an example of a man who had been told by a priest that having a vasectomy was a sin. The man had one anyway and then returned to confess it and receive absolution. Father Marty noted that some Catholics considered having a vasectomy a way of taking the burden of using birth control off the wife. Whereas she would be repeatedly sinning, the husband would commit only this "one-time" offense.

Father Charlie Bisgrove liked to say that a priest learned how to be a priest by being a priest. The atmosphere in the room — one of discomfort and anxiety in the face of what seemed like such a great burden — could not be lightened or dispersed with a simple solution. When the men fell silent, Father Marty described a circle with his hands, an ungraspable object. There were so many things that these new priests would have to consider: greater and lesser goods; the pastoral reality of finding one's community where it was, not where one would like it to be; the seesaw between those tense companions mercy and justice; the broken world itself, and the hard, patient, and tender work of being a man of God in such a world.

Father Marty dismissed the class. That night, there would a farewell party in the upstairs lounge for the men still fresh from the Rite of Sending. Nothing had been resolved. In a month or maybe two, anyone with any problem could walk into the confessional, and these new parish priests would have to come up with an answer between the opening blessing and the absolution.

Commencement exercises were held as part of Vespers, or evening prayer, on Saturday, May 2, 2003, at 4:30 P.M. Most of the seminarians and the families and friends of those graduating gathered in the pews of the Sacred Heart Chapel, where a jasmine tree in front of the baptismal font gave the air at the entrance a heady, sweet smell and the late-afternoon sun pouring through the windows bathed everything in yellow light. The faculty and the graduating seminarians gathered in the sacristy below. Father Brackin and his superior, the head of the SCJs, reviewed the order of the service at one of the tables. The graduates assembled on the side of the room where their gowns hung on racks.

"It's time, gentlemen," Mike Janowski said as he donned a robe. The other men followed his lead.

"Don't put your arms in," Don cautioned Craig. "Those sleeves — they stop."

Don felt out of sorts. He had just taken a dose of Benadryl for an allergy attack: maintenance had cut the grass.

The sacristy was a tumult of activity as faculty and clergy pressed together.

"There they are, all dressed up and nowhere to go," Father Mc-Lernon said with a smirk as he whisked past the graduates in search of his own academic garb, cutting a path through a throng of capes and mortarboards.

Don slapped Father Marty with the empty arms of his gown and moved through the milling group of faculty, graduates, and servers to the stairwell where Pat Murphy struggled to light the incense in the censer. Don listened to the organ prelude, "Praise to the Lord." He had composed the piece during his first year at Sacred Heart.

The ceremony was brief. Dr. Gallam delivered a heavily philosophical address peppered with well-turned phrases ("The Truth — God's Truth — is a single vast thing. We should fear no part of it"). Then the graduating seminarians approached the dais carrying their red-and-gray sashes. Father Raoul Gomez, the vice rector, put the sash over each man's head to signify the receipt of his master of divinity.

*Here it is,* Don Malin thought. When Father Raoul put the sash over his head, he felt energized. Father Marty told Don that he was proud of him, and Father Bob Schiavone gave him a bear hug. "You made it," Father Schiavone whispered.

Then everyone on the dais and in the pews extended their arms toward the graduates in a final blessing. A big meal followed. Heiser and Jim Pemberton begged off early — Heiser to finish a theology paper as he listened to the *World Café* and Jim to pack his clothes in plastic storage boxes. (Half of each seminarian's closet was to be left empty over the summer in the event someone needed the room.)

Downstairs, Don modeled a chasuble given to him by the Charismatic Renewal group. In profile, his Friar Tuck belly was evident. The Atkins diet had gone by the wayside.

"Three months?" Don asked, indicating the girth of his imagined pregnancy.

"Six," a woman said confidently.

As the gathering came to an end, people grew teary.

"Pueblo's not the end of the world," someone insisted.

"But you can see it from there," Don said with a laugh.

*  *  *

A black baseball cap sat on Dean Haley's desk. It read THIRTY FOR-
EVER. Dean had told no one back home about the diocese's decision
to drop him. He kept scrambling to put a positive slant on what had
happened, but from time to time, a sense of defeat would creep in.
He had had an interview at Elena's House and thought it had gone
well, but he was waiting to meet the board of directors. When he
told Father Tom Knoebel, the academic dean, that he had received
the letter from the diocese formally dropping its support, the priest
had said that it must finally have felt real. But the letter, with only a
few sentences, didn't make things real at all. The diocesan footer,
showing a green sun sinking into a southwestern landscape, only
goaded Dean with its embossed Gospel dictum: "Whoever follows
me will have the light of life." Dean thought, *I'm trying. I really am.*

One seminary wag liked to compare vocation recruitment to the
NFL and free agency. By this analogy, Dean was a top draft pick: single, young, charismatic, and Catholic. Dioceses should be knocking
one another down to court him. Dean had contacted a religious order and was happy to hear that they didn't want to talk to his bishop;
they wanted to talk to the rector at Sacred Heart instead. But no dioceses were tripping over themselves to recruit him.

Dean also fluctuated between wanting to return to the seminary
and feeling that the Church was missing the point with respect to
people like him. After classes finished for the semester, Dean and
Bob Brooks bought some scalped tickets to a Sugar Ray and Match-
box Twenty concert in downtown Milwaukee. As giant screens
flashed video images and light splintered across the capacity crowd,
Dean thought, *They've got it right. They know their audience. They understand the age group and the attention span. The Church could learn a lot
from this.*

Whenever Dean expressed such observations about the Church
and its mission to evangelize, he felt that people were inclined to
fault the audience and not the bearer of the message. But Dean believed that the bearer of the message had the responsibility to get the
message out to the people. If the people had short attention spans or

were geared toward video presentations, the Church had better acknowledge that. Didn't non–Roman Catholic churches use video and PowerPoint presentations to great effect? Bob and Dean left the concert thirty minutes early. Bob liked the line "I'm not crazy, I'm just a little unwell." Dean liked a song about teenage love. It was an "angry she ripped my heart apart" kind of song.

The last lines of the letter from the diocese were still hard for Dean to bear: "As of this date, you will no longer be a seminarian for th[is] diocese. May God be with you in whatever the future may hold for you."

When Dean looked around his room, he saw the accumulation of a year's work — a mess that would have to be moved somewhere soon. He thought he could buy a month or two more from Sacred Heart before he had to clear out. The Yakov Smirnoff ticket still hung on his bulletin board beside the photograph of the first-year students. A magnet from his chiropractor read, WHY ADJUST TO SUFFERING WHEN BETTER HEALTH IS ONLY AN ADJUSTMENT AWAY. The shelves were crammed with things: a self-help kit called *Attacking Anxiety;* another kit called *Advanced Mega Memory;* an Esteban guitar-playing video; several seasons of *The Sopranos* and *Buffy the Vampire Slayer* on DVD; a movie called *Sister Mary Explains It All* with Diane Keaton ("When it comes to sin, she's hell on wheels"); the Body-for-LIFE program that was intended to transform its owner physically, emotionally, and spiritually; a video game called Combat Medic; the plaster bust of Pope John Paul II; beside it, a teddy bear wearing a marine hat.

Dean's bag of medications was still nearly full.

"So this is the last time I'm going to see you?" Dean asked. He sat at lunch drinking tea and eating the sweet Korean biscuits that Philip Kim had passed around. Don Malin said that he would be leaving Tuesday.

Gary, the owner of the Cobblestone Inn, had given Don a Ford Explorer and taken Don's Jeep in exchange. Don couldn't believe Gary's generosity, or the generosity of so many of the people he was leaving behind in Milwaukee.

"So Don," Tom Mescall said as he turned toward Don, "it's been a five-year road for you?"

"Yep," Don confirmed. "Five years."

"Driving straight to Colorado?" Heiser asked.

Don nodded.

At the last rector's conference, Father Brackin had noted that someone was illegally opening the windows in the downstairs hallway with a crank and warned of dire penalties if this behavior continued.

"On my last day," Don vowed, "I'm going to crank all of those freakin' windows open and then ring that bell."

"I think he's a little excited," someone observed.

"Yeah, he's ready to go," someone else added.

A few of the men left the table, but Don lingered.

"Enjoy yourself," Don told people as they left, "but not too much."

"All my close friends are gone," Don said to the men who remained. His two closest friends at Sacred Heart had both decided they couldn't stay. His other friends had all been ordained. Don had never been good at keeping up with people. He was an extrovert. It was this quality that had helped him realize that celibacy could work for him. He could be involved with many people but wasn't devastated if someone let him down.

After lunch, he went up to his room and took out a CD that he'd had for years. It contained all of his work from nearly ten years of graduate school. He made a swift movement with the mouse, clicked once, and dropped the 2002–2003 academic year folder into the CD writer. He put the CD into the burner. In a few seconds, the work of two more semesters was saved. For the first time ever, Don locked the CD. This was the end of his studies.

This was the base of the "purple mountain majesties." This was the beginning of the "amber waves of grain." If Don had stepped off the porch and walked a mile up the road, he would have seen Pikes Peak, where "America the Beautiful" was composed. But he didn't. Later that day, he would drive up the highway into Pueblo, Colorado. He would pass roadside restaurants such as Taco Casa and Mi Ranchito, clusters of stucco and adobe homes, a HAY FOR SALE sign, a U-Pump-It gas station, a Sonic drive-in, and Patsy's, a biker bar. Then he would be in Pueblo proper and turn up Grand Avenue, past the bail bond office, with a cartoon jailbird looking out through cartoon bars, and the First Baptist Church. And finally he would arrive at the cathedral. There would be morning prayer and breakfast in the parish hall, a picnic in the park for his family and friends in the afternoon, and, that evening, a return to the cathedral for his ordination.

But at this moment, six in the morning on a chilly, partly cloudy day, he was alone, dressed in jeans, T-shirt, and loafers, swaying gently back and forth on the porch swing of a rectory down a country road. He was reading the Divine Office, as was required by virtue of his diaconate. Don had awoken an hour earlier with a song in his head. He often woke up that way, and the music became a sort of key for the day.

> As we lift up your name
> Let your fire fall
> Send your wind and your rain on your wings of love
> Pour down from heaven your passion and presence
> Bring down your burning desire.

Don prayed that he could receive all that God wanted for him that day. In the midst of that prayer, the details of what lay ahead — Masses to be said, the celebratory gatherings, some liturgical work he had promised a group of nuns — threatened to interrupt his contemplation. He remembered a retreat he had attended a few years before at a Benedictine hermitage. In the solitude of his own small cabin, Don had become overwhelmed by a sense that he was a dismal failure.

"I'm just a toad. Why do you want me to be a priest?" he'd asked

God as he looked out the window at the heavy snow falling onto a rich spread of piñon pine. It was so beautiful. "You see all that?" Don had heard a voice inside him say. "I made all that. Yeah. I made all that for you and everybody else on earth. Don't you think I'm smart enough to know what I'm doing with you?" Thirty years before, as a hormone-raging college student on another retreat, Don had been chastened by similar words addressed to Job: "Who is this that obscures my divine plan with his ignorance?" But at six in the morning on the day of his ordination, all Don felt was the peace that came with knowing he had made the right decision.

That night, the cathedral was filled a half hour before the Mass began. An ordination is believed to bring about an ontological change — a change in being — in the men ordained. It includes readings from the Old and New Testaments, the calling of the candidates, their presentation before the congregation, their election by the bishop, and the consent of the people. "We rely on the help of the Lord and our Savior Jesus Christ," the bishop announces, "and we choose these men, our brothers, for the priesthood in the presbyteral order." Then comes the homily, the examination of the candidates, and their profession of obedience. The men lie down, prostrating themselves before the congregation and the bishop, and the congregation and the bishop sing in a repetitive chant the Litany of the Saints:

> Saint Michael . . . Pray for us
> Holy Angels of God . . . Pray for us
> Saint John the Baptist . . . Pray for us

Saint after saint is named. Then comes the laying on of hands. The bishop does so in silence. He is followed by a line of other priests who file out of the pews to do the same. Then the bishop speaks the prayer of consecration. Next comes the Investiture with Stole and Chasuble of the priest candidates.

Before Don had left Sacred Heart, he had read something on the Internet about the unrealistic expectations people had of the priesthood. A priest was supposed to be available twenty-four hours a day: up at five-thirty in the morning, praying before the Blessed Sacrament, saying Mass at six, visiting the sick at seven — all without going to the bathroom or brushing his teeth. He was to dispense justice and mercy. He was to be absolutely strict with the rules of the Church and yet bend them for everybody. He was to be perfectly truthful and yet hide the truth from people when necessary; call a spade a spade but be diplomatic. He was supposed to be like everyone else but also otherworldly. In response, Don had thought: *Somewhere in the middle, I'm gonna be Don Malin, who's also Father Don Malin. I'm going to have to be who I am and at the same time be sensitive to all those expectations. So they want someone who's predictable but who's always doing something different; someone who has character or is a character. Well, they're going to get Don Malin.* Would Don Malin measure up? No — but he would do it anyway.

On this night, June 6, 2003, the men standing before the bishop are Don Malin and Martín Frías. The bishop is Arthur N. Tafoya of the Diocese of Pueblo, Colorado. The ordination takes close to three hours but passes quickly. Before the men really grasp what is happening, it is time for the anointing of the hands and the words "You are a priest forever in the Order of Melchizedek." At other times and in other places, the man standing before the bishop was Father Thomas Latham, Dean's mentor. The man was the mission priest lying in the coffin at Sacred Heart. The man was Father Charlie Bisgrove. The man was Saint Ignatius Loyola. The man was Father Karol Wojtyla. "You are a priest forever . . ."

The gifts are presented for the celebration of the Eucharist, and then the bishop embraces the newly ordained. The priests once again process to the altar and one by one embrace them as well. Don's mother, Diane B. Hallett, cries, as does one of his sisters and some of his friends. A few try to capture the ineffable on digital cameras.

Father Donald Philip Malin sits beside the bishop in the silence following Communion. His face reflects a profound joy. He is a changed man. Outside, thunderheads pile up along the Rockies, but the plains will have a perfectly clear night. Inside, the cathedral seems intimate, as if there were a fire burning in a hearth on the altar. No one else will be ordained in this diocese for the next two years.

Then the bishop hands Don an envelope containing his first assignment. The Diocese of Pueblo sprawls across the middle of Colorado, and Don may be placed far away from his friends and this cathedral.

"Do you want to know where you're going?" the bishop asks. The question might be directed at Don, but the smile on his face is for the people of the diocese filling the pews. Father Don Malin is their priest now.

Father Brackin served as rector for one more year and then headed to Hawaii for a six-month sabbatical. Father Tom Cassidy, a Milwaukee native, replaced him. The men took to their new rector quickly. The Archdiocese of Chicago reclaimed Father Marty Barnum and brought him back to teach at Mundelein seminary. Dr. Malchow retired.

Don Malin was assigned hundreds of miles away from Pueblo, in Grand Junction, a town on the opposite side of Colorado. He spent one year as a pastoral associate at St. Joseph Catholic Church there. Near the end of the year, Bishop Tafoya approached him with an offer to become the parochial administrator of St. Mary Catholic Church in Montrose, a parish of 1,050 families located sixty miles south of Grand Junction. As parish administrator, Don would be in control of the church. He would not hold the formal title of pastor, although he would do the same job. (The diocese requires that a priest must serve for several years before assuming the role of pastor.) The offer was more evidence of the priest shortage. The original candidate was pulled at the last minute because of an embezzling charge at his previous parish. Don said yes to the bishop, and by July 2004 he had taken up residence in Montrose on a three-year appointment. Even though he had four full-time employees and several part-timers, Don was the only priest in a large parish. As he approached the two-year mark as a priest, he was very busy and very happy.

After Philip Kim left Sacred Heart to be ordained, Jim Pemberton became the official patriarch, the oldest man at the seminary.

A few weeks before Heiser departed for a semester of study in Dublin, Ireland, he and Packy went swimming in Bass Lake, Wyoming. One of their favorite things was racing to a tennis ball that Heiser would throw into the lake. As Packy returned from fetching the ball, a rattlesnake bit him. Heiser killed the snake and raced Packy to the nearest vet, twenty minutes away. The vet did what he could, but Packy died the next morning. Heiser and Eric buried him with his tennis ball.

Heiser and Jim Pemberton were ordained deacons in the fall of 2004. Jim was ordained as a priest on May 21, 2005. More than a dozen of his friends from Sacred Heart attended his ordination, including David Placette and Philip Kim, both of whom had become priests the previous year; Wiggy, who would be entering his final year at Sacred Heart in the coming fall; Heiser; and many others. Don Malin had planned to come but had to cancel in the end because of the demands of parish life. Father Joe Scantlin's Most Blessed Sacrament Catholic Church was filled to overflowing.

The next morning Father Jim Pemberton celebrated his first Mass as a priest. Presenting gifts for the consecration, his four children and three grandchildren gathered in a circle around him. His youngest daughter handed him roses, representing Joy's presence. Jim returned to the altar and began the consecration, adding a special prayer for his wife, but as he spoke the words "Joy died" he began to cry. He paused. Tried again. There was a long silence. When Jim resumed speaking, his voice was at first soft with emotion, but it seemed to gather strength as the Mass progressed. He ended with the words of the general prayer, "All tears will be wiped away."

Less than a month later, Heiser was ordained in Wyoming. Craig, one of his hunting friends, bought him a German short-haired pointer in honor of his priesthood. Heiser named the dog Gromit.

Gromit sat in the front row at both his ordination and first Mass. At his ordination, an Indian drum group played at the beginning of the ceremony. There was a cedar smoke ritual and Heiser was presented with two eagle feathers. Dicky Ortiz blessed him and gave him an ornate Native American stole. The Ukrainian bishop of Chicago attended, as did Heiser's ex-wife. Heiser was posted to a church in Gillette, Wyoming, and Gromit had to spend Heiser's first year with Craig because Heiser wasn't allowed to bring a dog.

Heiser loved his new job. A few months after his arrival, he delivered a sermon one Sunday and in response received an e-mail from a parishioner that meant a lot to him: "Thanks so much for sharing your story and exposing your own suffering. Many people in the parish are going through similar things and it helps to know that someone has been through the same, will not criticize your suffering, and is showing there is a light at the end of a dark tunnel. I have been away from the church for many years. It is great to be back and to have such a wonderful, understanding priest."

Ron Kendzierski married Tina and settled in Cadillac, Michigan. He played his violin in local churches and launched a music program for students at an alternative high school. He also remained active in volunteer work, but marriage to Tina taught him about selflessness and thinking about the needs of others in a way that volunteerism didn't.

Despite ideological differences with the Catholic Church, Ron's dream of religious ministry did not go away. He found a group called the Ecumenical Catholic Communion, which, according to its Web site, is composed of "independent Catholic faith communities . . . not under the jurisdiction of the Pope [or] subject to the canon law or the guidelines of the Roman Catholic Church." For Ron, the Communion was a lifeboat floating next to the sinking ship. It enabled him to remain a Catholic while separating himself from the conservatism that he believed was strangling the Church. By the summer of 2005, he was on track to be ordained a priest with the Communion. Although he lost touch with the seminary after he left (aside from completing a few overdue papers for his classes), he sometimes thought back on his time at Sacred Heart and reflected on the men: *We all had good intentions, and we all wanted to make a difference in the world.*

Dean Haley returned to live in Texas. Some seminarians reported that Dean was still trying to find a diocese that would accept him as a seminarian. Almost a year passed without news, and then a curious report arrived at Hales Corners. It said that Dean had lost a finger while working on an oil rig in the Gulf of Mexico. Later, some of the men from Sacred Heart saw Dean at an ordination in Texas. He confirmed the story of the accident on the oil rig, but said he was looking forward. He was still intent on becoming a priest, especially now that the mandatory two-year freeze that had prevented other dioceses from considering him as a seminarian was about to expire.

Enrollments remained constant at Sacred Heart, and new men continued to arrive each fall and winter from across the country to study for the priesthood.

AUTHOR'S NOTE
AND ACKNOWLEDGMENTS


Fact is a journalist's currency. Getting a person's name right is important, and names shouldn't be sacrificed to some vague application of artistic truth. But there are times when identities have to be changed so that other facts — and the truth that these facts collectively reveal — may be told. I have changed a few names in this book in pursuit of that goal.

This project took five years and covered a lot of ground. As a result, many more people deserve thanks than I can possibly acknowledge here. But I'll make a start:

Most profoundly, I want to express my gratitude to the five men, my main "characters," whose spirit, vision, and generosity allowed me to tell the larger story of a vocation through the telling of their individual stories. Don Malin, Jim Heiser, Jim Pemberton, Dean Haley, and Ron Kendzierski — thank you.

And thank you:
Father Benedict Groeschel and the Franciscan Friars of the Renewal for early guidance; the Paulist Fathers for letting me observe their formation process up close; the unnamed seminarians, priests, and dioceses whose stories I haven't told here, who informed my understanding of a priestly vocation; Charles Michel and Father Andre

Papineau for showing me the way to Sacred Heart; Father Jim Brackin for granting access and displaying consistent fairness; the SCJs for openness and good humor; Peg Boyles for support and welcome; Father Charlie Bisgrove for relating many truths about priestly life; Father Marty Barnum and Father Paul Grizzelle-Reid for being accessible and wise; Brother Jim, about whom a whole book should be written; Father David Placette, Carl Hellwig, Father Philip Kim, Father Mike Mallard, Father Tom Mescall, Father Joe McDonald, Father Patrick Smith, John Schwall, Father Val Bradley, Father Gary Rottman, Chris McClellan, Hugo Morales, Father John Brosmer, and all the seminarians of Sacred Heart who sat around the dining tables while I taped their conversations and wrote in my notebook; Sister Marilyn and Sister Mary Carroll for their insights into seminary formation; Father Michael McLernon and Dr. Esther Warren; the faculty of Sacred Heart for opening your classrooms and putting up with my questions about the arcane and sometimes painfully obvious parts of your area of expertise; the Sacred Heart community. The support that I found extended to all corners of this place. It is difficult to conceive of a school or community that is more single-minded in its academic and spiritual purposes than Sacred Heart and of individuals more committed to turning out well-rounded priests. This is a place where secretarial, maintenance, and food services do much more than their job descriptions; the Louisville Institute and Dr. Jim Lewis for their generous support; Father Andrew O'Connor for offering workspace and the perspective of a young priest; Padre Pio; "Uncle" Tim Nolan; Neal Levy; George Gerdes for the use of his wonderful lyrics; Carlos Cuartas and Sister Pascal for their pastoral insights; Samuel Freedman for being a superb teacher and standard-bearer; Father Michael Hunt for being a wonderful reader, friend, and adviser; Charlie Scribner for supporting *The Collar* from the very beginning; Claudia Cross at Sterling Lord Literistic for being there throughout; Susan Stava for taking good pictures of an unwilling subject; Adam Dancy for his generous and learned assistance with my video footage; Anne Seiwerath for consistent pleasantness and sound answers to my questions; Barbara Jatkola; Martha Kennedy for her inspired cover; Lori Glazer, Bridget Marmion, Larry Cooper, Carla Gray, Walter Vatter, and Loren Isenberg for getting behind *The Collar.*

And a particular thanks to Eamon Dolan for being the kind of editor they say you can't find anymore.